T0347255

Interrogating Democracy in World Politics

It is often assumed that democracy is both desirable and possible in global politics. *Interrogating Democracy in World Politics* provides an important counter-argument to this assumption by questioning the history, meaning and concepts of democracy in contemporary international and global politics.

Combining viewpoints from the fields of international relations, political theory and history, the book includes:

- critical examinations of the concept of democracy as a political order and ethical ideal;
- assessment of the role and function of democracy in how contemporary political events are understood and evaluated;
- analysis of the relationship of democracy to international stability, liberalism and the emergence of capitalist economies.

The book focuses on the move from the concept of 'international politics' to 'world politics', recognising the equal importance of understanding democratic interaction both within and between states. It reviews current scholarly thinking in the field before providing a complex theoretical re-engagement with the meaning of democracy in contemporary world politics.

Interrogating Democracy in World Politics will be of interest to students and scholars of politics and international relations, democratisation studies and globalisation.

Joe Hoover, Meera Sabaratnam and Laust Schouenborg, Department of International Relations, London School of Economics, UK.

Routledge advances in international relations and global politics

Interrogating Democracy in World Politics

Edited by Joe Hoover, Meera Sabaratnam and Laust Schouenborg

Routledge
Taylor & Francis Group

LONDON AND NEW YORK

First published 2011
by Routledge
2 Park Square, Milton Park, Abingdon, Oxon OX14 4RN

Simultaneously published in the USA and Canada
by Routledge
711 Third Avenue, New York, NY 10017

Routledge is an imprint of the Taylor & Francis Group, an informa business

British Library Cataloguing in Publication Data
A catalogue record for this book is available from the British Library

Library of Congress Cataloging in Publication Data
Interrogating democracy in world politics / edited by Joe Hoover, Meera
Sabaratnam, and Laust Schouenborg.
    p. cm. – (Routledge advances in international relations and global
    politics; 93)
    Includes bibliographical references and index.
    1. World politics. 2. Democracy. 3. Cosmopolitanism. I. Hoover, Joe.
    II. Sabaratnam, Meera. III. Schouenborg, Laust.
    JZ1310.I58 2011
    327.1–dc22
                                            2010048176

ISBN: 978-0-415-59531-5 (hbk)
ISBN: 978-0-203-81594-6 (ebk)

Typeset in Times
by Wearset Ltd, Boldon, Tyne and Wear

Contents

Contributors

Claudia Aradau is Lecturer in International Studies in the Department of Politics and International Studies and Research Director for the Securities Programme of the Centre for Citizenship, Identities and Governance (CCIG) at the Open University (UK).

James Bohman holds the Danforth I Chair in the Humanities and is Professor of Philosophy and Professor of International Studies at Saint Louis University. His most recent book is *Democracy Across Borders: From Demos to Demoi* (MIT Press, 2007).

Daniel Bray is Lecturer in International Relations at La Trobe University.

David Chandler is Professor of International Relations, Department of Politics and International Relations, University of Westminster, London. He is the founding editor of the *Journal of Intervention and Statebuilding*. His recent books include *International Statebuilding: The Rise of Post-Liberal Governance* (Routledge, 2010) and *Hollow Hegemony: Rethinking Global Politics, Power and Resistance* (Pluto, 2009).

Ian Clark is E.H. Carr Professor of International Politics at Aberystwyth University. His most recent research has been a multi-volume study of international legitimacy. He has already published *Legitimacy in International Society* (OUP, 2005) and *International Legitimacy and World Society* (OUP, 2007), and his *Hegemony in International Society* will be published by Oxford University Press in 2011. He held a three-year UK ESRC Professorial Fellowship during 2007–10. He is a Fellow of the British Academy and an Honorary Fellow of Selwyn College, Cambridge.

Sandra Halperin is Professor of International Relations at Royal Holloway, University of London.

David Held holds the Graham Wallas Chair in Political Science, and is Co-Director of LSE Global Governance at the London School of Economics and Political Science. Among his most recent publications are *Cosmopolitanism: Ideals and Realities* (Polity, 2010), *Globalisation/Anti-Globalisation* (Polity, 2007), *Models of Democracy* (Polity, 2006), *Global Covenant* (Polity, 2004),

Global Transformations: Politics, Economics and Culture (Polity, 1999) and *Democracy and the Global Order: From the Modern State to Cosmopolitan Governance* (Polity, 1995). His main research interests include the study of globalisation, changing forms of democracy and the prospects of regional and global governance. He is a Director of Polity Press, which he co-founded in 1984, and General Editor of *Global Policy*.

Christopher Hobson is a Research Associate at the Institute for Sustainability and Peace, United Nations University.

Joe Hoover is an LSE Fellow in the Department of International Relations at the London School of Economics and Political Science. He formerly edited *Millennium: Journal of International Studies* and his work has appeared in *Human Rights Review, International Affairs* and *Millennium: Journal of International Studies*.

Jef Huysmans is Senior Lecturer in the Department of Politics and International Studies (POLIS) and Director of the Centre for Citizenship, Identities and Governance at the Open University (UK). He is author of *The Politics of Insecurity: Fear, Migration and Asylum in the EU* (Routledge, 2006); and *What is Politics?* (Edinburgh University Press, 2005). He edited with Andrew Dobson and Raia Prokhovnik *The Politics of Protection: Sites of Insecurity and Political Agency* (Routledge, 2006); and, with Patricia Noxolo, *Community, Citizenship, and the 'War on Terror': Security and Insecurity* (Palgrave, 2009).

Chantal Mouffe is Professor of Political Theory at the Centre for the Study of Democracy at the University of Westminster, London.

Nicholas Onuf is Professor Emeritus, Department of Politics and International Relations, Florida International University, and Professor Associado, Instituto de Relações Internacionais, Pontifícia Universidade Católica do Rio de Janeiro.

Peter Onuf is Thomas Jefferson Foundation Professor of History, University of Virginia.

Meera Sabaratnam is a PhD candidate in the Department of International Relations at the London School of Economics and Political Science. She has formerly edited *Millennium: Journal of International Studies* and currently teaches a Masters' course on conflict and post-war peacebuilding. Forthcoming is her co-edited collection *A Liberal Peace? The Problems and Practices of Peacebuilding* (Zed, 2011).

Saskia Sassen is the Robert S. Lynd Professor of Sociology and Co-Director, The Committee on Global Thought, Columbia University (www.saskiasassen.com). Recent books are *Territory, Authority, Rights: From Medieval to Global Assemblages* (Princeton University Press, 2008) and *A Sociology of Globalization* (W.W. Norton, 2007). For UNESCO she did a five-year project on sustainable human settlement with a network of researchers and activists in over 30 countries, as part of the 14-volume *Encyclopedia of Life Support Systems* (Oxford, UK: EOLSS Publishers, www.eolss.net).

Laust Schouenborg holds a PhD in International Relations from the London School of Economics and Political Science and is an external lecturer at the University of Copenhagen and Roskilde University. His articles have appeared in *Geopolitics*, *International Relations* and *Internasjonal Politikk*.

Preface

In world politics there are years that become symbols of dramatic and unexpected change, they can be stated simply as number: 1789, 1848, 1945 and 1989. It is possible that 2011 will come to represent an exceptional time as well, when democratic revolutions occurred throughout North Africa, a region that too many commentators had written off as unprepared for popular rule. As we were finishing this book, we joyfully watched authoritarian regimes in Tunisia and Egypt fall as protestors took to their streets and squares to demand fuller control over their own lives; we also apprehensively watched the autocrats and their security forces fight back in Libya and Bahrain. It is an important time to be thinking about democracy and its place in world politics. It is also an important time to be thinking about *how we think* about democracy – before we turn 2011 into a symbol of transformation, at which point the interpretation of these democratic revolutions will be more powerful than the events themselves.

While this collection of essays began as the theme for the annual conference for *Millennium: Journal of International Studies* in 2008, and was developed further throughout 2009 and 2010, we are glad to see it published at a moment when our central concern is made vital by ongoing political developments. Our goal was to challenge conventional understandings of democracy as a global phenomenon; to suggest that the idea of democracy is revolutionary and surprising, not easily contained in academic theses such as "the democratic peace" or "the end of history"; and to expose the thinness of historical narratives of democratic progress, which uncritically connect democracy to liberalism, to capitalism, to the West, to formal procedures of the rule of law, to the nation, as if these were essential pairings. The essays that make up this volume enrich our conception of democracy and challenge us to understand our present moment in its own unique terms.

As political unrest and change moved from one city to the next across North Africa and the Middle East, professional commentators scrambled to interpret events and hastily grabbed on to the most ready explanations to make sense of what they saw happening. Regime change in Tunis, protests in Cairo, violence in Libya were reduced to exonerations of the Bush administration's democracy promotion strategy in the region, or evidence for the progressive logic of liberal reforms, or an object lesson reminding hegemonic states that democracy is the solution to the problem of global instability. This is a distorted and partial view of contemporary events brought on by our dependence on myths, assumptions and half-truths that have accumulated around democracy as a privileged ideal in world politics.

The interrogations that our diverse contributors have pursued here push us to think about democracy differently, to see the tension it has with liberal capitalism, to see the disorder and violence inherent in popular rule, to see the challenge to world order presented by a sovereign people pushing against the boundaries and limits of the state system, to understand our solidarity with the protestors in critical ways, and, most importantly, to attend to the complexity, plurality and distinctiveness of democratic movements and institutions in world politics.

We do not pretend and could not hope to provide an alternative understanding of democracy that would make sense of the popular revolutions of 2011. Not only was that not the intention of this volume, but also such hopes, we think, are misguided. Critical academic study should dislodge our assumptions and expand our understanding of events, not predict, control or simplify them for easy consumption by the media, governments or a general public hungry for easy answers in complex times.

Joe Hoover, Meera Sabaratnam and Laust Schouenborg
London and New York

Acknowledgements

This book is the product of more than three years of work. It started out as a conference theme when the three of us were editing *Millennium: Journal of International Studies* as graduate students at LSE. That very successful conference and conversation culminated in the publication of a special issue of *Millennium* (vol. 37, no. 3, 2009), including earlier versions of several of the chapters that appear in this volume. We are extremely pleased that Routledge afforded us the opportunity to continue that conversation and expand our circle of interlocutors.

When engaged in a project like this over such a long time, you naturally incur many debts. At Routledge in particular we would like to thank both Heidi Bagtazo and Hannah Shakespeare for their responsive help and guidance.

At *Millennium*-central – D710 Clement House – everyone involved with that innovative intellectual institution also needs to be recognised, particularly our ever-helpful conference organisers Ramon Pacheco Pardo and Jorge Lasmar. Our warmest thanks go to David Mainwaring at SAGE who served as our liaison during the first year of *Millennium's* relationship with SAGE and who has remained immensely supportive in seeing this book through to publication.

Chapters 3, 4, 5, 7, 8, 10 and 11 are reproduced by permission of SAGE Publications, London, Los Angeles, New Delhi and Singapore, from *Millennium: Journal of International Studies*, Volume 37, Issue 3, 2009. Likewise, we recognise Wiley and Sons for allowing us to reproduce material for chapter 9 that first appeared in *International Political Sociology* (vol. 3, no. 1, 2009).

Finally, a deep felt thank you to our parents who taught us our first lessons in democracy.

Joe Hoover, Meera Sabaratnam and Laust Schouenborg
London and New York, March 2011

1 Introduction

Interrogating democracy in world politics

*Joe Hoover, Meera Sabaratnam and
Laust Schouenborg*

Democracy, as an ideal and a form of government, occupies a privileged position in world politics. In this volume, we aim to place both conventional understandings of democracy and its privilege under suspicion. This interrogation is important for understanding what democracy means beyond the nation-state and evaluating the historical narratives of progress that sustain these meanings. The goal of this introduction is to provide a framework for the multiple lines of questioning that are opened up in the chapters that follow. To do this we examine the privilege associated with democracy across multiple sites of world politics, drawing out three key assumptions. As we discuss these assumptions about democracy in world politics, we elaborate on the diverse ways that the contributions to this book challenge them. While the book is separated into historical and conceptual sections, reflecting different approaches to the topic, these different methods of interrogation share the goal of unsettling the assumptions supporting the privileged place of democracy in world politics – this provides a multi-dimensional critique that is radical but plural, revealing linkages, discrepancies and surprises, rather than leading to a single line of critique.

In an earlier period of world politics, suspicion was cast upon the very idea that democracy was important in such matters – either in relation to domestic government or the structure of international politics. A historical shift is evident across a range of issues in world politics. The democratic peace theory has a central place in International Relations (IR),[1] which gives democratic forms of government causal force in preventing wars. This builds upon a long-standing line of thought that accords pacific and moral virtues to democratic government. Related to this has been the infusion of a commitment to democracy into practices of development assistance and state-building, as well as the rise of a global apparatus of democracy promotion. These developments reflect not only the empirical claims regarding democracy's relation to peace and prosperity, but also a wider commitment to the universal moral value of democracy. The human rights regime defends the civil and political rights that are the cornerstone of the liberal democratic tradition, the discourse around the Responsibility to Protect (R2P) links sovereign legitimacy to a state's accountability to its citizens, and the fight to develop global governance through an international rule of law depends upon the presumed universality of democracy as a political good. This moral commitment to democracy culminates in the ideas of global civil society and cosmopolitan politics, which seek to use democracy to reform the international order directly. While these developments do not form a cohesive programme of thought, they do point to the privileged place democracy has in world politics.

Determining exactly how and why democracy became such a central concept in world politics is probably impossible. Undoubtedly, it has to do with the political dominance of liberal democratic powers, which in turn established a liberal international order that has defined world politics in the last century and the early part of our current one (Ikenberry 2009). Interesting as these debates may or may not be, our central concern is with the assumptions that give the discursive victory of democracy such seeming stability. A large choir sings the praises of democracy, but the simple force of the melody cannot cover the dissonance and tension, which calls out for acknowledgement if not resolution.

The privilege of democracy is made possible both by the histories we construct of its development and the conventional meanings that define an essentially contested concept. For this reason, our interrogation of the privilege of democracy proceeds on both historical and conceptual lines. The first section of the book focuses on the historical development of democracy and contests familiar narratives of progressive reform, essential linkages to liberal capitalism, the desirability of a democratic international order and the necessity of the nation-state as the key site of democracy. What emerges is a more ambiguous history that undermines many assumptions. The second section focuses on the meaning of democracy and undoes the necessary ties made between national citizenship and democracy, questions the universal moral value of democracy, and reconfigures the linkages between democratic government and peaceful world politics. To organise the diverse interrogations presented here, which pursue contrasting lines of critique in different domains of world politics, we focus on three key assumptions upon which democracy's privilege rests. First, we examine the assumption that democracy reduces violent conflict and supports peace and stability. Second, we question the belief in historical progress within societies that culminates in a liberal democratic capitalist state. Finally, we analyse the presumptions regarding democratic membership at various levels, looking to national citizens, cosmopolitan individuals and states as problematic democratic subjects.

Violence and stability

Perhaps what has contributed the most to establishing democracy as a universal good in world politics has been the idea that it is associated with peace and stability. This is a tradition of thought going back, at least, to Paine and Kant, and the latter's essay *Toward Perpetual Peace* from 1795 (Kant 1983). It became a real force in world politics when American president, Woodrow Wilson, made it a central element of his foreign policy in the final stages of the First World War – so much so that today the terms democracy promotion and Wilsonialism are often used interchangeably. However, if we look for the more recent causes of why the idea has risen to such prominence, it seems that the explanation is to be found in the work carried out by predominantly American IR scholars in the 1970s and 1980s on what came to be known as the 'Democratic Peace Thesis', namely the empirical proposition that democratic states do not go to war against each other. This research prompted Jack Levy to state in 1989 what had in effect become the consensus view in large parts of academia: that the 'absence of war between democratic states comes as close as anything we have to an empirical law in international relations' (Levy 1989: 270).

The year 1989 is important because it also signified the end of the Cold War, the start of an era of US dominance in world politics and – as we shall touch upon in the section on 'Historical Progress' below – the disappearance, in the view of some observers, of any systemic competitors to the liberal-capitalist-*democratic* way of life. The resulting material and ideological hegemony of the US was what allowed the first president Bush to proclaim a 'New World Order', president Clinton to follow this lead with his national security strategy of 'Engagement and Enlargement' and the second president Bush to embark on a full-scale military campaign in the name of democracy (and the eradication of WMDs), 'Iraqi Freedom', which had as its ultimate goal the democratisation of the entire Middle East, and perhaps, the world. As he expressed it in his State of the Union address in 2003 in the run-up to the invasion:

> Americans are a free people, who know that freedom is the right of every person and the future of every nation. The liberty we prize is not America's gift to the world, it is God's gift to humanity.
>
> (Bush 2003)

Or as he put it to the troops at Bagram Air Base, Afghanistan, in 2006:

> History has taught us democracies don't war. Democracies – you don't run for office in a democracy and say, please vote for me, I promise you war. (Laughter.) You run for office in democracies, and say, vote for me, I'll represent your interests; vote for me, I'll help your young girls go to school, or the health care you get improved [*sic*].
>
> (Bush 2006)

There are many different explanations in the academic literature for why democracies do not go to war – Bush's assertion that it is due to the check placed on decision-makers by the electorate, is only one of them.[2] However, the quote above, and numerous statements by his predecessors, is testimony to the fact that the democratic peace idea had successfully transplanted itself from academia to the real world of international politics.

Meanwhile, in the 1990s, and especially the 2000s, a number of academics started to question the idea of an unambiguous correlation between peace and democracy. In articles and a recent book, Edward D. Mansfield and Jack Snyder

(1995, 2001, 2005) have studied the propensity of democratising states to go to war, showing that they are just as, if not more, belligerent than non-democracies. If there is such a thing as the democratic peace, it only exists between so-called mature democracies. Amy Chua (2003) has developed a similarly critical argument in her US national bestseller *World on Fire*. Her key thesis is that exporting free-market democracy to countries with a market-dominant minority consistently leads to ethnic violence, when the newly enfranchised majority elects to possess what they believe is rightfully theirs to take. Finally, Roland Paris (2004), in the book *At War's End*, argues that prevailing peacebuilding strategies, based on comprehensive political and economic liberalisation, need to be rethought because they simply do not produce the positive outcomes originally ascribed to them.

However – and this is our key point – none of these authors question the fundamental value of democracy and whether it is *intrinsically* associated with peace and stability. Paris is especially clear on this:

> The purpose of this book, however, is not to reject the Wilsonian peacebuilding strategy in its entirety, but to expose the weaknesses of the naive version of Wilsonianism that informed the missions of the 1990s. Indeed, I shall argue that peacebuilders should preserve the broad goal of converting war-shattered states into liberal market democracies, because wellestablished liberal market democracies tend to be peaceful in both their domestic affairs and their relations with other states. The challenge, however, is to devise methods of achieving this Wilsonian goal without endangering the very peace that the liberalization process is supposed to consolidate.
>
> (Paris 2004: 7)

Rather, what they do is to question elements of the process of transition to democracy and whether these are associated or not with stability. The assumption is still that democracy constitutes the ideal, and most peaceful, way of life – if it is properly realised. In Amy Chua's words, 'the best political hope for these countries lies in some form of democracy' (Chua 2003: 263). This is not to give the impression that the contributions to this volume develop an anti-democratic programme, but to say that they do interrogate whether the idea of democracy is peaceful as such – both historically and conceptually. The result is a very different, and much more cautious, perspective on the presumed benefits of the democratic ideal.

Nicholas Onuf and Peter Onuf spearhead this charge with a provocative chapter on the emergence of modern international relations and the nation-state; exposing how both were partial expressions of the democratic principle, and their relationship to mass warfare. As they state at the start of the piece:

> Our purpose in this chapter is to show how emerging ideas of democratic self-government did not, and could not, lead to the republican millennium – a

new epoch of peace and prosperity – that revolutionaries once anticipated and peace theorists still await. To the contrary, democratization enabled the governments of modern nation-states to expand the coercive capacity of states in pursuit of interests they defined as vital for their nations' well-being. By doing so, democratization played an important part in unleashing 'the dogs of war'.

(Onuf and Onuf, this volume: 16)

Ian Clark is less blunt in his chapter titled 'Democracy in international society', He does not tie democracy directly to conflict, but he does suggest that democracy's manifestation in international society, in world politics, often appears as a form of exclusion when that society has traditionally been based on inclusion and pluralism. He traces this phenomenon through to contemporary proposals for establishing a league of democracies, enjoying special rights and duties, and the resistance to this, by states not sharing in these values. Chantal Mouffe brings this point home in her chapter 'Democracy in a multipolar world', in which she argues that this exclusion – politics in its *antagonistic* form – is likely to lead to violent confrontation. As a remedy to this, she defends an *agonistic* approach to democratic politics that treats other cultures and ways of organising political life as not intrinsically illegitimate. Her point is not that this will remove conflict, but merely that it will make it less likely and less uncompromising.

In their respective contributions, Christopher Hobson and Sandra Halperin offer analyses of democracy's relationship to liberalism and capitalism. Seeing that 'liberal' has almost become synonymous with 'democratic' in today's world (note the quote by Bush above), Hobson's argument, that most liberals in an earlier period of history were deeply suspicious of the democratic ideal, urges us to pause and reflect. Liberals tended to share in the general opinion that democracy was 'a dangerous and unstable form of rule which inevitably led to anarchy or despotism' (Hobson, this volume: 66). Similarly, Halperin unsettles the orthodox narrative of how free-market capitalism and open societies are stepping stones for the consolidation of democratic regimes. She reverses this causal link, and argues that it was in fact primarily the mobilisation of the working class for the First World War that led to democracy, embedded free-market economies and expanded political liberties. It was the threat of popular revolution that made the bourgeois classes compromise and give in to worker demands in these areas.

Further developing the destabilising role of democracy, in their chapter, 'Mobilising (global) democracy: a political reading of mobility between universal rights and the mob', Claudia Aradau and Jef Huysmans explore the democratic role of the mobile masses as agents of change that challenge established authority and structures. This challenge is not only domestic, as Halperin's piece documents, but global. Aradau and Huysman's political reading of mobility challenges the internationalist and cosmopolitan aspirations for a formalised and stable democratic politics by recapturing the disruptive elements of democratic mass participation.

Taken together, the contributions to this volume thus provide a much more comprehensive and multifaceted perspective on the value of democracy for peace and stability in world politics. They challenge one of the key arguments made for democracy promotion and interventionary politics in world politics, moving beyond the more limited focus on problems of transition that currently occupies much of the literature.

History and progress

The ways in which we understand the history of democracy fundamentally shape how we understand both its present and its future, which seems obvious but is often ignored, despite the reality that our historical understandings strongly limit the political possibilities that are considered legitimate across a wide range of states and other political communities today. The political force of these limits today is, in no small part, premised on the ideas both that it promotes peace and stability, as discussed above, and that it represents a historically advanced and stable form of government. Any critical interrogation of the meanings of democracy and democratic politics today must also interrogate and unsettle the dominant stories that are told about its emergence and apparent victories in the past.

The rapid ascendance to international prominence of Fukuyama's *End of History* thesis (1989) for example did not so much reflect a considered turn in the academy towards a neo-Hegelian theory of History and a Nietzschean reading of man's nihilistic condition in modernity. More simply it told the History of democracy in a way that a particular and powerful post-Cold War audience in the United States wanted to hear, and consequently provided an intellectual justification for the resurgent liberal thinking and policy-making that were pursued through the 1990s and 2000s that was expressed forcefully but was conceptually ambiguous. Its central contention – that the marriage of capitalism, liberalism and democracy expressed in the State represented the end of man's struggle for political recognition – was one eagerly seized upon, unsurprisingly, by supporters of American power to give their agenda momentum. What was startling and compelling about Fukuyama's argument was not simply that it endorsed the stability and supremacy of the American form of political community, but that the elimination of alternatives was a property of the Historical process itself, giving it not a parochial but universal significance.

While it may have been the neoconservative movement that took with most alacrity to Fukuyama's predictive claims and critique of political realism, a more minimalist version of the claim that capitalism, liberalism and democracy were stable, historically self-reinforcing and normatively desirable had long been broadly accepted across the mainstream of Western academic literature on world politics. The argument that liberal democracy was 'the only game in town' was popular among even those that had reservations about the obvious desirability of this powerful consensus (Cox 1998). The globalisation literature, both critical and supportive, that emerged from the early 1990s onwards also tended to view the growth of capitalism, liberalism and democracy as mutually reinforcing historical trajectories which were now, for various reasons accelerating and spreading at an exponential rate, as well as in ways which were making the territorial organisation of politics less primary in world politics (Scholte 2000).

The presumed historical naturalness of the relationship between capitalism, political liberalism and democracy in particular had informed US and Western European foreign policies both during and after the Cold War, that worked on the assumption that democracy in the rest of the world would emerge and eventually be consolidated through the process of further political and economic liberalisation and integration into multilateral and capitalist international institutions, as had seemed to happen with Europe and Japan. After the end of the Cold War, it became even easier to implicate the specific attributes of liberal democracy with inclusion into global capitalism under the more general developmental, technical rubric of 'good governance' (Williams and Young 1994), a principle which continues to animate many forms of co-operation and intervention with formerly colonised countries.

This strategy for democracy promotion considered elements such as performance legitimacy (Huntington 1991), the growth of a middle class (Inglehart and Welzel 2005), and the socialisation of elites as key factors in the emergence of democracy, all of which were compatible with the increasing influence of a market economy and liberal political values. For political scientists such as Huntington, the use of a liberal procedural version of democracy as the basis for analysis had the further benefit of allowing for comparison and evaluation from afar. As Skinner (1973) argued with regard to Dahl, however, the result of naturalising a very particular view of democracy with a view to its observability and processual character was a necessarily conservative ideological move couched in the language of 'neutral' inquiry.

It is against this background assumption of the naturalness of the relationship between capitalism, liberalism and democracy that apparent 'puzzles' in the study of world politics have emerged over the last two decades. Why did some states have only 'incomplete' transitions to democracy? Why were there 'reversals' in democratisation? How can we account for the spread of illiberal democracies? How has China managed not to democratise given its economic liberalisation? The structure of these questions reveals the deep way in which historical assumptions about the force and inevitability of this triadic relationship have dominated thinking about democracy.

Alternative, dissident literatures on democracy arose however, particularly out of historical and sociological approaches to the question of democracy, consideration of which was for a long time excluded from the dominant paradigms which sought to understand world politics, despite the attempts of some to bring them into the study of world politics (Halliday 1987; Rosenberg 1994). Core contributions to this included literatures on contentious politics (McAdam *et al.* 2001), structural violence and needs frustration (Galtung 1969; Burton 1990), and social conflict (Mann 1999). While these mostly focused on the relationship between democracy, politics and violence as expressions of modernity, they also offered some intellectual resources and inspiration for re-thinking the assumed historical relationship between democracy, liberalism and capitalism within and between states, the task taken up by the contributors in this volume.

In her chapter exploring the rise of democracy in two paradigmatic cases, Sassen argues that historically the industrialising classes, associated with the rise of the liberal rights-bearing subject of politics, pushed for the institutionalisation in law of a deeply unequal relationship between capital and labour, whereby the rights of capital to continue production systematically trumped claims made by workers for autonomy, better pay demands and working conditions. The ongoing inequalities of power and opportunity within liberal democracies, where all citizens are formally equal, relate specifically to the efforts during the evolution of capitalist liberal democracy to protect capital. This put restrictions on the kind of democracy that could be envisaged both at the time and in the present day. This argument complements that of Halperin's chapter, which argues that the aspects of mass participation in European democracies did not emerge as the gifts of a progressive liberalism, but rather were the somewhat inadvertent result of the working class being substantively mobilised for the purpose of industrial warfare and as a result improving their economic and political power. This created a platform from which various rights could be claimed. These chapters suggest that the assumption that the growth of capitalism and the ideal of the liberal subject were historically drivers of democracy is a deeply flawed one; indeed, the message seems to be that capitalist economic structures and the rapid development of property rights suppressed or at least did not encourage full and equal participation in the democracies that eventually emerged. This is a key argument particularly in terms of the contemporary attempts to link the promotion of capitalist growth automatically with the concept of democracy in 'transition' countries – the cautionary tale is that the concepts may well conflict, and indeed that the politics of emerging class interests condition the nature of the political settlement achieved in the name of democracy.

Key to all of these chapters is the conviction that historically democracy has primarily implied *struggle* and the making of substantive claims for the redistribution of power and legitimacy in a political system. Onuf and Onuf argue, reading the events through Tocqueville, that the emergence of democracy in America was only contingently associated with constitutional politics and liberal restraints on government. Rather, it gathered its force from the imaginary of a democratic nation, which itself was created through the processes of Revolution and War. This made it a force that could be highly destructive when challenged and one not tempered by various anti-democratic constraints, as the Civil War demonstrated.

The historical fear of being overwhelmed by the force of democratic struggle also comes across clearly in Hobson's piece which historicises the concept of democracy, and in particular the various ways in which it was perceived to conflict with and threaten established values of liberalism. By re-focusing our historical gaze on the rise of democracy as an embedded form of political struggle that produces its own momentum and force, the idea that democratisation can be brought about through mechanisms of internationally sponsored good governance is brought into question. More fundamentally, the question is raised as to whether the dominant contemporary conceptions of 'democracy' that inform world politics – that is, the equation with contested periodic elections and the rule of law – ultimately neuter the historically radical political potential of democracy to challenge distributions of power and legitimacy through the struggle for substantive rights and recognition beyond those offered by liberal capitalism.

Membership and the democratic subject

Because membership in a democratic polity is in theory maximally inclusive, the question of membership in such political community is inherently controversial. By enabling claims to political power based on equal rather than hierarchical status, democratic government generates social instability not as a simple historical fact, but as part of the inherent logic of the idea. For this reason discourses about stability and progress that surround our contemporary understanding of democracy are fundamental to its prestige. Yet, these assumptions also depend upon a further one, that the privileged subject of democracy, 'the people', is a coherent and identifiable political subject. Despite the invitation of universal participation, exclusions and limitations of membership undermine democratic openness, making it much easier for powerful political actors to take up the participatory mantle despite the persistence of hierarchy in the social order.

Aristotle grasped this tension and his rejection of democracy reflects this; it was not enough to limit democratic membership to citizens (already an exclusive category), it was necessary that political power be limited to the most virtuous in an ideal state (Aristotle 1996: Books III and IV). Closer to our own time and reflecting an early recognition of the linkage between domestic and international politics, Kant insisted that democratic participation be strictly limited by a rightful republican constitution and that each state be maintained as an independent body (Kant 1989). For Kant, the democratic subject was necessarily constrained by law and represented, rather than actually present, in political institutions. Yet, an important link was created between the people governed by a rightful constitution, as an expression of their rational autonomy, which in turn justified the independence of states, limiting republican government to the domestic sphere and making the international a distinct political space. In many ways this understanding of democratic membership and the political subjects of 'the people' and 'the state' are preserved today, as are Kant's reliance upon claims regarding the pacific nature of democratic government progressively realised.

The democratic citizen, as the individual rights-holder of liberal theory, bound in common cause with the nation, is assumed to be distinctly rational, opposed to wasteful and destructive wars, interested in prosperity and peace and able to hold the power of the state to account. Literature on the democratic peace is populated with such characters, assumed to be an adequate stand-in for actual citizens (Doyle 1986). Where membership in the nation is linked with less desirable results the democratic subject is seen as distracted and deluded by the forces of nationalism and ethnic identity, which prevent the realisation of democracy (Snyder 2000). Where deeper social ties of democratic politics are acknowledged, such that the character of the citizen is given context and history, national identity is tamed and made to serve the peace and prosperity promised by participatory government. The people become a social body linked by common cause, shared history and cultural identity and their power an expression of a general will.[3] This common identity is seen as vital to progress and development, as is exemplified again and again in literature on state-building and development where ethnic, religious and tribal conflict undermines the democratic collective identity necessary to the modern nation-state, which is taken to be the proper end of political development, the final embodiment of moral and stable government.

The democratic state in the international realm receives further privilege in liberal internationalist thought. Taking inspiration from Kant's dreams of a perpetual peace, liberal thinking has assigned self-determination moral and political power, which gives virtuous and powerful democratic states distinct privilege in world politics (Ikenberry and Slaughter 2006a). These liberal hopes gave birth first to the League of Nations, and then the United Nations – though in a conflicted form, as principles of sovereign equality sit uneasily with standards of legitimate government based on liberal democratic standards within the UN charter and through later developments. This democratic privilege justifies projects of intervention, development, state-building and human rights protection, which in turn attempt to replicate democratic subjects – citizens, peoples and nation-states – bringing political life to a harmonious resolution within and without state boundaries. The recent debates over R2P bring this into focus as the document is claimed to add no new responsibility to the UN charter while also clearly making states responsible to their people. While the privilege accorded to liberal democratic powers and the faith of internationalists in the power of multilateral institutions is often critiqued, these criticisms are rarely articulated in terms of the assumptions about democratic politics upon which they are based. Individual citizens are not actual parties to a contract, the people are never a given social identity and the state is not unambiguously the only or best space for democracy – but to admit these facts puts the privilege accorded to 'the people' within the state, as well as the 'nation-state' as their representative, into question.

Liberal cosmopolitans expose a tension in democratic thought by playing upon an important dissonance hidden in this harmonious score. If the individual's moral rights justify democratic government, how is the exclusion of national democracy legitimate? Especially in our contemporary age when the forces that affect individuals extend beyond the confines of the nation-state, it seems that democratic subjects and membership are evolving beyond nationalist and statist frames, or so cosmopolitans argue (Archibugi 2008). While cosmopolitanism remains a critical position, it has achieved a degree of dominance that warrants critical interrogation. This is all the more important because much cosmopolitan thinking depends upon questionable assumptions that there is a universal democratic subject, the rights-bearing individual, who is located, ultimately, in the political community of humanity. Both the universal citizen and the community of humanity are contested ideas that are all too often overwhelmed by the chorus of democracy's praises. David Held, in his chapter, reprises his influential defence of cosmopolitanism by challenging fundamental assumptions about the necessity of the state both in protecting individuals and enabling their political participation. While many of the chapters in this volume are critical of elements of Held's position, they share common ground on contesting fundamental assumptions of citizens, peoples and nation-states.

Chantal Mouffe provides a model for an alternative international politics, which has affinities with traditional pluralist international thinking but is a distinctive conclusion that advocates an agonistic understanding of democracy in world politics – moving beyond mere tolerance of different internal orders within states, which essentially drains international politics of ethical content, she encourages an agonistic democratic political orientation based in mutual respect through contestation. Following a related line of questioning Onuf and Onuf charge the democratic revolutions of the eighteenth and nineteenth centuries with fomenting a tempestuous and violent international politics caused by the inherent instability of democratic subjects. Citizenship, the people and the borders of the nation-state are all ambiguous and open to change, in a democracy failing to recognise that volatility is risky. For this reason they are critical of cosmopolitan thinkers who attempt to expand democracy without acknowledging that popular politics are almost never the rational and moral affair cosmopolitans predict. Likewise, Sassen looks to the historical emergence of democratic citizenship to reveal the revolutionary tendencies of democratic participation. Her chapter traces the formation of the legal subject in early democracies, highlighting that the initial democratic subject is much more a liberal bourgeoisie subject – a property owner, whose rights to ownership and contract are vital protections – than an equal democratic subject. She illustrates this point by highlighting the way in which the labouring class was disadvantaged by the construction of legal subjects in early democratic states.

Further, Aradau and Huysmans argue that the mobility of the masses, of the mob, was as important to the development of democracy as the establishment of a universal rights-bearing subject. The mob not only provides one of the key bases for the development of democracy by disrupting the political order before it can be tamed and institutionalised as 'the people' or 'the nation', but today the mobility of democratic masses retains its political force. The illegal movement of migrants and their attempts to exert democratic rights undermine the idea that the nation-state is natural or constant. In his chapter, Daniel Bray also undermines the territorial assumptions of democratic politics, but without resorting to conventional cosmopolitan strategies that presuppose a universal form of political community based on one's humanity. Instead, drawing on pragmatic philosophy, he points toward the development of democratic publics around particular issues and problems in world politics that either cannot be contained within state borders or by their nature exceed them. He looks at the way global responses to environmental crises generate concrete sites of democratic politics that are not tied to either the territorial state or a national identity. Finally, David Chandler provides a troubling critique of cosmopolitan approaches to democracy. In his chapter he faults both liberal and poststructuralist forms of cosmopolitanism for severing the democratic subject from any site of politics. While it might be the case that the assumed universality of the rights-bearing democratic subject is false and that the territorial state cannot effectively respond to social forces that shape contemporary life, the cosmopolitan response, Chandler suggests, is an evasion of the real question of what form and in what space will democratic politics take place if not within the sovereign state.

Conclusion

This critical project begins from the premise that ideas of democracy are not singular or simple, a prospect that does not sit comfortably with the contemporary role of democracy as a widely spread political currency that is exchanged for the political legitimacy to intervene, authorise, rule, excuse and defer in its name. Collectively, the pieces in the volume seek to show that the place and role of democracy in world politics is contingent, unstable and historically fragile, emerging through political struggle and disturbing the boundaries of world politics itself. As we have argued in this introduction, democracy and its emergence is both conceptually and historically associated with tumult and instability as well as peace, and has been suppressed by as well as survived alongside capitalism and liberalism, as its force and meaning have changed over time. Looking at the horizons of contemporary world politics, the new potential subjects of democracy – the agonistic mobs – emerge as simultaneously emancipatory and threatening in their demands, and the promises of progress and peace that were held out centuries ago look increasingly chimerical. Yet, it is this very instability and elusiveness that maintains democracy's perennial promise – that it may yet renew itself as a dynamic discourse of empowerment for the many and not the few. Through unsettling the ways in which power has appropriated the history and ideals of this agenda, we may yet be able to imagine alternatives.

Notes

1 We use the standard upper cases to denote the discipline as opposed to its subject matter.
2 Paradoxically, the war on terror was a key element in Bush's successful re-election campaign, suggesting that sometimes you can in fact be elected on the 'promise of war'.
3 A contemporary example of this line of thinking is found in Walzer (1983).

Part I
Historical interrogations

2 *Democracy in America* and democracy in the world today

Nicholas Onuf and Peter Onuf

What is the historical connection between contemporary conceptions of international relations and of democratic self-government? Scholars tend to treat the political relations of states and the political arrangements within states, including 'democracies', as distinct domains, subject to distinctive modes of analysis and assessment. We are hardly the first to contend that this distinction is untenable and misleading (see Gourevitch 2002 for a still useful summary). Beyond ritual affirmation of what has become a platitude of the moment, there has been some effort to show how these two domains relate to each other, chiefly through policy choices and constraints. Such analyses are consistent with the premises of positivist science, which presupposes that any observable whole consists of discriminate, causally connected parts. They disavow or disallow the possibility that some wholes are *made* whole and that their very existence gives them emergent properties. No analysis starting with parts can ever be complete; history confirms what analysis cannot show, that historicist scholarship can reassemble what positivist science must sunder.

New conceptions of politics, international and domestic, emerged at the same moment and as a whole. They began to do so in the 'Age of the Democratic Revolution', which took over the last decades of the eighteenth century, unleashed unimagined energies and redefined modernity. Having destroyed what contemporaries called the 'old regime', these same energies precipitated a political transformation that took additional decades for observers, such as Alexis de Tocqueville, to see clearly as a whole. A force to be reckoned with even after a century, the politics of transformation gave rise to claims of national self-determination and fostered democratic aspirations throughout the 'civilized' world and beyond (Palmer 1959–64; P. Onuf 2007). To this day, national and democratic aspirations constitute an indissoluble conceptual unity, however much betrayed in the political practices of leaders and misconstrued by scholars.

At the heart of this transformation was the emergence of the nation-state. Evident only in hindsight, conceptually without precedent, the nation-state consists of a particular people (or *nation*) with a territorially demarcated apparatus of impersonal rule (or *state*). The state is not just a container, as scholars often say, but functions as an exoskeleton for the nation as a 'living thing'. The functional fusion of nation and state simultaneously assured peoples their sovereignty by granting sovereignty to states in their relations and authorized governments to act on behalf of peoples formed into states. Nationalism and state-building are not transhistorical processes that happened to converge on the nineteenth century; neither is possible without the other.[1]

As long as governments can plausibly claim to enact the people's will, in the first instance by defending and promoting the state's vital interests, those governments may take a variety of forms. In the nineteenth century, these forms ranged from the revolutionary – in the case of the American and French republics – to the counter-revolutionary – the powers aligned against France and the reactionary regimes that sought to sustain a restored European peace after 1815. But all governments in the post-Revolutionary world had to meet the new 'national' and implicitly 'democratic' standard of legitimacy. Even as they sought to suppress Jacobins, 'red republicans', socialists and other professedly 'democratic' elements that endangered political and social stability, they appealed to a Rousseauian general will even as they ignored, repudiated or corrupted democratic procedures.

The counter-revolutionary outcome of revolutions in Europe obscures the profound impact of these upheavals on modern politics. States constituted a system – a liberal society of sorts – in the nineteenth century's early decades through their reciprocal recognition as independent states with rights and duties to each other.[2] The long nineteenth century confirmed the legitimacy of this system as governments behaved more or less predictably toward each other. How they behaved in the rest of the world also mattered, but only to the extent that other states, recognized as such, were adversely affected.[3] At least to a limited extent, these behaviours could be codified and controlled by the operations of the diplomatic system and according to the canons of international law because states were presumed to pursue their fundamental, long-term interests.

Because states and nations were (and still are) working wholes, state interests were understood to be those of their respective peoples. Less obviously, *interstate* relations were thought to become more lawful and predictable because they were *international* relations. Whatever liberal-minded jurists and tradition-bound diplomats envisioned later in the nineteenth century, these relations did not become more orderly and predictable. That the world of modern nation-states finally collapsed in general war and massive bloodshed in the next century has further obscured the common origins of modern conceptions of democracy and of international relations in the Revolutionary Age.

Our purpose in this chapter is to show how emerging ideas of democratic self-government did not, and could not, lead to the republican millennium – a new epoch of peace and prosperity – that revolutionaries once anticipated and peace theorists still await. To the contrary, democratization enabled the governments of modern nation-states to expand the coercive capacity of states in pursuit of interests they defined as vital for their nations' well-being. By doing so, democratization played an important part in unleashing 'the dogs of war' (D.A. Bell 2007). The history of the US, the first great self-professed modern democracy, illuminates the emergent properties of modern nations linked as states in a self-validating system of competitive, often hostile relations. As a visitor, Tocqueville understood that *Democracy in America* represented the shape of things to come as more and more peoples constituted themselves nations and nations became states.

Americans precociously embraced the characteristically modern idea of equality. These rights-conscious democrats were also nationalists, hyper-sensitive to slights and ever eager to assert their collective greatness (Tocqueville 2004: 106). Far from eschewing and transcending power, democratic Americans grasped the deeper logic of using government to mobilize abundant resources and turn them into coercive capabilities. It was no coincidence that the ascendancy of a militantly democratic political culture in Jacksonian America was also the era of 'manifest destiny'.

Tocqueville understood the connection: democracy made Americans a great and expansive nation, destined for continental, hemispheric and even global domination. 'There are today two great peoples on earth', he predicted, 'who, though they started from different points, seem to be advancing toward the same goal: the Russians and the Anglo-Americans.... Each seems called by a secret design of Providence some day to sway the destinies of half the globe' (Tocqueville 2004: 475–6). As a student of modern social psychology, Tocqueville recognized the deeper affinities between democracy and despotism. Human yearnings for equality could easily be 'degenerate' impelling 'the weak to bring the strong down to their own level' (Tocqueville 2003: 67). Modern democrats 'want equality in liberty', he concluded, 'but if they cannot have it, they want it still in slavery' (Tocqueville 2004: 584).

The aristocratic Tocqueville's forebodings about universal levelling and assertive foreign relations were leavened in America by republican principles and survivals of the old regime – decentralized constitutional government, the rule of law, the sway of preachers – that gave old liberties a new lease on life and suggested the broad outlines of his approach to the study of politics. The crucial point here is that Tocqueville agreed with democratic revolutionaries that they had wrought a fundamental political transformation, making the world modern by demolishing an old regime of hierarchy and privilege, but that he rejected their millennial hopes for the future. If equality was the defining fact of modern life, its ultimate implications were contingent, subject to various mitigating circumstances, 'hidden reefs' that might preserve the liberty of autonomous individuals (Tocqueville 2003: 306). In other words, Tocqueville recognized that democracy was the animating principle of modern nation-states, for better, as liberal internationalists hoped, and for worse, as political realists foresaw.

From Tocqueville's totalizing perspective, the Democratic Revolution transformed political life in and among the nation-states that constituted the civilized world. Like contemporary peace theorists and most liberals, Tocqueville linked the character of regimes with their behaviour in the sphere of interstate relations (*cf.* Waltz 1959: ch. 4). But the keen observer of American democracy was less sanguine – and more sanguinary – about the kind of world democratic nation-states would constitute, for he recognized the tremendous power they would be able to deploy.

In this as in so much else, Tocqueville was prescient. Consider the world we live in now. Efforts to foster democracy, whether in local communities or for the whole of humanity, founder on the indifference of their proponents to the conceptual unity of nation and state, democratic government and state system. It matters, but not enough, that many nations are imagined or indeed riven with genocidal violence, that many states are propped up or indeed fictions, that many governments are only nominally democratic or indeed exploited for personal gain, that the system is war-prone or indeed failing by virtue of its irrelevance to productive forces in the world economy, that the modern world has reached its limits or may indeed have already over-reached itself.

Disciplinary discourses

Political historians and scholars in International Relations (IR) look past the Revolutionary Age to discover the origins of their fields, whether in the post-Westphalian diplomatic system, Renaissance Italy or classical Greece. Similarly, students of democracy locate themselves in a field – one they call Political Theory and date back to the Greeks. Well before the Enlightenment, historians came to believe that writing about the past had to accord with a set of ruled practices making History a discipline; even before the discipline proclaimed itself a science, Enlightenment savants produced conjectural histories of human origins (Fasolt 2004; N. Onuf and P. Onuf 2006: 21–9). It is an open question whether IR has ever achieved disciplinary standing or remains, with Political Theory (a field that includes the history of political thought, normative political theory and so-called formal theory) a field of Political Science. While Political Science only became a discipline in the late decades of nineteenth century, IR emerged as an identifiable field of study only after the Second World War.[4]

As a broad generalization, scholars in the US who 'do' IR are trained in Political Science, and they share with most political scientists an attachment to the canons of positivist science. Scholars elsewhere are much more inclined to call IR a discipline, organize themselves into departments and forge alliances with Political Theorists who have historical and normative interests. Modern disciplines (or more precisely, modernist disciplines: Ross 1994) are more thoroughly institutionalized than fields and in some sense claim 'sovereignty' over their domains. They require pedigrees – 'invented traditions' that disguise their novelty, confer legitimacy and make disciplinary claims of independence credible (and thus make historians indispensable). By prescribing the proper subject of disciplined inquiry, genealogies proscribe other subjects and confirm a division of scholarly labour.[5] According to these disciplinary genealogies, the principles that define international relations were articulated *before* there were nations or states, properly speaking, just as democracy's conceptual underpinnings were articulated before the advent of modern democratic constitutions and governments.

The thrust of the new social sciences (we could just as well call them the new human sciences) was to develop general theories and test them with systematically gathered evidence. Historicist reservations were muted, and History was instead supposed to provide a comprehensive yet self-contained body of evidence to be mined for case studies and manipulated for statistical analyses. As positivist scholars searched for universal truths within disciplinary boundaries, they thought about History transhistorically, collapsing the distance between past and present, except insofar as they needed History for disciplinary validation. Paradoxically, new ways of thinking about History that were foundational to modern social science reinforced the tendency to minimize the significance of change in History: all effects have antecedent causes and their explanations are equivalent to predictions.

IR has exemplified these broad tendencies over the last few decades: in the name of science, the field (as we shall call it) is defined *theoretically* by reference to a set of conditions that must arise in a world of multiple sovereignties but could only arise in such a world. Scholars in the field call this condition anarchy; one measure of its theoretical significance is the striking inability of these scholars to imagine a significantly different history of international relations since the nineteenth century.[6] Not only does IR have a genealogy that supports its claim to uniqueness and independence by predating not just the field's late arrival (as we have remarked) but also the conditions that presumably warranted its development (Walker 1993: 26–49; N. Onuf 1998: 10–18). Even more, different versions of IR's genealogy support rival dominant theoretical orientations, or interpretive idioms, explaining how a system of nation-states actually works. One is political realism, which anchors its theorizing about anarchy's transhistorical effects in Thucydides, Machiavelli and Hobbes. The other is liberal institutionalism, which goes back to Grotius, Locke and Kant to show that anarchy is transhistorical but that the capacity to mitigate its effects is not.

Both idioms flourished in the nineteenth century, and liberalism even more in the aftermath of the First World War. Yet economic depression and another round of catastrophic war assured realism's dominance as IR emerged as a field. When realism had first emerged as an interpretive idiom in the wake of an earlier collapse of the European diplomatic system, it did so in a misleadingly 'conservative', even reactionary way. Just as old regime monarchies were ostensibly 'restored' after the French revolutionary wars, the axioms of old regime diplomacy gained a new lease on life. Yet appearances were fundamentally deceptive, for old forms and language fit awkwardly with liberal practices, national sentiments, revolutionary disturbances and democratic reforms.[7]

Monarchy could no longer be taken for granted as natural and legitimate in the post-Revolutionary era, but was increasingly seen as an 'old' and archaic form of rule, imposed on the peoples of Europe by force. Taught by experience, Tocqueville was acutely conscious that post-Revolutionary governments in France were artificial and ephemeral (Tocqueville 1987). He understood that old regime hierarchy and privilege had been demystified and demolished by the ascendant equality principle, and that the politics of class would have a chronically destabilizing effect in France and across Europe. He also recognized that states and societies could become realigned in ways that jeopardized liberty and subverted the virtues that had once flourished in the aristocratic old regime. Yet

Tocqueville was no reactionary, for he recognized that the Democratic Revolution was irreversible. Conservative efforts to 'restore' a lost world would necessarily fail.

By focusing obsessively on power relations among states, realist theorists and statesmen could succeed in imaginatively reviving and restoring the world that the French Revolution destroyed, if only for a time. Most crucial to this project was the characteristically modern move to draw a bright and impermeable line between domestic and foreign, a line that would be policed by the state. In the diplomatic domain, nation-states that commanded monopolies of force and legitimacy were in theory created equal, notwithstanding discrepancies in their actual power and domestic arrangements (ranging from the traditional monarchy to the liberal 'nightwatchman state'). Realists aspired to reconcile the tension between the rights of sovereign states and unequal state capacities. In doing so, they deployed the precepts of the old diplomacy in new ways: reason of state evolved from dynastic imperative into the enduring interest of a people or nation, represented by its government. The balance of power, once seen as the 'constitution' of an interdependent European republic or commonwealth, was now the tool of statecraft in an anarchic world. Finally, the 'law of nations', as natural law, was transformed into 'international law' – a minimal set of rules devised by governments to look like domestic law and make their day-to-day relations easier and more predictable (N. Onuf and P. Onuf 2006: 56–63).

The realists who did so much to foster IR's arrival as a field of study after the Second World War evinced a nostalgic affection for an era that stretched from Metternich to Bismarck. Realism has always drawn its support from Diplomatic History, which is to say, political history very narrowly construed. Conversely, diplomatic historians are typically realist in disposition and their acquaintance with IR as a field is largely confined to realist studies (Elman and Elman 2001). As realism's rival in making sense of international relations, liberal institutionalism has always turned to international legal scholarship for reinforcement. Just as diplomatic historians are realist in disposition, international lawyers are typically liberal in their assumptions and values.[8] However much realists may be surprised to learn that the nineteenth century was the 'golden age of international law' (Nussbaum 1954: 232), international lawyers have long indulged in this nostalgic sentiment.

That realists and liberals should be nostalgic for the same few decades has a simple explanation. Just as realists drew a bright and impermeable line between domestic and foreign, so too did liberals, and so must they both if they are to believe their joint claim that IR is an autonomous field. As we said, drawing the line is a characteristically modern move; in IR's genealogy, it is Hobbes's legacy. The bright line allows realists to carry on about Hobbesian insecurity from their refuge in liberal states and liberals to rationalize the uneven development of liberalism. For liberal legal scholars, states have rights and duties toward each other, just as people do within at least some states. Thanks to the liberal principle (correlative right and duty) of non-intervention, liberal states are protected from other states meddling in their affairs, in exchange for their not meddling in the affairs of those other states. Liberals assume the latter will become liberal as they benefit from a world economy operating on liberal premises and come to recognize the disproportionate benefits that liberal societies enjoy.

The liberal hope that free exchange will benefit everyone, however unevenly, and that prosperity will mitigate Hobbesian insecurity does not disallow some institutional support (even beyond the nightwatchman state we mentioned above). Within states, liberals codify the requisite institutional arrangements in constitutions, ideally consisting of a division and balance of powers – reflecting what is historically a republican preoccupation with the common good – to prevent governments from consolidating and abusing the power to interfere in people's individual pursuits. In such a constitution, itemized civil rights reinforce republican constitutional arrangements. Undergirding these rights is the principle of equality, however restricted in application, and its procedural entailments making people equal participants, in some way or another, in decisions on matters affecting them collectively. These procedures can vary considerably, but taken together they qualify a state's government as what we would call 'democratic' – or not.

The leading model for this liberal vision of a constitutional republic with a democratic government is the US and its Constitution, despite the complications arising from an elaborate federal design that raises questions about the 'fragmentation of sovereignty' and thus the very status of the federal union as a state (Tocqueville 2004: 187). As Tocqueville wrote in his discussion of the federal Constitution:

> The government of the Union rests almost entirely on legal fictions. The Union is an ideal nation that exists only in the mind, as it were,... for the sovereignty of the Union is so enmeshed with that of the states that it is impossible at first glance to see where the boundaries lie.
>
> (Tocqueville 2004: 186–7)

In this respect, the US blurs the line between the domestic and the international and therefore seems less than modern.

For realists, federal arrangements weaken the state in the modern world of states; for liberals, these arrangements may solve the size problem that republics have always faced but they also promote the uneven development of a modern liberal society.[9] In the liberal imagination, the appropriate model is a nation-state that takes the form of constitutional democratic republic. This is, needless to say, the grandest of legal fictions, subject to drastic simplification through the adoption of interchangeable and homogenizing labels: constitutional democracies, democratic nations, liberal democracies, democratic republics. If Britain has no formal constitution, then it is granted an informal constitution by inference. By contrast, the liberal international society of the nineteenth century had no constitution. To have said it is a republic would have been archaic. States are nations by stipulation. That states are equal stems from their being sovereign, and their participation in a liberal world of states is radically individuated. There is perhaps a crude sort of tribal democracy in their relations, but none of the democratic procedures that distinguish liberal societies in a civilized world.

Nineteenth-century liberals did, however, promote institutional developments to make a world of states a safe and prosperous place. International law was subject to codification and development, since the minimalist liberalism of the international system depended on an ordered set of unambiguous rules. Governments concluded bilateral trade agreements and extended most favoured nation status to counter the debilitating effects of unilateral mercantilist-realist policies. Governments also submitted themselves, if rarely, to the good offices and even the judgement of third parties. As the nineteenth century progressed and functional bureaucracies emerged within governments, these bureaucracies engaged in multilateral cooperation across state frontiers. By the end of the century, governments were assembling in highly visible public forums, giving some liberals hope that a world federal system was beginning to develop, with the primary organs of a modern republic incipient in periodic general conferences, arbitral panels and functional bureaucracies.

Whether the bright line thus compromised was a fantastic dream of multiplying fictions, or an inexorable feature of liberal prosperity, we shall never know. General war and great depression redirected liberalism domestically and so damaged it internationally that IR emerged as a realist enterprise. In this new field, international law ceased to be of interest, and international institutions were understood as instruments of or arenas for statecraft. Liberals who saw their own societies as constitutional democratic republican nation-states – or 'democracies', in the conventional shorthand – assumed other societies would adopt similar regimes as they 'modernized'. Even for liberals, the bright line hardly dimmed for half a century. There are democracies and there is a (more or less) liberal world stable enough for democracies to flourish.

This duality of democracies and liberal world ignores, even suppresses, the fundamental transformation of the Revolutionary Age: revolutions are popular events, the *demos* is unleashed; first come democratic nations; constitutions, republican institutions, and interlaced liberal economies follow in train; a still minimalist international system is anything but stable, even if the need for stability is the one thing realists and liberals seem to agree on. Nothing illustrates liberal amnesia better than democratic peace theory. In the 1980s, liberals suddenly discovered that democracies do not make war with each other (thanks mostly to Doyle 1983) and rather fancifully attributed this insight to Kant, who was, after all, no 'democrat' in any contemporary sense of the term. Not only does this claim run liberalism, republican arrangements and democratic procedures together, it presumes that they operate in tandem only *within* states; insofar as they do, then a minimalist liberal world will be safe for 'democracies' without any danger of becoming a constitutional democratic republic. The policy implications are clear enough: export democratic procedures, and the tail shall wag the dog and pacify the pack.

Democratic revolution, liberal world

Amnesiac democratic peace theorists betray their impatience with the modestly progressive, incrementalist predilections of liberal institutionalists. In their eagerness to proclaim the ascendancy of the liberal, capitalist democratic form of government and the new era of peace and prosperity that will inevitably follow, the peace theorists echo the millennial language of democratic revolutionaries two centuries earlier. These Revolutionaries also imagined that toppling the old regime of inequality, privilege and despotic power would bring history to an end. They were similarly impatient with the institutional infrastructure that stabilized relations and limited conflicts among the great powers, convinced as they were that the 'aristocratic' old regime was the root of all evil, including the chronic warfare that afflicted the poor peoples of Europe. Regime change was therefore their great panacea. In a new world of self-governing republics, war would no longer be the prime instrument of statecraft. As international boundaries ceased to be frontiers between belligerent powers, the bright line between foreign and domestic would disappear and old regime fiscal-military states would wither away.

Visions of world peace in the Revolutionary Age accompanied and justified the massive mobilization of military force that demolished the diplomatic system of the old European 'commonwealth' or 'republic' even as it transformed the regimes of revolutionary and counter-revolutionary states. Contemporary peace theorists honour their Revolutionary predecessors by embracing Kant, ripping him out of this revolutionary context and imagining that the conditions he stipulated for peace have finally emerged, however belatedly (Mattes, 2011). The result of postponing the democratic millennium to the late twentieth century is, yet again, to overlook the fundamental transformations of the Revolutionary Age and the connections between democratic experiments, nation-state formation and modern war. The Democratic Revolution is thus consigned to the dustbin of history, with its leading lights accorded places of honour in a long tradition of theorizing *toward* the democracy we have finally begun to achieve.

Teleological fantasies about democracy's triumph and the end of history are predicated on forgetting what was so clear to those who lived through the Revolutionary Age or to those who, in its aftermath, sought to make sense of the world it had made. For Tocqueville, 'democracy' – the ascendancy of the equality principle and the levelling of old regime hierarchies and distinctions it entailed – was the defining and irreversible fact of the modern world. Democracy was not a vision of a blessed future state, a work in progress to be realized by suitably civilized, enlightened and prosperous peoples in the fullness of time. The principle of equality was instead the defining, 'providential fact' of the modern world: 'it is universal, it is lasting and it constantly eludes human interference; its development is served equally by every event and every human being and all events as well as all men contribute to its progress' (Tocqueville 2003: 15). Democracy has never been a neutral term. Yet in Tocqueville's day, it did not carry the normative baggage that liberal institutionalists and constitutionalists now impute to it as they imagine an emergent condition, with equality linked to rights, rule of law and limited government.

Today's liberals may think themselves 'democrats', but this is only because they avert their gaze from the Democratic Revolution. They focus instead on contingent, epiphenomenal developments that were precociously modelled in the US, cherishing what were in fact survivals of the old regime. They fetishize constitutions, especially the federal Constitution, and the procedural entailments that *make* citizens equal under the law, overlooking the release of popular political energy that destroyed the old regime.

Despite his progressive sentiments, Tocqueville would have had little patience with these liberals.[10] He eschewed the top-down approach that comes naturally to IR theorists who *begin* their analysis – beyond the bright line – with the sovereign state, nominally equal to others, invoking notions of progress to imagine the ultimate emergence of their fantasy world. And it might be said of constitutionalists (on the other side of the line) that they begin with the 'fiction' of the sovereign people giving itself a higher, fundamental law, and therefore constraining its own revolutionary action against existing or future inequalities (Morgan 1988). In both cases, 'democracy' is immobilized, displaced to the future or to a founding moment in the past.

Democracy for Tocqueville was a dynamic, irresistible force, rising from the people. The US was destined to be a 'great nation' (a formula Tocqueville used repeatedly; see, e.g. Tocqueville 2003: 36, 44, 186, 777) because it was democratic, not because of the brilliant design of the federal Constitution drafted at Philadelphia in 1787. Travelling through the US during a period of escalating sectional tensions in the 1830s, Tocqueville recognized that the 'federal government is growing weaker by the day'. The union was 'an accident' and 'will last only as long as circumstances' remained favourable. 'By creating order and peace', the union had 'brought about its own decline' and 'a single revolution, a change in public opinion, might shatter it forever'.

Yet democracy would survive, he concluded, for 'the republic has deeper roots' (Tocqueville 2003: 464, 454, 464). The republican form of government was natural to the Americans ('every village is a kind of republic, used to self-government') and 'the current trend in American society seems to me increasingly toward democracy' (Tocqueville 2003: 454, 469).

> One should not, therefore, believe that it is possible to halt the rise of the English in the New World. The fragmentation of the Union and the ensuing war in this continent, the abolition of the republic and the resulting tyranny, may hold back their expansion, without being able to prevent the attainment of their inevitable destiny. No power on earth can block the advance of these immigrants to those fertile spaces which stand open everywhere to industry and which offer a refuge from every disaster. Future events of whatever kind will remove from Americans neither their climate, their inland waters, their great rivers, nor their fertile soil. Bad laws, revolutions, and anarchy

cannot destroy their taste for prosperity or that spirit of enterprise which seems the particular character of their race, nor can they snuff out completely the knowledge which lights their way.

(Tocqueville 2003: 482)

America was great because it was democratic, despite – not because of – the Constitution. The day would come, Tocqueville concluded,

> when North America will be home to 150,000,000 people, all equal to one another, all members of the same family, sharing the same point of departure, the same civilization, the same language, the same religion, the same habits, the same mores, and among whom thought will circulate in the same form and take on the same colors.
>
> (Tocqueville 2004: 475)

The equality principle, Tocqueville famously predicted, would give rise to mass society, an irresistible process of homogenization leading to unprecedented concentrations of power. This was what the advent of democracy meant for the modern world 'Everything else is doubtful, but this much is certain. And this is something entirely new in the world, the implications of which imagination itself cannot grasp' (Tocqueville 2004: 475).

That Tocqueville should give such short shrift to the federal Constitution exposes the conceptual incoherence at the heart of modern theorizing about democracy. Liberal institutionalists and democratic peace theorists confuse and conflate democracy and liberty, equality and rights. In Tocquevillian terms, they fail to grasp the implications of a Democratic Revolution that changed everything, focusing instead on the more or less rapid progress of free, constitutional and ultimately democratic government across the centuries – and across the great rupture of the Revolutionary Age. But as Tocqueville insisted, the history of liberty – the Whiggish narrative centring on the rule of law, constitutional limits on government and the vindication of rights – should *not* be confused with the history of democracy. Indeed, his fundamental point was that the convergence of these two narratives in America was fortuitous and contingent.

Long before independence, Anglo-American colonists enjoyed an extraordinary degree of liberty and equality under a community-based common law tradition and municipal institutions; they enjoyed 'the results of the democratic revolution which we are undergoing without having endured the revolution itself' (Tocqueville 2003: 23). In Tocqueville's France egalitarian impulses demolished the old regime and jeopardized the liberties that aristocrats had jealously defended against centralizing monarchs. But in America, the 'taste for freedom' was not a 'vague and ill-defined feeling for independence. It was not based upon the passions of disorder but on the contrary love of order and the law...' (Tocqueville 2003: 85).

The preservation of liberty was Tocqueville's great concern precisely because he recognized that it was at such risk under the new democratic dispensation.

The anatomist of modern democracy in its first great manifestation looked beneath America's constitutional exoskeleton for the fevered pustules of despotic power that followed so organically from the equality principle. Constitutional government, especially at the highest, federal level, was much less important than the ways in which the rule of law and associational, self-governing impulses arose from the people. The character of the people, not their constitutional contrivances, could alone explain the extraordinary coexistence and reciprocal reinforcement of equality and liberty in America. Tocqueville's analysis thus moved up, from political culture, to show how egalitarian impulses could be harnessed and 'the passions of disorder' channelled into productive enterprises. Liberty-loving Americans could be – or, rather, could think of themselves as being – 'equal' without turning their world upside down, or revolutionizing property relations, or murdering aristocrats – or emancipating their many slaves.

Tocqueville was the first great historian of the Democratic Revolution. His deeply personal sense of the profound and irrevocable change that had taken place in his own world inoculated him against both revolutionaries' millennial fantasies and reactionaries' restorationist nostalgia. More significantly, for our purposes, Tocqueville eschewed the complacent meliorism of liberal constitutionalists and institutionalists. Democracy would not emerge in the fullness – or at the end of – time. The genie was out of the bottle: 'equality of social conditions' was the 'factor which generated all others', the 'fundamental fact' shaping the history of America and the world, for better and for worse (Tocqueville 2003: 11). And the emergent democratic form was certainly not, as liberals imagined it, the antithesis of concentrated power. Even in the US, where for peculiar historical reasons 'individualism' flourished and ordinary citizens were jealous of their rights (Tocqueville 2003: 587–9), the equality principle facilitated unprecedented concentrations of power – as would become so abundantly clear in the carnage of the Civil War.

The age of the Democratic Revolution ushered in the world of modern 'democratic' nation-states, capable of wreaking unimaginable havoc on each other and on themselves. The bright line that Tocqueville drew between the lost world of the old regime and the new democratic world enabled him to see clearly how democracy changed everything, not only domestically – within increasingly competent and coercive nation-states – but also in the relations of states. In other words, Tocqueville could imagine a larger whole within which newly imagined and articulated parts – supposedly radically distinct and autonomous, but in fact reciprocally constituted – would emerge with such world-making clarity. It is ironic that Tocqueville's brilliant insights in *Democracy in America*, his vision of the simultaneous emergence of national-democratic regimes and a geopolitics of expansive 'great nations' contending for domination, should have been obscured and superseded by self-congratulatory – or now, more fashionably, self-loathing – American exceptionalists, obsessed with their own character.

Perhaps we can blame Abraham Lincoln for this outcome, for it was Lincoln who offered Americans a narrative of their history in which the cataclysmic rupture of the Civil War was smoothed over, mass slaughter justified and republican government – 'the last best, hope of earth' (Lincoln 1862) – vindicated. The nationalist Lincoln distinguished the nation from its purpose, pointing it toward a long-distant end of history when 'rivers of blood' would cease flowing and peace and prosperity would reign across the world. He famously urged his countrymen to identify the cause of the rump Union with the new nation's 'democratic' origins in 1776, when Jefferson penned the Declaration of Independence. 'From these honored dead', Lincoln told his audience on the battlefield of Gettysburg,

> we take increased devotion to that cause for which they here gave the last full measure of devotion; that we here highly resolve that the dead shall not have died in vain; that the nation shall, under God, have a new birth of freedom; and that Governments of the people, by the people, and for the people, shall not perish from the earth.
>
> (Lincoln 1863)

Americans could tell themselves that their democratic experiment – exceptional, precocious, endangered, but emerging victorious in a great war – defined them as a people. They did not constitute a mere 'nation' among other nations, but instead embodied and represented those hopes for a more peaceful, freer, better world that the founding fathers imagined and liberals still cherish. Lincoln thus defined democracy and saving the Union in millennial terms, casting himself as the 'humble instrument in the hands of the Almighty, and of this, his almost chosen people, for perpetuating the object of that great struggle', the American Revolution (Lincoln 1861).

What Americans do not tell themselves is that the Civil War itself expressed the genius of their democracy, unleashing the disorderly 'passions' of a deeply fractured, liberty-loving people. The price of northern victory was the destruction of 'the Union as it was' and the violation of democratic procedures and of the expressed will of the peoples of the seceding states. That these things should be done in the name of a people that no longer existed is the defining fiction, the central myth, of American self-understanding. And this idea of the democratic nation subordinated liberty to power: 'let us have faith that Right, Eternal Right makes might', Lincoln exhorted his fellow Americans before the war began, 'and as we understand our duty, so do it!' (Lincoln 1860).

Democracy today

In the last twenty years, 'democracy' has been a byword, or perhaps a catchword, in public discourse. As related developments, the demise of the Soviet Union and the rediscovery of 'civil society' contributed to this phenomenon. The alleged triumph of liberalism and apparent democratization of many states fuelled it, as did the policy, adopted by the US government, of exporting democracy (understood, of course, as democratic procedures). Many commentators believe globalization has given democratization its impetus. The globalization of civil society seems to have enabled the human rights movement, long stalled by government resistance, to punch holes finally in the legal wall between domestic and international affairs. Liberal lawyers began advocating 'democratic governance' as a human right (Franck 1992); liberal scholars in IR could worry about 'democracy-enhancing multilateralism' (Keohane *et al.* 2009).

In light of these developments, quite a few scholars – both liberal and critical – in IR and Political Theory turned their attention to ethical issues transcending national frontiers, in the process talking to each other as never before. Civil war and intervention gave longstanding ethical concerns a fresh urgency. So did all the talk prompted by globalization about the decline of the state and 'erosion' of sovereignty. When Chris Brown published *Sovereignty, Rights and Justice: International Political Theory Today* (2002), he could intimate that 'international political theory' had achieved the recognition he had called for in *International Relations Theory: New Normative Approaches* (1992). Today, recognition of International Political Theory (IPT) as a (sub)field has led, as a measure of institutionalization, to a biennial conference and eponymous journal, where a new generation of scholars is finding its voice.

As we have emphasized, scholars create genealogies to legitimate newly proclaimed fields of study. Brown seized on a particularly attractive possibility by tracing cosmopolitan and communitarian threads in the history of political thought and presenting them as alternative ways of thinking about the reach of ethical responsibilities in a world of states (C. Brown 1992: Part I; also see Thompson 1992, Boucher 1998). The cosmopolitan-communitarian binary gives IPT some historical heft and situates its concerns in the familiar framework of a debate (C. Brown 1999; Cochran 1999). Globalization provided an incentive for doing so: with the presumed erosion of sovereignty, the global and the local offer up competing points of departure as well as a novel dynamic displacing the relations of states in a minimally liberal international society with the thicker flows of a pluralist civil society now global in scale.

No less a figure than Aristotle anchors cosmopolitanism and communitarianism as entwined genealogies and endows the cosmopolitan-communitarian debate with a suitably grand stage. On the one side is the Aristotelian mantra that the whole is greater than the sum of the parts; on the other is Aristotle's conviction that the size of the whole always matters in politics. Thus staged, the possibility, properties and limits of democracy are inescapable themes for debate, given Aristotle's compelling claim that democracies must have few enough citizens that they can all knowledgeably participate, as equals, in public life. If the *demos* is a self-sufficient whole, a community fixed in place and scale, a republic is an institution first, subject to imaginative extension not by Aristotle but by his Stoic successors.

Standard treatments of cosmopolitanism start with the universal city of the Stoics and Stoicism's early modern florescence but skirt seventeenth-century humanist utopians before moving on to Kant. Not only do contemporary cosmopolitans dwell on a few sparse passages in Kant's work, they insist on Kant, not

Locke, Constant or Mill, as liberalism's most authentic voice – one that is globally aware and ethically arresting (Bohman and Lutz-Bachmann 1997). Leaping from Kant to the present avoids any pressure to consider liberalism's vicissitudes over the intervening two centuries. Even more conveniently, it affords cosmopolitan liberals an opportunity to bring democracy into the picture, as if the preceding two centuries had settled any possible question of what democracy entailed. Today we see global democracy held up as a worthy goal in political practice and the inevitable end of history.[11] As always, liberal instrumentalism and progressive teleology fold together in righteous certainty.

Cosmopolitanism is the stronger thread in IPT's entwined genealogy, communitarianism the weaker thread. The Stoics had no counterpart; tribalism and the hordes of Asiatic despoilers had no defenders. Early modern republicans rediscovered the size problem, but it is Rousseau's conception of the general will that exposes Political Theory to the full implications of the size problem: beyond a certain size and without established procedures for participation, consent can only be imputed. The republican Rousseau is to communitarianism what the republican Kant is to cosmopolitanism, but with greater justification. Yet Rousseau thought democracy was impractical – indeed 'impossible' – at any scale.

> In the strict sense of the term, a genuine Democracy has never existed, and never will exist. It is against the natural order that the greater number govern and the smaller number be governed.... Besides, how many things impossible to combine does not this Government presuppose? First, a very small State where the people is easily assembled, and where every citizen can easily know the rest; second, great simplicity of morals to preclude excessive business and thorny discussions; next, much equality of ranks and fortunes, without which equality of rights and authority could not long subsist: Finally, little or no luxury...
>
> (Rousseau 1997: 91)

After Rousseau, the communitarian genealogy typically turns to Hegel, the *Volk* and the Romantic German idealism of *Gemeinschaft*, whether expressed in reactionary or radical terms, and ends there. While this genealogy may give critical theory an entrée to IPT, its large effect is to focus attention on the nation as a fictive community but eliminate any sense that such a nation is, as a product of the Democratic Revolution, necessarily an embodiment of the *demos*. The Rousseauian Tocqueville would have provided just this sense, yet he is conspicuously missing from IPT's communitarian genealogy. Meanwhile, Political Theory has itself seen a communitarian revival, dating from the 1980s (Bellah *et al.* 1985; Etzioni 1998). In this movement, Tocqueville is more honoured than read (but see Taylor 1998 for an exception), the excesses of liberalism provide a foil, democracy is held up as an appealingly unspecific ideal and the nation is taken for granted as a frame of reference.

To the extent international relations come into view, it does so as a warrant for claims that a 'global normative synthesis' is under way (Etzioni 2004). The communitarian revival thus provides IPT with a ready-made rationale for a debate with cosmopolitanism but few resources for staking out a distinctive position. Instead contemporary cosmopolitans and communitarians read the state of the world in strikingly similar terms. Their genealogies converge and their debate – a cosmopolitan affair, it must be said – shows little sign of intercommunal incommensurability.

Seyla Benhabib's debate with Jeremy Waldron, Bonnie Honig and Will Kymlicka (Benhabib 2006) offers a telling illustration. Benhabib is a leading cosmopolitan thinker with a deep background in critical theory; her Tanner lectures afforded Honig an opportunity to put forward a variant of the cosmopolitan position and Waldron and Kymlicka communitarian critiques. Yet the second of Benhabib's two lectures pre-empted her interlocutors by emphasizing the interaction of 'democratic iterations' and universally valid cosmopolitan norms (2006: 47–9) *and* 'the interdependence – never frictionless but ever promising – of the local, the national, and the global' (2006: 74). In Benhabib's synthesis, the local and global are conceptually anchored by their respective genealogies. By contrast, the national is, conceptually speaking, an empty set, into which popular concerns and government responses are relegated for inconclusive discussion.

What does '*L'Affaire du Foulard*' (Benhabib 2006: 51–61) say about the effects of democratic iterations on France as a constitutional democratic nation-state? 'We have to learn to live with the otherness of others whose ways of being may be threatening to our own', Benhabib answers. 'How else can moral and political learning take place, except through such encounters in civil society?' (Benhabib 2006: 60). The cosmopolitan-communitarian synthesis encourages a familiar kind of liberal utopianism. As such it reinforces realist scepticism. More to the point, it ignores the normative power and lasting effects of the Democratic Revolution. World-making is an historical process, marked by utopian dreams, liberal escapism, revolutions few and far between. The Democratic Revolution may have ended in 1815, or perhaps not until 1848, or 1917 when Lenin came to power, or 1949 when the Chinese Peoples' Republic was formed. Yet its great achievement – a world of popular republics, of constitutionally democratic nation-states – lives on. Every democratic iteration invokes the Revolution and affirms its power.

Democratic nations are here to stay, but they are hardly stable or secure in their constitutional arrangements. As Tocqueville saw so clearly, they are susceptible to factionalism, sectionalism, sectarianism, and what we have come to call class struggle. Republican institutions and liberal ways can reduce these fevers, but plebiscitary democracy and inter-nation tensions can make them worse. Just as civil society flourishes in good times, the breakdown of the civil order too often accompanies hard times and frightening social changes. We remind ourselves, *sub voce*, that the *demos* is vulnerable to demagoguery and despotism. We forget that civil war is a recurring feature of political life in democratic nations and, not just coincidentally, the liberal world (N. Onuf and P. Onuf 2006: 343–52).

Rousseau saw this at the dawn of the Democratic Revolution: 'there is no government as subject to civil wars and intestine turmoil as Democratic or popular Government, because there is none which tends so constantly to change its form' (Rousseau 1997: 92). Tocqueville anticipated civil war in the US. The *demos* unleashed in 1848, he walked the streets of Paris a frustrated politician amid 'scenes of civil war' (1987: 167). To paraphrase one of Tocqueville's contemporaries, we might even say that civil war is a mere continuation of democratic politics by other means.

Notes

1 The literature on nations and nation-building is voluminous. For further discussion and citations see P. Onuf (2004). Much of the literature on the state is not just critical but denies its conceptual relevance to modern political theory. Here see Bartelson (2001). Also of interest is recent discussion of the state (implicitly, nation-state) as a person. See 'Forum on the State as a Person' (2004).

2 See further N. Onuf and P. Onuf (2006), where we argue that the liberal society of nations served as a model for incipiently liberal societies, and not the other way around.

3 Again there is a vast literature, in this case much of it partisan. A good place to start is Bull and Watson (1984).

4 On Political Science, and the social sciences generally, see Porter and Ross (2003), Part II; on Political Theory, see Gunnell (1993); on International Relations, see Schmidt (1997).

5 It should be clear that we use the term *genealogy* in a general way, and not to signal an affinity for Michel Foucault's Nietzschean conception of genealogy.

6 No one makes this clearer than Waltz (1979). Against anarchy as an interpretive key, see N. Onuf (1989). On the unwillingness to imagine a different history, see Lebow (2010).

7 Here, of course, we follow Henry Kissinger (1957). For the decades following see Schroeder (1994).

8 See Koskenniemi (1989), where the genealogy of international law is presented as a 'doctrinal history' tied to liberal political thought from the seventeenth century on. We should also point out that the field of International Law and the subject of international law were so thoroughly co-constituted, at least in the nineteenth century, as to be indistinguishable.

9 On the size problem in republican theory, see P. Onuf and N. Onuf (1993: 74–87). For Tocqueville's perceptive comments on the size problem, see (2004: 179–85). On uneven development in the antebellum US, see N. Onuf and P. Onuf (2006: Part II).

10 The best modern study is Brogan (2006). Wolin (2001) is invaluable as an intellectual biography.

11 Indicatively, there is a vast recent literature on global democracy. In addition to what can be found in this volume, see Bohman (2007), Archibugi (2008).

3 Democracy in international society

Promotion or exclusion?

Ian Clark

Historically, international society's attitude towards democracy has been highly ambivalent. To the extent that it has acknowledged its significance at all, it has held that democracy is a 'unit level' phenomenon, applicable to the states as members, rather than a feature to be incorporated directly at the 'system level'. This ambivalence has, no doubt, reflected an appreciation that otherwise democracy creates acute tensions for international society. It is prone to manifest itself as a form of exclusion, even when international society might have a preference for inclusion. This chapter addresses the sources of international society's reticence, and the tensions to which its promotion of democracy currently gives rise. It is now commonplace for national governments routinely to affirm their intent to 'continue to promote and support the spread of democracy' (UK Cabinet Office 2008: 49), and to act collectively to do so. Is this wholly unproblematic?

This theme, in addition, provides an interesting case study of the complex interplay between normative development, and the role within this of shifts in the material and ideological balance of power. It raises intriguing questions about the extent to which democracy has become a more widespread, and potentially universal, norm within international society, as a result of a process of normative deepening and integration. Alternatively, does its current dissemination rather reflect favourable balances of power that have allowed the core states of the western system to socialize international society into their own preferred value system, both by encouraging and rewarding emulation, and also by punishing via forms of social exclusion?

In a stimulating piece written a decade ago, James Mayall explored 'Democracy and International Society', and asked two key questions: 'Can the internal constitution of states be determined by international society, and can international society itself be democratized' (Mayall 2000: 62)? This discussion is narrower – democracy *in* international society – and is confined to how it has itself practised concerns about democracy. To that extent, it addresses the first question only, since international society has largely eschewed the second, or at best offered a half-hearted response through the terms of the former. International society, by addressing democracy *within* states, has seemed to hope that the issue of democracy *among* them might become redundant. There are, of course, many other concerns about democracy that impact on international relations: whether 'domestic' democracy is being eroded by transnational conditions, and may be in need of 'cosmopolitan' supplements (Held 1995; Holden 2000; Marchetti 2008), or about the potential for 'transnational discursive democracy' (Dryzek 2006). These are not the focus of this chapter.

Membership and exclusion

International society's initial commitment to a sovereignty-based pluralism precluded any overt expression of interest in the domestic constitution of states, democratic or otherwise. However, even as these concerns did first begin to impinge internationally during the nineteenth century, international society remained diffident. So robust was its reticence, that its great charters of the twentieth century – the League Covenant and the UN Charter – made no explicit mention of democracy (Rich 2001: 20). However, this certainly does not mean that a commitment to democracy had no impact on the conception of the League, or on its practice. On the contrary, its membership policy was deeply imbued with this concern, and for the first time the resulting tension became apparent. Persuaded that autocracy was the source of war, and that only democracies could be receptive to the judgement of world public opinion – and so able to honour their commitments as members – Wilson initially sought the application of a de facto criterion of democracy as a test for League membership. There were suggestions that the new organization be named a League of Democracies (on its recent reincarnation, see below). On 28 December 1918, Wilson had voiced his view that the League should support the spread of democracy, 'and, eventually, comprise only democratic nation-states' (Cohrs 2006: 32). The French, unusually, were happy enough to concur with this particular principle, and set out in their own blueprint for the League the condition that 'no nations can be admitted to the League other than those which are constituted as States and provided with representative institutions such as will permit their being themselves considered responsible for the acts of their own Governments' (R. S. Baker 1923: 153). This conveniently rationalized the exclusion of Germany (until its future bona fides could be demonstrated), as well as Bolshevik Russia. Unfortunately, the League's new project of collective security (replacing a balance of power by a community of power) required an *inclusive* principle to have any hope of effectiveness. The League could work only if all were on the inside, otherwise the outsiders would simply reconstitute a balance of power (as, indeed, they promptly did). The sotto voce implementation of a preferential policy of democratic membership had at once cut across this fundamental logic of the new security system.

Wilson's policy heralded a new trend for the twentieth century. I have previously referred to this as 'another double movement' (Clark 2001b). As a counterpart to Karl Polanyi's analysis of the exposure to the market, and the reactive quest for forms of social and political protection, a similar movement can be discerned within the geopolitical arena (Polanyi 1944). For Polanyi, the great formative force during the nineteenth century had been the vulnerability of society, under industrial capitalism, to the full effects of the unregulated market. In reaction, forms of state welfarism and interventionism were developed by the middle of the twentieth century to cushion its effects. The 'double movement' thus consisted in the fact that 'markets spread all over the face of the globe', but then, in response, 'a network of measures and policies was integrated into powerful institutions designed to check the action of the market' (Polanyi 1944: 76).

An analogous development took place in international relations. The first movement was the creation during the late nineteenth and first two-thirds of the twentieth centuries of an international society that had become fully global in scope. However, as a 'double movement' in reaction to this more inclusive society, there emerged also from within a thicker version, committed to a distinctive set of economic and political values. This alternative vision has, at least since 1919 but more vigorously since 1990, sought to fashion a solidarist international society, committed to the market and to liberal democratic principles. Arguably, these political principles were actively to be promoted as a form of 'protection' for the bloc of Western states now increasingly exposed to the vagaries and inconveniences of the open global political 'market', as it developed during the twentieth century.

What this brought out is the increasingly deep-seated tension between 'rule rationality' and 'value rationality' in international society. It highlights the growing incompatibility between international society's more overt commitment to a certain form of state, as appropriate for membership, and the divergent basis of its own pragmatic and pluralistic activities. The conundrum was how international society was to profess faith in a solidarist view of rightful membership, while simultaneously continuing to adhere to pluralist procedures for sanctioning collective international action. On the former, the explicit doctrine of international society now much more pointedly privileges state capacity for good governance, and democratic accountability and responsibility, and this is incorporated in a number of regional charters. On the latter, however, it tends still to operate on the pragmatic search for consensus, blind to the constitutional make-up of the individual states that form part of it. In this way, the substantive criteria for rightful membership now present a greater challenge to the procedural norms that continue to underpin international society. This magnifies the looming tension between international society's rhetorical preference for democracy as the constitutive form of the state, and its own inability to operate on that basis in undertaking international action. This connects with the idea, in Jack Donnelly's terminology, that there are now two categories of outlaw states: 'behavioural outlaws', who violate norms, and 'ontological outlaws' who are outlaws 'more for who they are than what they have done' (Donnelly 2006: 147). In its recent deployments, democracy has been used to foster the category of 'ontological outlaws', those found deficient for what they are rather than for what they have done. In that sense, some might emphasize the aggregate condition that 'there is no fully satisfactory Arab model of democracy' (Albright 2006: 219), rather than disaggregate the actual foreign policies pursued by individual Arab states.

The end of the Cold War: democracy and regulation

The end of the Cold War needs to be understood in this context, as one important stage in the attempted advancement towards a more overtly normative style of international society, as defined by the core states within it. It remains to be seen how successful this attempt will be in the longer term. An interesting question is how far this trend should be regarded as evidence of normative integration, or more as the consequence of the uneven distribution of state power resulting from the Cold War's end. The way democracy has manifested itself in this new situation is as a revised standard of civilization, as the appropriate test for recognition for membership (Gong 1984; C. Hobson 2008a; Keene 2002; Murphy 1999). In short, the geographical extension of international society that accompanied the zenith and subsequent decline of the imperial age has evoked a second and counter tendency in its normative intensification, emanating from its core. Thus viewed, international society is subject to an attempted 'reinvention' (Dunne 1998), and the end of the Cold War marked a critical phase in that development.

In an earlier work, the author suggested that the adoption of democracy as a fundamental norm of international society was part of the post-Cold War 'regulative' peace settlement: it provided evidence '*both* for normative change *and* for the exercise of state power' (Clark 2001a: 223). Collective subscription to liberal democratic principles was intended to entrench the new peace by regulating 'not simply the international behaviour of states, but the very nature of the states themselves, as the best guarantee of their compliance with the norms of the new order' (Clark 2001a: 235). Democracy promotion within the newly emerging states would thereby help consolidate the fortuitous pro-western shift delivered by the collapse of its Soviet protagonist.

There had been little possibility of elevating liberal democracy as a norm of international society during the course of the Cold War. By the early 1990s, however, a considerable transformation was visible. 'Today', we were told, 'democracy constitutes the ideological core of world order' (Olesen 2005: 109). Principles of liberal democracy had come routinely to be transfused to the periphery through international society's post-Cold War peacebuilding missions in conflict zones (Paris 2002). It was not just that democracy was more prevalent: it came to enjoy a new status as a now authoritative principle of international life. To illustrate the point, in the period from 1993 to 2000, the Security Council referred to democracy in fifty-three of its resolutions (Fox 2004: 69). In one ringing endorsement, it was typically suggested that the 'norm of democracy has achieved striking universality in the current international system' (McFaul 2004–5: 148). So much was this so that some began to speak confidently of an emerging norm of 'constitutional democracy as the only legitimate form of government' (M. H. Halperin 1993: 105).

The evidence for this promulgation of a more pronounced set of domestic legitimacy tests at the end of the Cold War is overwhelming. The concern with good governance went to the heart of the increasingly clear affirmation by international society of its belief in the liberal peace, not just as academic theory, but also as the basis of international policy. This was no sudden or radical innovation. Political conditionality, as a test for development aid, had already become established as part of the European Union's policy discourse during the 1980s, and was now presented as an explicit form of promotion of democratic and human rights norms (Youngs 2001). Such liberal democratic ideals became deeply embedded in international policies on economic development, in post-conflict reconstruction and nation-building, and also explicitly in those actual admissions that were to take place, to bodies such as NATO and the European Union (Stivachtis 2008). In these various cases, tests of an explicitly democratic nature were to be imposed on would-be members. There was evidence also that, in some regional settings, democracy was becoming more 'legalised' (Hawkins and Shaw 2008).

When the bell finally tolled for the end of the Cold War, the 'Charter of Paris for a New Europe' was agreed at a summit of the Conference on Security and Cooperation in Europe (CSCE) in 1990 (Clark 2007: ch. 7). It affirmed the intention of its signatories 'to build and strengthen *democracy as the only system of government of our nations*' (CSCE 1990: 3, emphasis added). This was a striking international declaration. In one memorable evocation, a prominent US delegate to the CSCE process pronounced 'a new public order for Europe' was being born (Buergenthal 1990). While the declaration palpably concerned the constitutional order *within* states, what was so momentous was that it took the form of a statement agreed *among* states. If there were thereafter to be an onus upon individual states to comply, it followed that there would be also an onus upon international society to hold them to account.

The Charter was symptomatic of much that was to come later, and heralded what the US National Security Strategy (2002) later called 'a single sustainable model for national success'. Other regional charters pronounced similarly. The Constitutive Act of African Union declared its objective to 'promote democratic principles and institutions'. The Inter-American Democratic Charter, adopted by the Organization of American States in 2001, declared in Article 1 that 'the peoples of the Americas have a right to democracy and their governments have an obligation to promote and defend it'. These statements seemed to vindicate the perception that the end of the Cold War had witnessed the advance of liberal democracy, not just as a political fact, but also as an authoritative normative principle, incurring commensurate international responsibilities for its protection.

Many commentators certainly viewed the major symbolic importance of the Paris summit in this light. It has been described as providing 'the source of an overarching constitutional order that sets the standard to which all national legal and political institutions must conform' (Bobbitt 2002: 638). According to its prescriptions, domestic political arrangements would henceforth be 'linked to international legitimacy': these could no longer be left to the individual states themselves to determine (B. Cronin 2003: 129). Compliance with the wishes of international society on the matter of implementing democratic practices now provided 'the international standard for regimes wishing to integrate into the global order' (Schmitz and Sell 1999: 36), and hence the Charter was regarded as an 'attempt to make the quality of a state a precondition for its participation in European international society' (Flynn and Farrell 1999: 531). In this way, international society would take on the responsibility directly to monitor the 'rightful membership' of the individual states. Even more graphically, the norm of democracy agreed at Paris has been depicted in the following historical terms:

> The resulting Charter of Paris for a New Europe was notable not only for officially ending the Cold War, but also for establishing new standards on internal governance and domestic politics. In particular, the Charter's declaration [on democracy] ... suggested a consensus around principles of state organization unseen since the Congress of Vienna in 1815.
>
> (B. Cronin 2003: 128)

What was the source of this transition? Was it normative, or merely power political? One suggestion links it to developments in thinking about international law, and especially with respect to a legal entitlement to democratic access. This was a conspicuous development of the rules of rightful membership in a democratic direction (Clark 2005: 181). It rested on the argument developed by a number of writers, but in particular by Thomas Franck. 'Both textually and in practice', he had contended, 'the international system is moving towards a clearly defined democratic entitlement, with national governance validated by international standards and systematic monitoring of compliance' (Franck 1995: 139).

Franck had noted the expression of such a norm within the regional setting, but was at that time unprepared to maintain that it applied globally (Franck 1992: 78). In contrast, writing subsequently of the Vienna Declaration of 1993, Buergenthal was by then adamant that this amounted precisely to such an extension:

> Whereas [the Copenhagen] document laid the foundation for the establishment of a democratic European public order, the Vienna Declaration can be read to have done the same for the world as a whole ... [T]he absence of democracy in a state is today in itself a violation of the human rights of its population and ... the international community has the right for that very reason to concern itself with efforts designed to remove obstacles to its democratisation.
>
> (Buergenthal 1997: 714–15)

To the extent that this interpretation was valid, it suggested transmutation of a principle of domestic legitimacy into a principle of international legitimacy: it is because of the individual's right to democracy that international society has a duty to prescribe and monitor its implementation. The degree to which it does so is a measure of its own adherence to international norms.

In seeking to adopt a norm of universal democracy in the constitution of states, international society was venturing into a terrain that was alien, and potentially hostile, to it. Unsurprisingly, it has tried to sweeten this bitter pill by packaging it within the more traditional normative preferences of international society. It can therefore serve as a good example, with respect to dissemination of new norms, of the 'finding that such efforts are more likely to be successful to the extent they can be grafted on to previously accepted norms' (Price 2003: 584). While the advocacy of democracy may be rooted in an increasingly accepted claim to an entitlement to it (as Franck and others attest), it remains the case that international society has largely explained this acceptance of an international duty to monitor democracy as arising from its fundamental need to ensure peace and security. In Franck's words, 'the right to democracy can readily be shown to be an important subsidiary of the community's most important norm: the right to peace' (Franck 1992: 87). Accordingly, the logical sequence is that 'the legitimacy of the democratic entitlement is augmented by its hierarchic relation to the peremptory norm of global peaceability' (Franck 1992: 89). To this extent, democracy is presented as an adjunct norm, validated by its contribution to the attainment of peace. The suggestion is that the basic thesis of the democratic peace has now been internalized in international law, and accordingly the extension of the zone of democracy will contribute to this goal (Clark 2001a: 225). The Charter of Paris had explicitly appealed to this important connection:

> [o]ur relations will rest on our common adherence to democratic values and to human rights and fundamental freedoms. We are convinced that in order to strengthen peace and security among our States, the advancement of democracy and respect for and effective exercise of human rights, are indispensable.
>
> (CSCE 1990: 5)

This development reflected also the greater post-Cold War concern with intra-state conflict and civil war, and democracy was regarded as a particularly pertinent palliative in this context. In 2001, Kofi Annan had attested his belief that 'the work undertaken by the United Nations to support democracy in its Member States contributes significantly to conflict prevention' (Fox 2004: 74).

Underpinning this, there was evidently a new configuration of power favourable to the United States, and upon which it was believed the new norm could be securely established. This interacted with the new normative agenda. Francis Fukuyama vividly presented the unfolding drama of the end of the Cold War within such a frame of reference:

> The intimate connection that exists between power and concepts of legitimacy is nowhere better illustrated than in Eastern Europe. The years 1989 and 1990 saw one of the most massive shifts in the balance of power that has ever occurred in peacetime ... There was no change in the material balance of power ... This shift occurred entirely as a result of a change in standards of legitimacy ... Legitimacy constituted, in Vaclav Havel's phrase, 'the power of the powerless'.
>
> (Fukuyama 1992: 258)

The claimed causal sequence is that the shift in standards of legitimacy issued in the revolutionary new balance of power, not vice versa. This is partly correct, insofar as the tide of domestic legitimacy evidently turned against the prevailing regimes in Eastern Europe, and contributed to the collapse of the old order. It was demonstratively this normative shift that ushered in the transformation of the balance of power in its wake. However, when we turn specifically to the adoption of democracy as a principle of international legitimacy, as enshrined in the Charter of Paris and elsewhere, the causal sequence is not quite so straight-forward. It would be hard to maintain that the new international consensus that coalesced around this norm was itself innocent of the altered distribution of power: to a considerable degree, adoption of the norm became possible only because that balance had already shifted. It was the new equilibrium that opened up the prospect of a consensually agreed international norm of democracy.

Pluralism and concerts of democracies

After a generation during which the formal rationale of international society had been one of equality and universality, it has appeared since 1990 that its core members would prefer to revert to a more limited, and certainly unequal, concept of membership. Either some states are potentially to be excluded, or, if they belong at all, they do so on qualitatively different terms from the remainder. What were formerly considered external differences between groups of states – those inside and those outside international society – have now been internalized: all may be members of international society, but not equally so. In Keene's terms, the task is now to pursue the goal of 'civilization', not 'toleration', even among the insiders (Keene 2002).

This is occurring because of a clash between two concepts that are wholly at odds with each other. The one postulates legitimacy as the product of 'domestic' political values; the other sees it as something conferred by international norms and decisions, expressed through agreed procedures. In the former, international institutions derive their legitimacy from the democratic credentials of the individual states; in the latter, the actions of individual states working collectively derive their legitimacy from adherence to international society's procedures.

The logical extension of this polarization is that – pending the creation of Wilson's preference for an international society composed entirely of democratic states – the pertinent international society should be considered, not as its totality, but rather as the more restricted grouping of democratic states within it. What we are witnessing is not so much the abandonment of international society as a yet further attempt at reinvention to a more restricted form, confined for some purposes to its thicker democratic core. The corollary of international society's expressed preference for democratic government domestically, on this logic, is that this particular section of international society must have a greater entitlement to speak on behalf of the whole. This would represent the final colonization of a principle of international legitimacy (rule rationality) by one emanating from domestic legitimacy (value rationality).

Such views have been gaining in some prominence, especially in the United States, even if 'there is very little sign of their reflecting any political or legal consensus within international society as a whole' (Hurrell 2007: 156). The central idea was embraced by the advisory teams to each of the contenders in the 2008 US Presidential election. Advisors on both sides endorsed calls for a Concert or League of Democracies (Alessandri 2008; Diehl 2008), and it is the bipartisan nature of these proposals that is interesting, regardless of their final political outcome. Strikingly, it has been suggested that what they share in common is the view that 'undemocratic governments are members of the international community at our sufferance' (Shorr 2007).

There had, of course, been indicative precedents going back to the Clinton administration. We are now told that Phillip Bobbitt, while serving in that administration, had (unsuccessfully) recommended adoption by an alliance of democracies of an explicit doctrine of intervention, specifying three conditions under which it might take place (Bobbitt 2008: 445–6). What this indicates is that, from their inception, such proposals have been associated with the quest for a new 'legitimacy constituency' by which international action might be authorized. There were reports in the late 1990s of US encouragement of India to participate in such a developing community of democracies (Mohan 1999). Clinton's Secretary of State, Madeleine Albright, had then sponsored the setting up, after a meeting held in Warsaw in 2000, of the Community of Democracies (Albright 2003; Council for a Community of Democracies (CCD) 2006). Although this body had since made some efforts to organize itself into a 'democratic caucus' in the UN, its main focus has instead been on democracy promotion, rather than on forming a group of democratic states to act in combination on specific international issues. The proposals for a Concert that were more recently surfacing appeared to take this initiative to a new level. In one formulation, the US and EU are urged to form 'a kind of G2' as an 'energizing force in creating a global alliance of democracies and in animating joint action by the G8' (Bobbitt 2008: 482–3).

This idea for a Concert had initially been floated in two main quarters: the first was the Princeton Project, and the other a series of writings by Ivo Daalder and James Lindsay. Both, however, had direct or indirect links to the Obama campaign through those acting as his advisors, even if Obama himself did not publicly adopt the proposals. The co-directors of the Princeton Project, Anne-Marie Slaughter and G. John Ikenberry, emphasized their study's view that a key problem was the current inability of the UN Security Council to act in crises, and, as a partial solution, they floated the suggestion that the veto be curtailed in these situations. On the back of this, they recommended also 'creating a Concert of Democracies to lobby for effective reform and to create a possible alternative decision-making body if such reform ultimately proves impossible' (Ikenberry and Slaughter 2006b). These became the central elements of the final Princeton Report. This recommended, inter alia, that the United States 'should assist and encourage Popular, Accountable, and Rights-regarding (PAR) governments worldwide', as well as outlining their concept for a Concert of Democracies:

While pushing for reform of the United Nations and other major global institutions, the United States should work with its friends and allies to develop a global 'Concert of Democracies' – a new institution designed to strengthen security cooperation among the world's liberal democracies. This Concert would institutionalize and ratify the 'democratic peace'. If the United Nations cannot be reformed, the Concert would provide an alternative forum for liberal democracies to authorize collective action, including the use of force, by a supermajority vote. *Its membership would be selective, but self-selected.*

(Ikenberry and Slaughter 2006a, emphasis added)

They also set out a Charter for this Concert (Ikenberry and Slaughter 2006a: 61). Some might see in this a none-too-veiled threat: while the focus was evidently on reform of the UNSC (United Nations Security Council), a putative alternative was being readied just in case. Moreover, it was clear that the policy actions that might most concern the Concert were exactly those of a possibly interventionist – and hence politically highly sensitive – character. Their Charter was explicit that its members were indeed signing up to a commitment that the responsibility to protect falls to the international community in cases where state governments are themselves unable or unwilling to fulfil this obligation. As a corollary, and in another formulation,

a state of terror can never be sovereign … To be assured of sovereignty, and of the protection of the international community … a state need only become transparently a state of consent. International law should be reformed to recognize this rule as a fundamental element in the constitution of the society of states.

(Bobbitt 2008: 481–2)

In short, if the Concert were to act as an alternative source of authority for collective action, it would of course be called upon to act on precisely those issues most likely to divide the Security Council. At the same time, those outside the Concert would be offered, at best, a conditional sovereignty.

The other source of the Concert idea has been Ivo H. Daalder, writing in partnership with James Lindsay and other co-authors (including Robert Kagan). Daalder was also known to have links to the Obama campaign, and is now US ambassador to NATO. He had first mooted the suggestion of an alliance of democracies back in 2004. In this proposal, the Alliance was clearly envisaged as taking on a variety of major security roles. Unlike the existing Community of Democracies, with its relatively narrow agenda of democratization, the Alliance 'would by necessity be far more ambitious: it would unite democracies to confront their common security challenges', and, militarily, 'that means emulating NATO' (Daalder and Lindsay 2004). They then brought a reworked proposal to the fore again during 2006 and 2007, now adopting the common nomenclature of a Concert of Democracies. What they had in mind was a proper organization 'with a full-time secretariat, a budget, ministerial meetings and regular summits'. It would operate in the three areas of security, economic/development and demo-cracy/human rights. As with the Princeton Project, it highlighted the current difficulties in mounting actions through the UNSC, but it went on to develop a much more fundamental rationale for the Concert, drawing a sharp contrast in *legitimacy* between it and the Security Council:

> But should international legitimacy rest on universalism...? This notion reduces the criterion of legitimacy to a procedural question: the number of states or votes one can marshal in support of a given action will determine that action's legitimacy. The nature of the action itself – or the nature of the states consenting to it – matters little, if at all ... This is a deeply flawed conception of legitimacy ... States may be equal in a procedural sense, but they are not equal in fact ... [W]hy should states with no legitimacy at home have an equal say as states with such legitimacy? Real legitimacy ... resides in the people rather than the states – which is why state decisions to confer international legitimacy must rest in the democratically chosen representatives of the people, not in the personal whims of autocrats or oligarchs.
>
> (Daalder and Lindsay 2007: 52–3)

Strikingly, this replicated those arguments previously set out in the context of NATO's Kosovo campaign in 1999, and those espoused by commentators such as Charles Krauthammer in the context of the Iraq War in late 2002 and early 2003 (Clark 2005: 185–7). These had, in various ways, been deeply critical of the status and role of the Security Council, and had endorsed the greater legiti-macy attached to NATO's action in 1999, on account of its claimed expression of a democratic consensus. The proposal resulted from a mixture of motives: both to tie the USA into a new form of multilateralism, and also to facilitate humanitarian interventionism, while threatening to circumvent the existing mul-tilateralism expressed through UNSC procedures on the law of armed force.

For these reasons, commentators were not surprised to detect considerable overlap with similar proposals emanating from the Republican side. Prominent among these have been the contributions of Robert Kagan, known to be an advisor to the McCain campaign. Kagan also has championed the cause of a League of Democracies (Kagan 2008b; Werth 2008). His diagnosis in his latest book is that 'the new era ... will be one of growing tensions and sometimes con-frontations between the forces of democracy and the forces of autocracy' (Kagan 2008a: 58). Russia and China do not just practice autocracy but 'believe in autocracy' (Kagan 2008a: 59). As a result, 'autocracy is making a comeback' (Kagan 2008a: 68). In this more hostile environment, democracies must look to themselves, and form a concert or league, not least because they need 'new means of gauging and granting international legitimacy to actions', especially to those that 'democratic nations deem necessary but autocratic nations refuse to countenance' (Kagan 2008a: 97). What had so recently seemed as the inevitable victory of the democratic form rested on a more precarious balance of global forces, and already that is shifting in directions hostile to democratic states. Kagan's League is thus presented, not as the voice of democratic triumphalism, but as a seemingly rearguard defensive action.

It is no part of the present discussion to suggest that such a project will come to fruition: indeed, as a specific proposal, it is now quiescent. The point, instead, is simply to draw attention to this tendency, and to explore its significance in the context of previous attempts to socialize democracy into international society, and to render it a more explicit criterion of full membership. The proposal, on the basis of what has been sketched so far, carries a number of implications, and these have already been seized upon in the diverse, and far from universally supportive, reactions to it.

There has been relatively little positive commentary from outside the United States. The Australian government under Kevin Rudd quickly distanced itself from a 'mini' Asian version, the so-called 'quad' involving the US, Japan, and India, for fear that it seemed anti-Chinese (Ching 2008). British Foreign Secretary, David Miliband, chose to sit firmly on the fence:

> You can see the dangers. You don't want to set up something which undermines the ability of the international system to get to grips with difficult issues. Equally though ... should people with the same values work effectively together? The answer must be yes.
>
> (Lustig 2008)

Some have noted a 'complete absence of any welcoming responses from outside the United States' (Carnegie Endowment 2008; Carothers 2008). There have, however, been some notably high profile detractors. Speaking in the United States, Mikhail Gorbachev referred to it as a 'mistake'. 'We must not, instead of the United Nations, propose NATO or some kind of a coalition of democratic countries', he said (All Headline News (AHN) 2008). Revealingly, Lord Hannay, Britain's former UN ambassador, drew attention to the 'undesirability ... of systematising the divide in the world between democratic sheep and undemocratic goats', and the government's spokesman in the Lords, Lord Bach, conceded in response that 'we would not want any multilateral organisations to undermine the United Nations,' because its 'universal membership gives it an unparalleled political legitimacy' (House of Lords Debates 2008).

The problem that has exercised many about these Concert and League proposals is that their prescriptions seem to stand in sharp contradiction to their description of prevailing trends, and as such to be a recipe for great-power conflict, rather than any means to redress it. François Heisbourg was therefore concerned about 'a systematic polarization between the West and the Rest' (Heisbourg 2007), Robert Skidelsky about 'a new Cold War between states labelled democracies and autocracies' (Skidelsky 2008) and Shashi Tharoor about a 'self-fulfilling prophecy of the emergence of a league of autocracies' (Tharoor 2008). For these reasons, the Concert has been dismissed as a 'classic version of American escapism', predicated on the wishful thinking that 'the

United States need not negotiate with countries that hold different values and political systems' (Stedman 2007: 943). The reality it evades is the need to 'deal with, and work out a modus vivendi among, the many different types of political system that exist in a plural world' (Roberts and Zaum 2008: 66). As *The Economist* was to put it on 3 July 2008, 'the whole point of global talking-shops is that they include everybody, not just your friends'.

This is not the place to enter into this debate, but simply to tease out its implications for the wider argument. Pervasive in this discussion to date has been the (proponents') view that the Concert would be a useful complement to a stalled UNSC, against which is offset the (critics') view that this would be corrosive of the UN, and in effect establish a 'private' force-authorizing body, in lieu of the existing 'public' one. Who should authorize such action, if not the Security Council? The answer, Daalder and Kagan tell us, 'is the world's democracies' (Daalder and Kagan 2007). Although it is abundantly clear that the authors of the Princeton Project bear no malign intent against the UN, and nor for that matter does Ivo Daalder, their cause was clearly not helped by others who did endorse the initiative for such a League on explicitly anti-UN grounds. Charles Krauthammer was disarmingly candid on this very issue:

> Well, I like the idea of the league of democracies ... What I like about it, it's got a hidden agenda. It looks as if it's all about listening and joining with the allies ... except that the idea here, which McCain can't say, but I can, is to essentially kill the U.N.'
>
> (Clemons 2008)

The (solidarist) democratic sector of international society, on this account, has a greater entitlement to speak on behalf of the whole, and should be promoted as a conscious alternative to the deficient (pluralist) UN system. The intended substitution of 'value rationality' for 'rule rationality' in the framing of international legitimacy is once again transparent, and gives rise to the concern that any such grouping 'would face the same credibility problems as coalitions of the willing' (Abramowitz and Pickering 2008).

Conclusion

This policy debate has been but the latest instance of that recurring dilemma about international society as an inclusive or exclusive body. The core appeal of a Concert of Democracies is as a pole of attraction (like the post-Cold War European Union or NATO), and as a model for emulation. However, to be fully effective in such socialization, it must also act robustly to reward those who sign up and, as a corollary, exclude (and diminish) those who do not. Intriguingly, Ivo Daalder has used the EU analogy, and its capacity to effect regime change, in his own advocacy of the Concert: 'if you want to be a member, here's what you have to do. That's how you change regimes, by having benefits of membership' (Carnegie Endowment 2008). Were such a Concert to eventuate, it would come to represent the tangibly hybrid character of contemporary international society, partly pluralist and inclusive, while also partly solidarist and exclusive, the latter representing the vanguard who currently seek to reinvent international society in their own image. The sceptics, for their part, view this as little more than a final rearguard action to perpetuate a fragile Anglo-American/Atlanticist leadership of international society, in the face of its encroachment from Asia (Lind 2007; Mahbubani 2007). At the very least, it fits a pattern stretching back to the League debates in 1919, when, first confronted by an expanding and intractable international society, the Anglo-American core began to promote an alternative version from within. This has throughout been predicated upon a sub-version of pluralism and universalism. In its place, international society is encouraged, cajoled, and if necessary, coerced to subscribe to a value rationality that privileges liberal democracy, and to a revised rule rationality that reflects that new priority, and in which consensual legitimacy within the democratic world would be taken to trump any expression of consensual legitimacy in the deformed international society that reaches beyond it. Even within international society, democracy's mission is to 'civilize', not to 'tolerate'.

This contemporary debate captures also the rich and complex interplay between normative integration and state political action in the context of shifting distributions of power. There is little gainsaying that democracy, as a value, is now more deeply embedded in international society than it was fifty years ago, and stands as a major commitment for a broad cross-section of its members, representing possibly one half of the total. As a result, 'democratic legitimacy today contends for hegemony in the international system within a broader shared framework centered on popular sovereignty' (Bukovansky 2002: 10). However, that reminds us that it yet falls some way short of a universal value, and those who refuse to subscribe to it are arguably engaged in a more active counter-offensive than was the case even a decade ago. The reason, in part, is no doubt that the forms of democracy promotion pursued after the end of the Cold War have come to be viewed more sharply by those on the receiving end as simply extensions of western state power, and ways of exploiting and perpetuating the imbalance of power that the end of the Cold War had inaugurated. The saga of military interventions in Kosovo, Afghanistan and Iraq has no doubt done much to reinforce these perceptions. Instrumentally, resistance to liberal democracy (and its associated international rights' agendas) has now become the continuation of international politics by other means. Those who feel excluded now make appeal instead to national sovereignty, and to the virtues of pluralism in international society. The century-old Wilsonian programme for making the world safe for democracy by turning it into a principle of international society has, for the moment at least, become considerably more hazardous.

4 Power to the people

Nationally embedded development and mass armies in the making of democracy

Sandra Halperin

Introduction

Misconceptions about the factors that made possible the achievement of democracy in Europe continue to influence our view of the requisites for and prospects of democracy in the contemporary 'developing' world. For instance, the notion that a capitalist bourgeoisie played the decisive role in democratizing Europe still informs a great deal of historical and theoretical writing,[1] despite increasing evidence that it was the working classes that played the decisive role in this outcome (see e.g. Collier and Collier 1991; Rueschemeyer *et al.* 1992; Hall 1993; Downing 1997; Collier 1999). Furthermore, those scholars who do recognize the crucial role of the working class in European democracy, nonetheless tend to misunderstand why and how this occurred and, consequently, why workers have not played a similar role in contemporary 'developing' countries.

The achievement of democracy depends on increasing working-class political power and this, many argue, has been effectively foreclosed by policies that have fragmented national labour forces. According to this argument, the post-Second World War compromise was concluded with permanently employed full-time workers represented by national industrial unions. Today, globalization has restructured the labour market in ways that erode the permanent, full-time employment that characterized the labour force with which the compromise was concluded. By producing increased heterogeneity and inequality within labour markets, globalization has eroded the economic conditions for labour solidarity. Moreover, as Erik Wright argues, firms are increasingly oriented towards global rather than nationally based markets and, thus, are no longer dependent on the purchasing power of workers in the countries within which those firms are located (Wright 2000; see also Teeple 1995).

However, contrary to these claims, the struggle between labour and capital today is not being waged under fundamentally different conditions. First, labour did not become largely permanent and full-time until after the Second World War and as a result of the compromise that it entered into with capital: thus permanent, full-time labour was not a precondition but a *result* of the compromise. Second, while increased capital mobility and the subsequent downward pressure on wages may be pitting workers against each other worldwide today, historically, this appears to be 'normal'. Attempts to forge solidarity internationally among labour forces have not been, on the whole, successful. Before 1914, British employers confronted with workers' demands to reduce hours and raise wages threatened to bring in workers from France, Belgium and Germany at a cheaper wage. Continental wages were substantially lower than in England, and English labour leaders feared competition of goods produced by low-wage industries, and threats by employers to replace striking English workers with Europeans (Collins and Abramsky 1965: 39). Nor did the conditions of labour before 1914 facilitate the development of strong unions and high solidarity within national workforces. As shall be argued here, (1) industrial development in Europe before 1914 was characterized by atomized labour forces with relatively low wages and low skills; (2) labour became unified through its mobilization, not for industry, but for war; and (3) this was decisive to the achievement of democracy.

'Democracy' is here defined as a political system characterized by (1) free and fair elections of representatives with universal and equal suffrage; and (2) the institutionalization of opposition rights (freedom of association and expression, protection of individual rights against arbitrary state action). This definition borrows from Rueschemeyer *et al.* (1992: 43–4). Inclusive participation in the political process, participation that transcends class boundaries, as Rueschemeyer and his co-authors rightly point out, though often treated as secondary to other dimensions, is the central feature of democracy.

While Europe's industrial bourgeoisie, like its landed elite, was 'generally supportive of the installation of constitutional and representative government', it was 'opposed to extending political inclusion to the lower classes' (Rueschemeyer *et al.* 1992: 8). This was only achieved when working-class mobilization, not for industrialization but for war, set in motion processes that simultaneously increased working-class political power relative to that of other classes, and increased pressures for a relatively more nationally 'embedded' economy – one characterized by the territorial coincidence of production and consumption and the expansion of domestic markets. It was these socioeconomic changes that ensured that extensions of the franchise would combine with free and fair elections and the institutionalization of opposition rights to produce durable, substantive democracy.

The argument of this chapter proceeds as follows. Until the world wars, it was the traditional landowning elite that formed the basis of Britain's 'capitalist class', dominated the state apparatus and led Britain's capitalist development. Political institutions were designed to maintain the power of traditional forces against the lower classes; and, in general, they were successful in achieving that end (first section). It was the increase in working-class power due, not to its mobilization for large-scale industrial production, as is usually assumed, but to the mass mobilizations for the world wars, that made possible the achievement of democracy in Europe. Before the Second World War, European industrialization was sectorally and geographically limited, largely carried out by atomized, low-wage and low-skilled labour forces; based on production, not for local mass consumption, but for export to governments, elites and ruling groups in other states and territories (second section). It was not until the world wars created a unified and powerful labour force in Europe that stable, full democracy became part of the European political landscape. The third section discusses the circumstances that made possible the growth of labour power in Europe and, as a result, the achievement of democracy and a broadening of the social base of development. The fourth section considers the implications of the analysis of previous sections for how we understand globally constituted relations of power, and their relationship to democratic struggles throughout the world today.

The bourgeoisie and political development in nineteenth and early twentieth century Europe

Many scholars claim that, in contrast to the third world, where the indigenous bourgeoisie failed to acquire either political or economic hegemony, in Britain 'an independent capitalist middle class' emerged by the eighteenth century sufficiently strong to fight and win a battle for state power against the merchant and financial monopolists that had originated in the feudal land aristocracy (see e.g. Moore 1966; Chirot 1977). But it was the aristocracy that formed the basis of Britain's 'capitalist class', and, despite granting concessions to wealthy non-aristocratic industrialists after the 1848 revolutions, remained the dominant faction of the bourgeoisie throughout the nineteenth and early twentieth centuries.

Europe's liberal bourgeoisie[2]

Distinctions are conventionally drawn between class structures in those European societies that were supposedly dominated by an indigenous, independent capitalist bourgeoisie, and those that were not. This distinction is the basis of various schemas that define 'two roads' to industrial capitalism and democracy in Europe. One road, exemplified by Britain, is characterized by the emergence of a relatively open political space – the result of a bourgeois revolution having displaced the old landed aristocracy and the absolutist state; while the second road, exemplified by Germany and other 'late' developers, is distinguished by its relatively closed political space, the result of the continuing dominance of an agrarian class able to block industrialization and resist democracy (see e.g. Moore 1966; van der Pijl 1998; Coates 2000).

But nowhere in Europe was there a clear division between industrial and landed capital; in fact, everywhere industrial capitalist development was characterized by their fusion. In Britain, as elsewhere, the nature of industrial capitalist development was shaped by the political convergence of a landed aristocracy and large capitalist manufacturers.

Many have argued that this elite had become bourgeoisified by the eighteenth or nineteenth century. However, either the aristocracy absorbed the industrial bourgeoisie and dominated it; or they resisted the industrial bourgeoisie and dominated it. Despite all that has been written about industrialists replacing landowners as the dominant element in the ruling elite, until 1914, non-industrial

Britain could easily outvote industrial Britain (Hobsbawm 1968: 96). Before then, industrialists 'were not sufficiently organized to formulate broad policies or exert more than occasional influence over the direction of national affairs' (Boyce 1987: 8). Land in Britain, as elsewhere in Europe, was highly concentrated, as were its financial and industrial sectors, and these became increasingly so throughout the nineteenth century. Traditional corporatist structures – guilds, patronage and clientelist networks –survived in some places and grew stronger, and new ones were created. By 1914, these formed part of the complex of privileged corporations and vested interests in Europe that were 'quite as formidable as those of the Old Regime' (McNeil 1974: 164–5).

These were neither peripheral aspects of Britain's industrialization, nor a dying 'feudal' substance. The traditional landowning elite was able to channel industrial expansion into dualistic and monopolistic forms. Dualism preserved the political and economic bases of traditional groups by restricting growth to within the constraints posed by the concentration of capital and land ownership.[3] As a result, industrial expansion in Europe was shaped, not by the liberal, competitive ethos emphasized in most accounts, but by feudal forms of organization, and by rural, pre-industrial, and autocratic power structures.[4]

Democracy in Europe

It is often claimed that '[i]n the early part of the twentieth century' most Western European societies 'were either political democracies, or well on the way toward becoming so' (Chirot 1997: 222). However, before 1945, Europe, in common with parts of the contemporary third world, experienced partial democratization and reversals of democratic rule. Political participation was severely limited; and where liberal electoral politics were introduced, governments had difficulty in maintaining them for sustained periods of time. Parliaments were dissolved, election results disregarded, and constitutions and democratic civil liberties continually thwarted by extra-legal patronage systems, corruption and violence.

Democracy in Europe first arose as democracy for male members of the ruling class. As the urban, industrial bourgeoisie grew in wealth and numbers, it sought to wrest a share of political power from the *ancien régime*. When they showed themselves willing to ally with the lower classes in order to achieve this objective, the representatives of the landed elites granted them representation in Parliament. Once this was accomplished, industrialists and landed elites closed ranks to prevent further extensions of the franchise.

On occasion, landed elites favoured extensions of the suffrage that would increase their weight relative to that of industrial interests. Thus, in Norway, the suffrage was extended to the property-owning stratum of peasantry prior to its being achieved by the urban working class. Bismarck favoured an extension of the suffrage to strengthen landed interests against financial interests, since the landed elite controlled the behaviour of their dependents and their workers at the polls (Weiss 1977: 76). Similarly, in Belgium, the right wing could secure the vote of the mass of peasant voters who were Catholics, and so had less to fear from universal manhood suffrage than the Liberals (Carstairs 1980: 51). The liberal bourgeoisie, however, almost always resisted democracy.[5] As Karl Polanyi noted, 'From Macauley to Mises, from Spencer to Sumner, there was not a militant liberal who did not express the conviction that popular democracy was a danger to capitalism' (Polanyi 1944: 226).

European 'democracy' before 1945 was a severely limited form of representative government, based on a highly restricted, means-tested suffrage that excluded the great majority of adults from participation: men below the age of 25 or 35, and women. Since the life expectancy in Europe before the First World War was between 41 (Austria, Spain) and 55 (Sweden, Denmark, Norway) years of age, those who had the vote were men in the last third of their life. If the same system prevailed in the west today, the vote would be restricted to men over 54 years of age.

Universal adult suffrage would have enfranchised 40–50 per cent of each country's population. However, in 1910, only some 14–22 per cent of the population was enfranchised in Britain, Sweden, Switzerland, Belgium, Denmark, the Netherlands and Germany. Where the suffrage included members of the poorer classes, three-class and other weighted and plural voting systems, open balloting, and restrictions on and biases against working-class organizations and parties made it futile for poor people to vote.

Until 1918, Britain's suffrage qualifications were so complicated that determining the number of qualified voters was difficult. Lodgers had to make an annual claim in order to keep on the register; and claims and objections were heard by barristers in the presence of party agents, a method that did not guarantee accuracy or completeness. 'Though 88 percent of the adult male population would have qualified to vote in 1911 were it not for complications and limitations in the registration procedures which were biased against the working class, less than two-thirds were on the voting polls.' Moreover, half a million of the eight million voters that year were plural voters 'and needless to say not many of them were working-class' (Rueschemeyer *et al.* 1992: 97). The Representation of the People Act of 1918 nearly tripled the size of the electorate by simplifying the requirements for male voters and by extending the suffrage to women 30 years and over who qualified as occupants. However, plural voting persisted. In 1931, the Labour Party received 9 per cent of the seats in parliament with 30 per cent of the vote (Carstairs 1980: 197). It was not until 1948 that the Representation of the People Bill abolished plural voting.

Table 4.1 Europe in 1910

	Life expectancy	Voting age
Belgium	47	25
Germany	47	25
Denmark	55	35
Norway	55	25

Throughout the century, weighted voting was designed to grossly under-represent urban areas. In Britain, scores of depopulated constituencies ('rotten boroughs') existed under the control of large landowners who were able to manipulate the votes of the inhabitants; until 1914, the stagnant or declining small towns and rural areas of Prussia that supported conservatives were vastly over-represented in the Reichstag. In Denmark, the peasants were enfranchised in 1849, but until 1915 the votes of noble landowners and wealthy burghers were weighted to give them a majority of the seats in the upper chamber of parliament.[6] Universal suffrage was introduced in Belgium in 1893, but extra votes were given on *capacitaire* criteria (literacy, formal education or appointment to public office) and to heads of families upon reaching 35 years of age.

In addition to weighted suffrage and plural voting, open balloting, usually by oral voting or by a show of hands, restricted the suffrage by allowing governmental officials and local elites to use pressure and manipulation, especially in rural areas. Open balloting was used in Hungary and Prussia as late as 1914, in Denmark until 1901 and in Austria until 1906 (see Goldstein 1983: 15–17).

Many agricultural labourers were given the vote in Britain in 1884, but they remained dependent upon the goodwill and charity of landlords and farmers. Farm labourers attending Labour meetings were subject to prosecution;[7] and the aristocracy, clergy and the squires in rural areas put pressure upon tenants and farm workers to support Conservative candidates (Gosnell 1930: 24–5). Until 1945, priests and large landed proprietors in France saw to it that working farmers and the peasantry voted 'appropriately' (Gosnell 1930: 55). In Prussia, where there was no secret ballot, landowners controlled the vote of the landless labourers who depended on them for incomes, homes and food. Squires led their peasants to the polls and watched them carefully. Owners of large estates withdrew their trade from merchants or artisans who voted for liberals (Weiss 1977: 76). Liberals or radicals were not allowed onto estates to canvass or pass around their ballot papers. Right up to 1914 'the only ballot paper an estate labourer was likely to see was the Conservative one, handed to him by his foreman outside the polling booth' (Lieven 1992: 222).

Given these restrictions on the suffrage the figures listed below do not reflect the actual number of people who were permitted to vote freely under the systems existing at the time.

On the eve of the First World War, Norway was the only European country with universal and equal suffrage. If we count only male suffrage, then France too can be counted. After the war, Denmark, Finland, the Netherlands and Sweden established full suffrage. Germany and Austria briefly did too. By the eve of the Second World War, Britain can be added to the list, though instances of plural voting remained. Only after the Second World War did universal, equal, direct and secret suffrage become the norm throughout Western Europe.

Before the First World War, parliamentary institutions in Europe functioned more like royal courts than the parliaments and other legislative bodies that exist today in the West. Hereditary transmission of socio-political status was still widespread.[8] Political institutions were continually compromised and undermined by

Table 4.2 Per cent of European population enfranchised, 1910

Country	Percentage
Finland	45
Norway	33
France	29
Spain	24
Bulgaria	23
Greece	23
Serbia	23
Germany	22
Belgium	22
Switzerland	22
Austria	21
Sweden	19
UK	18
Denmark	17
Portugal	12
Romania	16
Russia	15
Netherlands	14
Italy	8
Hungary	6

Source: Lieven (1992: 222).

efforts to preserve privilege and to forestall the acquisition of power by subordinate groups and classes.[9] Where liberal electoral politics were introduced, governments had difficulty in maintaining them for sustained periods of time. Constitutions and democratic civil liberties were continually thwarted by extra-legal patronage systems, by corruption and violence. In general, political institutions were designed to increase the power of traditional forces against the lower classes; and they were generally successful in achieving that end. Though Labour governments came to power in Scandinavia, Britain, France and Spain, a broad spectrum of public opinion still considered them essentially illegitimate. This contributed to the manipulation of parliamentary politics by authoritarian movements during the interwar years. During the interwar years, and throughout Europe, the chief political objective for most conservative parties or interest groups was the exclusion of the socialists from any decisive influence on the state. As Charles Maier observes,

> If the socialist left seriously presented its own economic objectives on the national level, alarmed conservatives fought back. They resorted either to decentralized but simultaneous boycotts of government bonds and money (as in France), or to concerted political opposition to taxation within the terms of coalition politics (as in Germany), or to extra-legal coercion (as in Italy).

(1975: 581)

The first Labour government took office in Britain in 1923, but fell two years later because it failed to prosecute an alleged Communist editor charged with sedition. During the election campaign which followed, a 'red' scare aroused by the Foreign Office contributed decisively to Labour's defeat. The Party made a comeback in 1929, but in 1931 a new government was formed by a coalition of Liberals and Conservatives after a campaign which convinced a majority of voters that the Labour Party represented 'Bolshevism run mad' (McHenry 1940: 16–17). In 1936, a Popular Front Government dominated by socialists was elected in France. After introducing labour reforms, Leon Blum, who headed the government, was denounced as an agent of Moscow (Carr 1947: 264). French capitalists boycotted government bonds and money, forcing Blum to resign in 1937. The entrance of the German SPD into coalition governments, and the refusal of non-socialist parties, organized business interests and the military to cooperate with them, caused the collapse of Germany's Weimar Republic (Breitman 1981). During the interwar years, socialist parties were shut down by right-wing governments in Italy, Germany, Austria and Spain, and outlawed in Portugal, Hungary, Poland and the Balkan countries. In most of Europe, socialist and communist parties' participation in the political process was extremely fragile until after the Second World War.

The trans-local structure of industrial capitalist expansion

States in Europe were built up within a pre-existing, region-wide system of social institutions, relationships and norms. For centuries, and with the Church acting as a unifying agent, political development, class struggles, social change, ideology and culture remained essentially trans-European (see e.g. Pirenne 1966; Mann 1988). The expansion of industrial production in Europe brought groups across states into closer relations of interdependence. While the properties of dominant groups in different parts of Europe varied, the connections and interactions among them produced a set of common solutions to the problems of organizing production along new lines.

The most acute problem that arose with the expansion of industrial production was how to mobilize a mass of workers while at the same time maintaining their subordination to capital. The dominant 'solution' to this problem was to slowly and selectively introduce mechanization while retaining methods of production that deskilled workers and kept labour, as a whole, fragmented and poorly paid.[10] However, this raised an additional problem: if the standard of consumption of the masses remained the same or was reduced, where would consumers be found for the products of expanded production?[11] The *overall solution*, therefore, was to expand production principally for export to other countries. This enabled ruling groups to limit the development of mass purchasing power at home, while developing it among foreign groups and ruling bodies through the creation of public debt, and investment in infrastructure, railroads and armaments. As a result, the expansion of production, both within and outside Europe, involved, not whole societies, but the advanced sectors of dualistic economies in interaction with others in Europe, Latin America, Asia and elsewhere.

Elites are generally interested in adopting the most up-to-date methods of multiplying their revenue, wealth and power. They follow the leaders, emulate their goals and adopt their policies.[12] Consequently, common problems arising from the establishment of a capitalist labour market and new labour processes were generally resolved throughout the world in broadly similar ways. In Britain, dominant classes ensured that the conditions for realizing profit were met by using methods of absolute surplus value production at home and expanding production largely for export to other ruling groups. This became the model for industrial organization throughout Europe (S. Halperin 2004: chapter 3).

Europe emerged into its first century of industrial capitalism from the crucible of the French Revolution and the Napoleonic Wars. A quarter century of war and revolutionary turmoil had made clear the central dilemma for dominant groups tempted by the possibilities of great profits from the expansion of production: how to mobilize (train, educate and, in other ways, empower) labour while, at the same time, maintaining the subordination of labour to capital. Many analogies were drawn between the mass army of soldiers created in the Napoleonic Wars and the mass industrial army of workers needed for industrial capitalist production. At the same time, the socialism born in the French Revolution seemed, in combination with the revolutionary ferment unleashed by the war, to threaten an anti-capitalist revolt of the masses. This was the context within which elites throughout Europe undertook to mobilize labour for industrial production.

Elites were cohesive and had much to gain. They either controlled the apparatus of the state directly or had access to political leaders and could trade their political support, or the withdrawal of political opposition, for concessions from them. They were therefore able to carry out, throughout the nineteenth century, a purposive, determined and essentially coherent legislative, legal, military and political assault on artisans, labourers and peasants. However, these policies had unintended consequences: by generating the imperialist conflicts that eventually led to multilateral great power war in Europe, external expansion ultimately forced governments and ruling elites to mobilize (organize, train and, in other ways, empower) the masses. This is precisely what a century of external expansion had enabled them to avoid. As a number of scholars have shown, war often produces social levelling, revolution and shifts in the balance of social forces (see e.g. Andreski 1968: 33–8; and Marwick 1980, chapter 11). In the course of the world wars this is what happened in Europe.

The 'European model' of industrial capitalist expansion: a reinterpretation

Foreign trade was the primary engine of economic growth in England in the nineteenth century; but it was the home market, and the 'democratization of consumption' that initially gave the impetus to England's industrial growth. Britain's industrial output quadrupled during the eighteenth century, and the bulk of this output was mass consumption goods (Eversley 1967: 22). In the nineteenth century, however, and long before it had been exhausted as a market for goods and capital, Britain's domestic economy ceased to expand; so much so, that by 1914 it had become under-mechanized and poorly integrated relative to those of other advanced countries. Numerous scholars have pointed out that British investors under-invested in the domestic economy and that funds used for British foreign investment could have helped to develop a domestic market for the expanded output of the British economy.[13] Moreover, between 1880 and 1914 returns from overseas investment were far below what might have been earned by devoting the same resources to the expansion of domestic industry.[14]

Why, then, did investors neglect opportunities for profitable home investment and, instead, pursue investments overseas that were more difficult and costly to acquire and, in some cases, not as lucrative? The usual explanation is that domestic markets were not yet developed enough to provide profitable investment opportunities for surplus capital and that capitalists were consequently forced to seek for more profitable investments abroad.[15] But domestic economies were not then, and tend not to be now, capital saturated. Britain, and other European economies, did not, as is usually assumed, develop initially on the basis of the expansion of the internal market and then, subsequently, expand into world markets: they expanded production for foreign markets long before the opportunities for profitable investment had been exhausted at home (see, e.g. Trebilcock 1981). The market that was 'saturated' in Britain in 1902 and before, as John Hobson made clear, was one constituted solely by the wealthy classes. He argued that whatever England produced could be consumed in England, provided that there was a proper distribution of 'the "income" or power to demand commodities' (J.A. Hobson 1902: 88). However, as Hobson noted, more than a quarter of the population of British towns was living at that time at a standard 'below bare physical efficiency' (J.A. Hobson 1902: 86).

Some theorists argue that while capital exports may not have been necessary as a means of securing markets for surplus goods, they were necessary to Europe's industrialization as a means of acquiring raw materials and accumulating capital. However, Paul Bairoch has argued that the 'core' countries had an abundance of the minerals of the Industrial Revolution, were almost totally self-sufficient in raw materials and, in fact, exported energy to the 'third world'. In fact, non-colonial European countries had, as a rule, a more rapid economic development than colonial ones during the nineteenth century (Bairoch 1993: 77, 172). Given the difficulties with standard interpretations of British investment, it seems reasonable to look elsewhere for an explanation.

Britain's consumer revolution in the eighteenth century had important implications for the structure of British society. Mass consumption is associated with democracy. The economic power workers would have exercised as consumers would have enabled them to exercise power over wages and prices.[16] In Britain, the real wage per head was raised as the product per worker was raised. However, the share of this product handed over to the worker in wages did not rise (E.H.P. Brown 1968: 31). Consequently, the standard of consumption of labour bore no relation to its productivity. As long as the vast mass of workers remained solely a factor of production, their increased productivity did not provide them with the purchasing power needed for a higher standard of consumption. Consequently, while wages rose with increases in productivity, they declined in relation to the wealth of society and the ruling class.

Had the 'democratization of consumption' of the eighteenth century continued, and had a broad-based industrial growth developed, along with the mass purchasing power and internal market needed to support it, the class, land and income structures on which the existing structure of social power in Britain rested would have been destroyed. The consumer revolution and the emergence of a domestic market for mass-produced consumer goods, because it worked to undermine class distinctions and increase social mobility, was politically threatening and, thus, was not encouraged. Moreover, a fully industrialized economy, as distinct from the more circumscribed industrialization-for-export that was pursued in Britain, requires mass mobilization. Mass mobilization for industry (as for war) creates, out of the relatively disadvantaged majority of the population, a compact and potentially dangerous force; thus, elites were concerned to limit industrial expansion.[17] Marx was perhaps only reflecting a general perception of his times when he wrote that

> The advance of industry ... replaces the isolation of the labourers ... by their revolutionary combination, due to association. The development of Modern Industry, therefore, cuts from under its feet the very foundation on which the bourgeoisie produces and appropriates products.[18]
>
> (Marx 1967: 93–4)

The development of exogenous demand and consumption through the export of capital and goods provided the basis for a limited industrial expansion, and one whose benefits would be retained solely by the property-owning classes. In 1914, British industrialization was as sectorally and geographically limited as dualistic colonial economies. Landed and industrial property had become increasingly concentrated. Mechanization, skilled labour and rising productivity and real wages were found only in sectors producing for export. Little attempt was made to expand or mechanize industries producing goods for domestic household consumption. Even Britain's export industries were slow to adopt new techniques or improvements, not only in textiles, but also in coal, iron, steel, railways and shipbuilding (see S. Halperin 2004: chapter 3).

The circuit of capital

Europe's economy before the Second World War was based on the development of external markets for heavy industry and high-cost consumption goods. By expanding its shipbuilding, boiler-making, gun and ammunition industries, Britain was able to penetrate and defend markets overseas; this, in turn, provided opportunities for Britain to build foreign railways, canals and other public works, including banks, telegraphs and other public services owned or dependent upon governments. British exports of capital provided purchasing power among foreign governments and elites for these goods and services, and funded the development and transport of food and raw materials exports to Europe, thus creating additional foreign purchasing power and demand for British goods, as well as decreasing the price of food, and thereby the value of labour, in Britain.[19] At the centre of this circuit was the City of London, which like the advanced sector of a 'dependent' economy depended 'only slightly' on Britain's economic performance (Boyce 1987: 18–19).

The bulk of Britain's capital exports between 1880 and 1913 went to the Dominions, Europe and the USA. Almost 70 per cent of it went into docks, tramways, telegraphs and telephones, gas and electric works and, in particular, the enormously capital-absorbing railways. Only the production of modern armaments is more capital absorbing (the mass production and export of armaments began with the United States in the 1860s).[20] Increasing blocs of territory throughout the world became covered with networks of British built and financed railroads, provisioned by British steamships and defended by British warships.

It was the conviction of 'many authors' that the prosperity and political and social stability enjoyed by the great colonial powers was connected with their overseas possessions (Wesseling 1997: 41). However, by 1914 the extremes of wealth and poverty created by dualistic economic expansion were generating more or less continual conflicts (S. Halperin 2004: chapters 4 and 5). Britain, in 1914, 'was a divided country, in which extremes of wealth and poverty coexisted, often in a state of mutual fear and incomprehension' (Floud 1997: 7). In 1913, less than 5 per cent of Britain's population over 25 years of age possessed over 60 per cent of the wealth of the country (Clough 1940: 672–3). Though the population of Britain had become on average nearly three and a half times richer between 1830 and 1914, 'up to a third of the population in 1914 had incomes which did not provide them with sufficient food to sustain health throughout the year' (Floud 1997: 3, 15). Wages rose sharply between 1905 and 1913, but the gain was offset by a strong increase in the cost of living and by a wide range of social and economic factors (Benson 1989: 56).

By 1914, tensions were rising not only within European states, but also among them. As more and more countries began pursuing dualistic, externally oriented economic expansion, expansionist aims began increasingly to focus on Europe itself and, as they did, Europe's balance of power and imperialist regimes began to dissolve.

What changed and why

The threat of an imperialist war in Europe forced governments and ruling elites to do precisely what a century of *overseas* imperialist expansion had enabled them to avoid: mobilize the masses.

In the eighteenth century, governments relied on the social elite to pay for mercenary troops and to provide military leaders to fight professional wars. The impact of these wars on the social order had been relatively limited. However, participation of the lower classes in the wars fought by Napoleon's mass 'citizen' armies and in the mass armies mobilized to fight against them, as well as in areas of work and social life usually barred to them, worked to enhance the power of labour and to strengthen its market position. It also compelled governments to ensure their loyalty by extending to them various rights.[21] Thus, after the Napoleonic Wars, there was a return to old-style armies of paid professionals, mercenaries and 'gentlemen' (Silver and Slater 1999: 190). The new weapon introduced by Napoleon (mass armies) was used in 1870 by France and Germany, also with frightening consequences (the rising of the Paris commune), and then not again until 1914.[22]

In 1914, aggressive imperialist threats on their frontiers forced European states, once again, to use what was then still the most powerful weapon of mass destruction: the *lévee en masse*. The mass mobilizations for the First World War set in motion a social revolution that, between 1917 and 1939, swept through Europe. Efforts to prevent its further spread and escalation led directly to the Second World War. At its end, the region was wholly transformed. Previous regional conflagrations had been followed by restorations (e.g. the Napoleonic Wars, the revolutions of 1830 and 1848 and the First World War); however, the Second World War, by shifting the balance of class power throughout Europe, made restoration impossible. Instead, the vastly increased organizational strength and power of working classes and peasant masses,[23] and the decline of the aristocracy as a result of wartime changes, created the conditions for an historic class compromise and for the achievement in Western Europe both of a relatively more nationally embedded capitalism (i.e. a more balanced and internally oriented development) and of democracy.

The class compromise concluded in Western Europe after the Second World War was based on social democratic and Keynesian goals and policy instruments. It required that social democrats consent to private ownership of the means of production and that capitalists use the profits they realized from this to increase productive capacity and partly for distribution as gains to other groups (Przeworski 1979). Wages rose with profits, so that labour shared in productivity gains, making higher mass consumption possible for new mass consumer goods industries. Parties representing labour became legitimate participants in the political process.

Post-Second World War development in Europe was characterized by sustained growth rather than short-lived windfalls, and by a more equitable distribution of income. No longer based on dualistic expansion, it was the outcome of the performance largely of the society itself rather than of foreign islands of capital.[24] There is near unanimity that, in Britain, income after the Second World War was distributed more equally than in 1938. Before the First World War, the top 5 per cent of the population owned 87 per cent of personal wealth, the bottom 90 per cent, 8 per cent. In 1960, the figures were 75 per cent and 17 per cent (Hobsbawm 1968: 274). In contrast to pre-war policies, post-war policies were characterized by a more equitable distribution of income as well as rising income per head. Very large wage increases were conceded by many governments as one of their first acts following the war; and raising the level of employment was treated as a very high priority in the formulation of development strategies and plans, and in the laying down of investment criteria. Sustained investment, balanced growth, the elimination of monopoly and the production of higher levels of welfare for the population produced broad-based development and unprecedented growth.

Western Europe's phenomenal post-war growth has been attributed to a variety of factors: Marshall aid, the creation of regional institutions, trade liberalization, foreign labour, war-induced institutional and technological changes, and 'learning'.

Marshall funds played a prominent role in Western Europe's post-war recovery, but investment capital had not been lacking before the war: Britain, France, Germany and Austria made enormous amounts of capital available to each other and to other European countries; and Eastern Europe, which received no Marshall funds, also experienced unprecedented rapid industrial development and increasing affluence from the early 1950s until around 1970. By the time regional and international organizations had abolished trade restrictions among its members, Europe's post-war 'take-off' was well under way. Charles Kindleberger (1964) attributes Europe's rapid post-war growth to the availability of large supplies of labour. But Western Europe had suffered, not from insufficient labour before the war, but from persistent unemployment (Landes 1969: 390–1); and large numbers of foreign workers had been available and used in significant numbers (Strikwerda 1993: 1122).

Some scholars have argued that the world wars did not create, but only accelerated, the trends that produced Europe's relatively more nationally embedded economies (Kuznets 1964); that, as a result of their wartime role in managing economies and encouraging industrial expansion, governments had 'learned' how to create the mass demand necessary to base industrialization on the expansion of the internal market. But government-induced demand creation was a key feature in Europe's nineteenth-century industrial expansion. Almost universally, government demand substituted for missing developmental 'prerequisites' such as capital, skills and a home market for industrial goods.[25] And if the post-war shift that oriented investment and production towards the domestic market was the result of 'learning', i.e. of gaining a better or different understanding of demand management, then why hasn't this learning benefited growth in the contemporary developing world?

Moreover, arguments about 'learning' misunderstand the nature of the changes that occurred throughout Europe following the Second World War. These changes, as Joseph Schumpeter and others have observed, represented not a further evolution of nineteenth-century trends, but 'a massive capitulation' to social democracy. As Schumpeter noted, a decisive shift in the balance of class power had occurred throughout Europe as a result of the Second World War, and this explained, not only the transformation that had taken place there, but its apparent permanence:

> The business class has accepted 'gadgets of regulation' and 'new fiscal burdens', a mere fraction of which it would have felt to be unbearable fifty years ago.... And *it does not matter whether the business class accepts this*

new situation or not. The power of labour is almost strong enough in itself – and amply so in alliance with the other groups that have in fact, if not in words, renounced allegiance to the scheme of values of the private-profit economy *– to prevent any reversal* which goes beyond an occasional scaling off of rough edges.

(1976: 419–20; my emphasis)

We might further consider the link between the shift in the balance of class power and Europe's post-Second World War transformation by reflecting on today's advanced industrial democracies. These are countries which (1) never had an entrenched landed elite (Canada, New Zealand and Australia); (2) saw a significant decline in the power of landowners as a result of civil war (the United States); (3) experienced a breakdown of their traditional social structures and massive land reforms as a result of devastating wars (most of Europe); or (4) had a massive land reform imposed by external forces and experienced, as a consequence, the breakdown of their traditional class structures (Japan).

Implications for democracy today

The discussion of preceding sections raises questions about the adequacy of current initiatives for achieving full participatory democracy. In particular, it challenges their association of economic openness with democratization. The focus of a vast literature, as well as the rationale for most, if not all, major democracy promotion proposals and programmes, is the association of the achievement of democracy with the development of more open economies. But, as previous sections argued, the achievement of Western democracy is associated, not with greater economic openness, but with the emergence of a relatively more nationally 'embedded' capitalism, involving greater restrictions on capital and an increase in state regulatory and welfare functions. The emergence of democracy, historically, is associated with a breakdown of traditional class structures, an increase in the power of working classes relative to that of other classes, a relatively more nationally embedded capitalism, the development of purchasing power among a mass domestic citizen workforce, and the extension and integration of domestic markets. It is associated with state policies that ensure that wages rise with profits, so that labour shares in productivity gains, making higher mass consumption possible for new mass consumer goods industries. None of these changes feature prominently in the vast qualitative and quantitative literature devoted to exploring 'requisites' of democracy'; nor are they outcomes envisioned or promoted by the democracy promotion efforts of Western governments, NGOs and international organizations.

In fact, it is frequently argued that globalization and, in particular, unrestricted international transactions, potentially contributes to democratization. In a widely cited recent study, Daron Acemoglu and James Robinson argue that, if capital owners can more easily take their money out of a given country, they will be more secure about democratic politics and less inclined to use repression to prevent a transition to democracy; and since trade opening increases rewards to the relatively abundant factors of production in each country, in less developed countries which have an excess of labour and a shortage of capital, international trade will work to reduce the gap between the incomes of labour and capital and thus change the extent of inequality between capital owners and labour owners (Acemoglu and Robinson 2006: 20–1). The basic dynamic that this implies involves the maintenance of a balance of class power. Acemoglu and Robinson reinforce this point by arguing that the rich consent to democracy and redistribution when they deem the costs of continued repression or the threat of revolution to be too high and that, consequently, 'a relatively effective threat of revolution from the citizens is important for democratisation'. When 'citizens are not well organised, the system will not be challenged and transition to democracy will be delayed infinitely' (2006: 31).

Establishing and maintaining a balance of class power has long been recognized as a requisite of stable democracy (see, e.g. Przeworski and Wallerstein 1992). In the post-Second World War 'class compromise' in Western Europe, the relatively poorer majority gave up revolution and consented to private ownership of the means of production, while the relatively wealthier minority consented to democracy and redistribution, i.e. to using the profits they realize from private ownership of the means of production to increase productive capacity and for distribution as gains to other groups. The need for a balance of class power to maintain democracy suggests that countries that are more unequal will tend to be less democratic; and Acemoglu and Robinson find, in fact, that democracy is positively associated with a relatively higher labour share of GDP than is found in non-democratic countries (2006: 59).

But if democracy requires a balance of class power, then democracy depends on constraints that limit the possibility of the threat of massive disinvestment, as a means of swaying the balance of class power in favour of employers. This requires restrictions on the ability of capital owners to take their money out of a given country. It also requires restrictions on the ability of employers to undermine local labour by relocating or outsourcing production abroad where labour regulations are less stringent and more difficult to enforce.

However, structural adjustment programmes, which are designed to more widely open up economies to foreign capital and foreign trade, have been persistently promoted as inextricably linked to democracy and the expansion of civil society. The demise of the Washington Consensus that promotes this view may be, as Charles Gore argues, 'inevitable'. But what Gore noted in 2000 probably also remains the case today: that it is still too early yet to announce its fall (Gore 2000: 800). Evidence of its persistence can be seen in the fact that the measures these programmes prescribe are also found with almost unvarying regularity at the heart of a variety of other programmes and initiatives, including fast-track transitions from socialist systems, 'shock therapy', post-war and post-disaster (e.g. tsunami, hurricane) reconstructions, civil society initiatives, good governance proposals, stabilization measures and democratization promotion programmes.[26] In aggregate, they are also associated with the pre-conditions or exigencies of 'globalization'.[27]

But these measures stand in direct opposition to the changes associated with the achievement of democracy in the West, including the resumption by states of the welfare and regulatory functions that they had relinquished in the nineteenth century and the pursuit of policies designed to increase domestic investment, produce a more equitable distribution of income and expand domestic markets. Getting this history right is important. Misconceptions about how democracy was achieved in the past informs not only academic research and writing: it also shapes expectations in the third world, the democratization and development initiatives promoted by Western agencies, and our understanding of globalization and its relationship to democratic struggles throughout the world today.

Notes

1 Arguments in the dependency and the traditional development literature maintain that, while in Europe the industrial bourgeoisie challenged the political power of traditional elites and was a prime force in the achievement of both industrial development and democracy, in third world countries, the local bourgeoisie is crippled by the domination exerted by international capital and too weak and dependent to act as an effective agent of national industrial and democratic development. See e.g. Gerschenkron (1962), Evans (1979), O'Donnell (1979) and Portes (1985)).

2 The discussion that follows often focuses, not on Europe, but only on Britain, as Britain represents the 'hardest case' for the arguments elaborated in this chapter.

3 'Dualism' is used here in the sense that dependency theorists use the term: to describe a lack of integration of various parts of the domestic economy due to strong linkages between portions of the economy and foreign economies. Dependency theorists argue that this sort of 'dualism' is a result of the colonial and imperial policies of European powers who recast third world economies in a specialized, export-producing mould, thus creating fundamental and interrelated structural distortions that continue to thwart development. See e.g. Amin (1977), Cardoso and Faletto (1979), Williams (1979), Murdoch (1980), Sunkel (1993). While the discussion that follows adopts this term, it rejects the notion that 'dependent development' describes an idiosyncratic contemporary third world development, and that it is an outcome largely of the domination of external powers.

4 See, for an elaboration, S. Halperin (1997 and 2004). For a summary of the arguments concerning Britain see S. Halperin (2004: 83–4).

5 Rueschemeyer et al. contend that Switzerland was an exception; in France and Britain segments of this class perhaps also played a positive role (1992: 98).

6 Goldstein 1983: 18–19. Urban areas were generally over-represented to ensure the political dominance of urbanized elements in legislatures in Austria, Germany and the Scandinavian countries.

7 See, e.g. Labour Organizer, March 1924, 9.

8 Britain's House of Lords, a hereditary body monopolized by the great landowning families, had absolute veto power over legislation proposed by the House of Commons until 1911 (Lieven 1992: 205).

9 In addition to the electoral abuses previously discussed, European governments suspended parliaments after the First World War, outlawed opposition parties, censored the press and limited assemblies. Parliamentary democracy was destroyed in Italy (1922), Portugal (1926), the Baltic states (1926), Hungary (1919), Poland (1926), the Balkan countries (1923, 1926, 1929), Belgium (1926, 1935), Germany (1934), Austria (1934), the Netherlands (1935), Switzerland (1935) and Spain (1936).

10 Britain's labour market exhibited a sharp dualism. In the export sectors, there developed a 'labour aristocracy' consisting of 'a maximum of 15%, and probably less', of the work force (Hobsbawm 1968: 161). The other 85 per cent of the workforce, including women, children, rural labourers and migrants, worked in low-wage unskilled jobs with little security, and in poor working conditions. Throughout the century earnings for these workers remained insecure and insufficient. See S. Halperin (2004: 91–9).

11 Mass consumption is associated with democracy. Its corrosive effects were recognized in the laws regulating consumption throughout history. Sumptuary laws restricted the personal consumption of goods based on class and income and were enacted in Europe between the fifteenth and eighteenth centuries, as in other places and times, to preserve and reinforce lines of distinction between classes. They were aimed largely at the masses and 'uppity' middle-class elements. Laws forbidding the common people from clothing themselves like their betters were retained by many states well into the nineteenth century. See e.g. Baldwin (1926) and Hunt (1996).

12 That is why nationalist policies and rhetoric emerged across different societies. As Liah Greenfeld (1992) shows, groups in different countries were facing problems similar to those that, in England, had given rise to nationalism and, with modifications, copied the model developed in England. Solutions developed in one country were, thus, observed and copied, with modifications relevant to the specific context. As Charles Tilly notes, developments in some countries 'created visible, prestigious, transferable models for exploitation and opportunity hoarding'. Consequently, 'Throughout the world, administrative structures, constitutions, and declared commitments of regimes to development, stability, and democracy came to resemble each other far more than did the diversity of their material conditions and actual accomplishments' (1991: 180).

13 Barratt Brown (1970: x). On Germany and France see Wehler (1969) and Wesseling (1997).

14 Davis and Huttenback (1988: 67). It might be argued that capitalists *thought* that profit margins were higher abroad. We cannot definitively know. However, given the overall context in which investment and other decisions were made, which included widespread fears of proletarian radicalism, it is reasonable to argue that this context influences a reorganization of production which limited industrialization and the distribution of its gains and which shifted 'the composition of output in favor of capital goods, exports and goods and services for upper-class consumption' (Deane 1979: 270).

15 See, e.g. Lenin (1939). The notion that advanced countries had capital-saturated economies was current at the time Lenin wrote and later was embraced by a wide variety of theorists and historians.

16 In previous centuries, when the production of goods in Europe had been largely for local markets, the masses had been able to exercise power through consumer choice or boycott. Consequently, there was a 'highly sensitive consumer-consciousness' among working people and a tradition of popular action to gain fair prices. In the eighteenth century, workers also acted to gain fair wages and to regulate their work time (Thompson 1993: 189).

17 As Tom Nairn argued, Britain's elite opposed any 'aggressive development of industrialism' and the social transformation necessary to it (1981: 21). German elites also feared that industrial expansion would increase the danger of socialism. This was much in evidence in the opinions expressed in *Kreuzeitung*, the most influential organ of German conservatism. Friedrich Richter, *Preussiche Wirtschaftspolitik in den Ostprovinzen* (Köningsberg: Ost Europa, 1938: 48–52; cited in Tipton 1976: 115–16). And the opposition of these elites was successful in hampering industrial development plans in Germany in the 1890s and preventing their revival after 1902. See, also, Weiner (1982: 1–10).

18 It might be argued that owners of wealth were not conscious of the social externalities associated with the application of large masses of labour to production. While this seems hardly plausible, they would have been after Marx spelled it out for them in the widely read and cited *Communist Manifesto*. Britain's industrialization kept 85 per cent of its workforce (those working outside the export sector) in low-wage, unskilled jobs with little security, and poor working conditions; the bulk of labour worked in agriculture, the largest branch of the British economy in employment terms until 1901 (Hobsbawm 1968: 195). Before the Second World War, British agriculture was largely unmechanized: the majority of farms in England and Wales did not possess either a tractor or a milking machine, despite their having been available for some thirty years or more (Benson 1989: 19). Landowners' control over the countryside and the rural populations ensured that rural workers did not join the ranks of organized labour until the First World War. It was mobilization for the world wars that united urban and rural, skilled and unskilled labour for the first time. More on this, below.

19 Britain's industrial wage earners realized 55–60 per cent of their wage in the form of food; the steady fall in prices of staple food imports after 1874 allowed real wages in Britain to rise until the First World War (Mathias 1983: 343).

20 Dobb (1963: 296). Hobsbawm argues that 'many of the railways constructed were and remained quite irrational by any transport criterion'. However, investors were looking 'for any investment likely to yield more than the 3.4 percent of public stocks' (1968: 111).

21 Serfdom was abolished in Prussia concurrently with Stein's military reforms, as it was in Russia when Alexander II transformed the army from a professional into a conscript force. In Austria, the adoption of universal military service coincided with reforms that established a constitutional monarchy (Andreski 1968: 69).

22 See, for an overview of this issue, Howard (1961: 8–39). Russia conscripted large numbers of men for the Crimean War; but contrast an account of the forces raised for that war (Royle 1999: 91–2) with an account of the French mobilization in 1870–1 (Taithe 2001: esp. 6–13, 22–8, 38–47).

23 Unskilled labour joined the ranks of organized labour for the first time between 1914 and 1921. James Cronin observes that, before the war, the distinction within the working class 'between "rough" and "respectable," between the skilled and organized and the unskilled and unorganized', had been 'very real to contemporaries and was reflected in many aspects of politics and collective action'. Following the war, however, 'a variety of technical, social and economic processes conjoined to produce a working class that was ... less sharply divided within itself, and also more culturally distinct from middle and upper class society'. After the war, skilled and unskilled workers, workers of different occupations, anarchists and socialists, Social Democrats and Communists, revolutionaries and reformists closed ranks to press for change (J. Cronin 1982: 121, 139).

24 The dualistic, 'dis-embedded' economic expansion discussed throughout this chapter involves both capital and trade mobility: the dispersal of capital investment and production, and production for international trade at the expense of the expansion of domestic markets.

25 Morris and Adelman (1988: 123–4). During the First World War, the machinery of government vastly expanded in Britain: it nationalized industries, raised taxes, limited profits, controlled labour relations, and imposed rationing and price controls to effect equitable distribution. However, after 1918, forces of resistance worked 'to restore the social and economic conditions of 1914' (Abrams 1963: 58).

26 See, for instance, *The Greater Middle East Initiative* (GMEI), and the *Broader Middle East and North Africa Initiative* (BMENAI). These focus on a combination of democratization measures linked to the adoption of more effective investment and trade policies.

27 See, for a review of recent, and inconclusive, empirical research on the effect of economic and financial globalization on democracy, Eichengreen and Leblang (2006). Empirical evidence does suggest, however, 'that greater integration of deregulated trade and capital flows over the last two decades has likely undermined efforts to raise living standards for the world's poor' (Hersh *et al.* (2001)). By maintaining or increasing inequalities, this might be assumed to negatively impact prospects for democracy.

5 Escaping the liberal straitjacket
Re-examining democracy's history

Christopher Hobson

> If you establish democracy, you must in due time reap the fruits of a democracy.
> Benjamin Disraeli (Hansard 1859: 1245)

Introduction[1]

Disraeli's observation is one that the current British Prime Minister would surely agree with. Where the two would diverge is over what exactly these 'fruits' are. For the present-day leader, it would no doubt entail a mixture of goods: freedom, liberty, prosperity, stability, peace and a range of other positives. Disraeli, however, was not particularly keen on reaping democracy's harvest, which he viewed as consisting of rotten fruit. The above quotation continues:

> You will in due season have wars entered into from passion and not from reason; and you will in due season submit to peace ignominiously sought and ignominiously obtained, which will diminish your authority and perhaps endanger your independence. You will in due season find your property is less valuable, and our freedom less complete.
>
> (Hansard 1859: 1245)

For the majority of democracy's past, opinion has generally sided with Disraeli, regarding it as a dangerous and unstable form of rule which inevitably led to anarchy or despotism. Yet democracy's present-day ascendency has led to this historically more prevalent viewpoint being lost.

As part of this history of forgetting, it is a *liberal* vision that largely structures our mental horizons of what democracy is, and can be. With the final collapse of the people's and one-party models of democracy in the 1980s, liberal democracy emerged as dominant, almost by default (Burgess 2001: 59–63). For many observers, though, the defeat of communism did vindicate the liberal model. Fukuyama (1989: 3) boldly proposed that:

> What we may be witnessing is not just the end of the Cold War, or the passing of a particular period of postwar history, but the end of history as

such: that is, the end point of mankind's ideological evolution and the universalization of Western liberal democracy as the final form of human government.

In such accounts, democracy's uneven and contested past is replaced by a Whiggish narrative of progress. This is representative of a more general tendency by liberal scholars to conceive of democracy in universal terms, abstracting it from history and in so doing, taking it as something relatively unproblematic and settled.

The central argument of this chapter is that to properly comprehend democracy's present and future, we must cultivate a much deeper and more nuanced reading of its past. Needed is 'a radical historicisation of democracy', in Frank Ankersmit's (2002: 10–11) words, which foregrounds that it is a contingent historical fact, and something that is far from inevitable. This position inverts the standard account provided by liberalism. Rather than comfortably accepting the current prominence of democracy, this chapter instead considers the much longer tradition of thought which saw it as something deeply problematic, and very distinct from liberalism. In so doing, the approach taken highlights the historical contingency of the present democratic moment, questioning whether this state of affairs is actually much less secure than many presume. At the same time, such a perspective also promotes a much more reflexive position, one that can point the way towards a considered case *for* democracy.

The argument will proceed as follows. First, democracy's current place in international relations will be considered, focusing on the liberal argument that democracy is universal as a value, and increasingly also in practice. Second, it is suggested that the liberal reading of democracy's history downplays or excludes the majority of its past, much of which contradicts a simplistic progressive narrative. Building on these observations, an alternative account is presented, one which explores the historically conditioned nature of both the liberal democratic model and democracy's present normative positioning. In the penultimate section, a reconsideration of democracy in light of this 'radical historicisation' will be undertaken, noting that it points towards a more cautious stance, highly cognisant of democracy's limits and fragility. In concluding, the consequences of the argument for understanding democracy's role in contemporary politics will be considered.

Democracy at the 'end of history'

A defining feature of the post-Cold War era has been the ideological ascendancy of democracy. As Larry Diamond (2003a) observes, democracy 'came during the 1990s to be a *global* phenomenon, the predominant form of government, and the only broadly legitimate form of government in the world'. Indeed, the widespread acceptance and growth of democracy across the world suggests it is fast becoming a 'universal value', something akin to a default position for humanity (Sen 1999). In the speeches and thought of world leaders, policy-makers and observers, democracy is regularly equated with the lofty ideals of freedom, liberty and equality. The rhetoric of George W. Bush (2008b) offers a particularly clear and significant case of this:

> The United States appreciates that democratic progress requires tough choices. Our own history teaches us that the road to freedom is not always even, and democracy does not come overnight. Yet we also know that for all the difficulties, a society based on liberty is worth the sacrifice. We know that democracy is the only form of government that treats individuals with the dignity and equality that is their right. We know from experience that democracy is the only system of government that yields lasting peace and stability.

This strong faith in democracy is perhaps one of the few things many would be willing to agree with Bush on. One could continue listing examples, but the basic point, namely, that there has been a remarkable consensus over the normative and political desirability of democracy in the post-Cold War world, is relatively uncontroversial.[2]

The above quote from Bush also reveals a distinct understanding of the relationship between history and democracy. It is premised on a linear, teleological account of history, whereby developments and changes over time have an underlying logic or purpose, and an ultimate end point can be identified and potentially reached. This perspective is by no means limited to Bush; it has been a hallmark of many liberal scholars and practitioners. The clearest, and most influential, enunciation of this position has been provided by Fukuyama (1992: 48), who proposed that, 'there is a fundamental process at work that dictates a common evolutionary pattern for *all* human societies – in short, something like a Universal History of mankind in the direction of liberal democracy'. While the triumphalist narrative has been heavily critiqued, it would be a mistake to discount this thesis. Few have agreed wholesale, but many continue to accept the argument in a qualified form, with the assertion of liberal democracy's superiority resonating especially widely (Marks 2000: 534–5). As Žižek (2008: 421) observes, 'it is easy to make fun of Fukuyama's notion of the End of History, but the dominant ethos today is "Fukuyamaian": liberal-democratic capitalism is accepted as the finally found formula of the best possible society'. It is also a position that Fukuyama (2008; 2010) continues to strongly maintain, even if the language is now a bit more cautious.

Fukuyama's influential account of democracy and its past forms an important component of 'liberal millenarianism', a prominent intellectual movement that emerged in the liberal zeitgeist of the 1990s. Marks (2000: 538–9) identifies the defining characteristics of this position as: (1) a teleological conception of history; (2) an understanding that this *telos* is liberal democracy; (3) a belief that 'we', the West, have essentially reached this end point of liberal democracy, in comparison to a non-liberal 'they' that have yet to progress; and (4) an overriding sense of optimism and confidence about democracy's present and future. Liberal millenarianism is notably found in the works of some of the most prominent thinkers on democratisation, democratic peace theory, democracy promotion and international law.[3] What makes this movement significant is precisely the close links that exist between academic and policy-making circles in these fields (Guilhot 2005; Robinson 1996).[4] This has been recently evidenced in the thought and practice of the Bush administration and their neo-conservative backers, whereby the advancement of democracy abroad was at the heart of American foreign policy. Indeed, Tony Smith (2007) has strongly argued that liberal millenarianism was influential in shaping and giving justification to Bush's 'liberal imperialism'.

For liberal millenarians – academics and policy-makers alike – democracy's merits and universality have been amply demonstrated, ethically and empirically. In terms of its normative validity, 'democracy', in George W. Bush's (2008a) words, 'leads to a better life'. Liberal democracy is seen as the form of government most capable of providing for basic human rights and needs, such as freedom, liberty, stability and equality. Robert Dahl (1998: 45) comes up with a condensed list of ten desirable consequences of democracy: '(1) avoiding tyranny, (2) essential rights, (3) general freedom, (4) self determination, (5) moral autonomy, (6) human development, (7) protecting essential personal interests, (8) political equality,... (9) peace-seeking, (10) prosperity.' Existing liberal democracies are seen to provide these goods – in either absolute or relative terms – both domestically and internationally. And its continued spread is taken as evidence that (liberal) democracy is something that transcends cultural boundaries. Regularly cited are opinion polls, such as the Pew Center and Barometer surveys, indicating that democracy is the preferred form of government in all regions of the world (e.g. Diamond 2008: 32–3). In this sense, the demand for democracy is taken as universal. Increasingly so is the supply, according to the influential Freedom House and Polity data sets, which show a slow, but clear, global movement towards democracy over the last century. This trend became more noticeable with the third wave of democratisation, with its breadth seen as further proof that the desire for, and possibility of, democracy is universal (Gershman 2005: 20–2; McFaul 2004–5). From this perspective, this kind of government may have emerged from a historically and culturally specific context, but it has transcended those localised beginnings to become truly universal in its aspirations, scope and applicability (Diamond 2008; Fukuyama 1992).

A 'radical historicisation' of democracy

The dominant liberal millenarian vision universalises a historically specific understanding of what democracy is, and should be. Underwriting the account is a linear, teleological reading of democracy's past, which operates to validate this problematic truth claim. Indeed, one of the most significant dimensions of democracy in world politics today is the extent to which a Whig reading of its history, as exemplified by – though crucially not limited to – the liberal millenarians, has been naturalised, and the basic idea of democracy as a good goes unquestioned.

As Ankersmit (2002: 10–11) observes, 'since we are all democrats (or so one may hope!), we tend to see democracy as the fulfillment of our political destiny and as the political system that will remain with us for the rest of human history'. There is, however, nothing fixed or eternal about democracy, or any other method of governing for that matter. In previous epochs religious or monarchic conceptions dominated; today these are anachronisms that have long since disappeared from our world-view. In much the same way, there is little to suggest that democracy will inevitably endure. Even if liberal democracy represents the only viable state form at present – a highly contentious claim – this does not preclude the possibility that non-democratic or post-democratic alternatives will emerge in the future. Yet the liberal millenarian framework inhibits our ability to recognise if such changes are occurring.

Opposed to this self-defeating tendency of conceiving of democracy in abstracted, universal terms, a 'radical historicisation' of democracy consciously foregrounds its historically conditioned and variable nature. Ankersmit (2002: 11) explains the consequences of adopting this alternative perspective:

> On the one hand, it obviously entails a relativisation of democracy: we should not see it as the epiphany of the ultimate political Truth, as we so often tend to do. On the other hand, such thinking may stimulate a more realistic attitude toward democracy than customarily is the case, an attitude that may be more beneficial to the cause of democracy than ahistoricist adoration and blind glorification.

Building on these reflections, it is argued that this kind of approach is better equipped to comprehend the contemporary nature of democracy.

Simply put, it is time to break free of the liberal straitjacket that constrains our democratic horizons. To demonstrate this central claim, a brief conceptual history of democracy will be sketched in two parts.[5] First, the dominant liberal democratic model will be considered, and second, the historical development of the present normative consensus on democracy will be explored. This discussion is motivated by Quentin Skinner's (1998: 116–17) important suggestion that:

> The intellectual historian can help us appreciate how far the values embodied in our present way of life, and our present ways of thinking about those values, reflect a series of choices made at different times between different possible worlds. This awareness can help to liberate us from the grip of any one hegemonal account of those values and how they should be interpreted and understood.

With this in mind, recovering the way the concept of democracy has changed over time illustrates that there is nothing essential in its present shape and meaning. In addition, it highlights that the liberal model now dominant is not natural, but born of historical contingencies, and as circumstances change it could be superseded or disappear.

Liberal democracy: liberalism and democracy

> I passionately love liberty, the rule of law, and respect for rights, but not democracy.
>
> (Tocqueville, quoted in Canfora 2006: 18–19)

Liberal democracy is of relatively recent vintage, having emerged only in the second half of the nineteenth century. Before their unlikely marriage, liberalism and democracy had long been separate doctrines, respectively concerned with liberty and equality. In this regard, democracy and liberalism each took a different emphasis from the banner of the French Revolution – '*Liberté, Egalité, Fraternité*'.[6] Schmitt (1988: 13, 17) extends this distinction further to a separation in theory between 'liberal individualism' and 'democratic homogeneity', but notes that 'modern mass democracy rests on the confused combination of both'. This 'confusion' stems from democracy and liberalism sharing the same starting point, the individual, but 'the individual of the former is not the same as the individual of the latter' (Bobbio 2005: 42). Put crudely, liberalism's individual is essentially atomistic, whereas democracy's individual is more directly societal. The initial, if somewhat banal, conclusion is that the relationship between liberalism and democracy is highly complex, one open to multiple interpretations.

Given that liberalism and democracy are – historically and theoretically – distinct, this suggests that liberal democracy is far from being a logical, let alone necessary, form.[7] Indeed, at first glance the potentially conflicting concerns with liberty and equality would seem to work against combining the two doctrines. In this regard, Bobbio (2005: 48–9) usefully identifies three possible relationships between the two components that make up liberal democracy: (1) liberalism and democracy are compatible; (2) liberalism and democracy are antithetical; (3) liberalism and democracy are necessarily interlinked. Theoretically, the first of these is the most plausible: democracy and liberalism do share some similar concerns, and thus have the potential to join, but this is not preordained. This differs, however, from the dominant perspective in liberal internationalist scholarship, where it is the third relationship – one of necessity – that prevails. Editor of the influential *Journal of Democracy*, Marc Plattner (1998) strongly argues that a 'profound kinship' exists between liberalism and democracy, and that even if the two doctrines were separate in the past, they are now inextricably linked. Plattner was writing in response to Fareed Zakaria's (1997) now seminal article, 'The Rise of Illiberal Democracy'. While Zakaria carefully distinguishes liberalism and democracy, his concern is precisely that illiberal democracies are deficient in one of the two 'necessary' components. The underlying premise ultimately remains the same: liberalism and democracy are interlinked. Instead, the problem is that many new democracies are lacking the required element of liberalism.

In the thought of nineteenth-century liberals, it was the second relationship – one of incompatibility – that dominated. Given the tendency by liberals today to naturalise the contemporary liberal democratic model, it is instructive reflecting on this contradictory position held by their predecessors. Liberals strongly advocated popular sovereignty against monarchy and aristocracy, but were much more reticent about popular government. This was especially evident during the 1848 Revolutions, as liberals soon sided with conservatives against the more revolutionary – and democratic – demands of socialists and communists. Reflecting on events in Paris, Alexander Herzen acutely identified the halfway position of liberals: 'they want freedom and even a republic provided that it is confined to their own cultivated circle. Beyond the limits of their moderate circle they become conservatives' (quoted in Ellis 2000: 49). This cautious response was motivated by a fear that the levelling instincts of democracy threatened the liberties which had only just been wrestled from monarchs and aristocrats. As Herbert Spencer put it, 'the function of Liberalism in the past was that of putting a limit to the powers of kings. The function of true Liberalism in the future will be that of putting a limit to the powers of Parliaments' (quoted in Christophersen 1966: 174).

At the heart of liberal fears was the belief that in a democracy the liberties of the individual would be sacrificed at the altar of equality. An excellent representation of this position can be found in Lecky's *Democracy and Liberty*, published in 1899:

> ...strong arguments may be adduced, both from history and from the nature of things, to show that democracy may often prove the direct opposite of liberty.... Equality is the idol of democracy, but, with the infinitely various capabilities and energies of men, this can only be attained by a constant, systematic, stringent repression of their natural development. Whenever natural forces have unrestricted play, inequality is certain to ensure. Democracy destroys the balance of opinions, interests, and classes, on which constitutional liberty mainly depends, and its constant tendency is to impair the efficiency and authority of parliaments, which have hitherto proved the chief organs of political liberty.
>
> (Lecky 1899: 256–7)

The growing sense of democracy's inevitability made liberals all the more worried about limiting and controlling it. Writing in the 1860s, Matthew Arnold observed that: 'at the present time, almost everyone believes in the growth of democracy, almost everyone talks of it, almost everyone laments it' (quoted in D. Bell 2007: 31). Indeed, when Tocqueville had earlier travelled to America, it was partly to assess whether the 'rising tide' of democracy would engulf Europe, or if it could be managed. And one significant consequence of Tocqueville's (2003) widely read study was a growth in concern with democracy's perceived susceptibility to the 'tyranny of the majority', whereby the rights of the minority are subject to the caprice of the unrestrained majority. Given the tremendous socio-economic changes taking place, the majority would necessarily be the poorer, less educated working classes. Partly for this reason, liberals were against the institution of universal suffrage, regarding it as having the potential to facilitate the destruction of constitutional barriers protecting individual rights, while also leading to the voices of the enlightened few being drowned out by the uneducated masses.

The contradiction underlying the programme of nineteenth-century liberals was that the universalist language used to claim and secure constitutions simultaneously made it difficult to indefinitely ignore calls for the extension of basic rights and the franchise. In this sense, the subsequent appearance of liberal democracy was not so much due to most liberals wishing for it. Rather, it partly emerged from a miscalculation in the strategy used to entrench liberal rights, combined with a gradual recognition by liberals that the best way to manage democracy's seemingly unavoidable rise was to control it as best they could. As it happened, the advent of extensive, and eventually universal, suffrage did not result in the calamities that many liberals had worried about. Writing at the turn of the century, the author of *Unforeseen Tendencies of Democracy* observed that before universal suffrage 'there were many fears about the bad influence of their ['the excluded masses'] vote on the government, but there were no fears that they would not immediately and fully exercise the privilege conferred on them' (Godkin 1898: 60–1). Liberals only became more convinced supporters of democracy once it was demonstrated that it was not the great threat to individual rights it was thought to be. Placed in a longer historical context, it can be seen that there was little preordained in the creation of 'liberal democracy'. It is a relatively recent construction, one that only emerged in the late nineteenth and early twentieth centuries.

In considering the historically conditioned nature of liberal democracy, one must further note that this union was not, by any means, an even one. It may be the case that democracy can be traced back to ancient Greece and beyond, but in the modern era it was liberalism that came first, and would structure the subsequent reappearance of democracy. As a result, in the liberal democratic model to emerge in the West, 'liberalism is its absolute premise and foundation and penetrates and shapes its democratic character' (Parekh 1993: 157). This point is fundamental. Even if one accepts the position that democracy and liberalism are necessary partners – which is questionable on both historical and theoretical grounds – the way the two components have been reconciled was historically determined. Within the prevailing model of liberal democracy, liberalism has been the dominant partner and provides the confines within which democracy exists. Yet there is no reason, logically speaking, why this should be the case. The composite nature of liberal democracy suggests it is open to various possible formations, depending on how each of its two parts is understood and incorporated. For example, alternate liberal democratic models could be based on an equal weighting between the two components, or democracy instead playing the hegemonic role. Indeed, it is most likely that different forms of liberal democracy would garner more support and traction in non-Western environments, where different conceptions of the individual and community exist (Parekh 1993: 169).

By appreciating the historically conditioned nature of the dominant liberal democratic model, the simplistic teleology and universalism that informs the liberal millenarian position is challenged. Like all other forms of rule, liberal democracy is a system of government that emerged in a particular context to answer a set of political questions unique to that time (Ankersmit 2002: 92–3). The dominant liberal democratic model emerged in the West over the last centuries and necessarily reflects this heritage. Notably, the strong emphasis on the liberties and freedom of the individual is the result of a specific set of historical contingencies, where liberalism was fighting the prevailing collectivist worldview that had preceded it (Niebuhr and Sigmund 1969: 79–80). Liberalism's conception of the individual and society is very distinctive, different from historically prevalent understandings, even within the West (Arblaster 1984: 8). In this regard, Parekh (1993: 169) observes that 'different societies define and individuate people differently. They also therefore define freedom, equality, rights, property, justice, loyalty, power and authority differently.' The Western tradition of liberalism, and thus the liberal democratic model that stems from it, provides just one set of answers to these questions.

Democracy before liberalism

Democracy has always been the naughty boy in the School of Ages, so he has had to bear the blame of anything done wrong, as a king beheaded or a city burnt; but he is getting old enough to defend himself, and will probably give us some new versions.

(Harwood 1882: 40)

Harwood's observation reflects the shift that occurred at the close of the nineteenth century: the historically dominant verdict against democracy was slowly being overthrown, and a new, liberal conception was emerging. This movement proved so successful that the longstanding interpretation of democracy as unworkable and undesirable has been almost totally eclipsed. Yet over the *longue durée* it is this narrative of democracy as deeply flawed and problematic that has generally prevailed. From this perspective the liberal interpretation is inverted: the contemporary situation is not the normal state of affairs, quite the opposite – it is the ascendency of democracy that is the historical aberration. Through this reading, the liberal millenarian vision is replaced with a much more sensitive and nuanced perspective, founded on an awareness that for much of democracy's long life it has been ignored, derided and denounced.

After the fleeting appearance of *dēmokratia* in ancient Greece, democracy effectively disappeared for the greater part of two millennia. Athens, taken as the birthplace of democracy and the fullest embodiment of its meaning, seemingly left behind a long list of reasons advising against it: democracy was a violent, chaotic, unstable form of rule where those least capable of ruling wisely exercised power in a wilful and selfish manner. Athens would cast a very long shadow over democracy. When Edmund Burke (1999: 94) castigated the French revolutionaries, he would recall the Athenian experience: 'until now, we have seen no examples of considerable democracies. The ancients were better acquainted with them.... If I recollect rightly, Aristotle observes, that a democracy has many striking points of resemblance with a tyranny.' Indeed, the writings of Aristotle, as well as Thucydides and Plato, proved influential, as they were taken as reliable, insightful eyewitnesses to democracy's many failings (Roberts 1994). Even if their thought was much more ambiguous on the matter, it was collectively read as providing strong evidence against democracy. One clear example of this can be found in Hobbes' (1975: 13–14) introduction to his translation of the *History of the Peloponnesian War*: 'for his [Thucydides'] opinion touching the government of the state ... it is manifest that he least of all liked the democracy'.

In considering the Athenian legacy, it is crucial to recover the original connotations of the term *dēmokratia*, which have been obscured by the tendency to translate it simply as the people (*dēmos*) exercising power (*kratos*). While *dēmos* can be read as being the whole political community, it was generally understood in a more narrow sense as one class of people: the poor multitude. This interpretation was found in authors such as Plato and Aristotle, and would structure the concept of democracy well into the nineteenth century (Godkin 1898: 24; Wood 1996: 126). *Kratos*, meanwhile, has a forceful and almost violent dimension to its meaning that has been wholly lost. The term *kratos* 'referred to might, strength, triumphant power and victory over others, especially through the application of force' (Keane 2009: 59). Thus, when these terms were combined, what *dēmokratia* essentially conveyed was the direct and forceful exercise of power in a small polity by the poor many. This was the understanding of democracy that helped condemn it to irrelevance for centuries.

In the late eighteenth century there was still a near universal consensus over democracy being unfeasible and undesirable. It remained little more than a scholarly and antiquarian idea that had little purchase or relevance in politics (Rosanvallon 1995). Considering this state of affairs, it is not surprising that the American and French Revolutions were not primarily about democracy, despite the retrospective significance given to them as 'democratic revolutions' (e.g. Palmer 1959–64). Democracy still meant *dēmokratia*: a direct form of social rule, inapplicable and inappropriate to the modern context these revolutions were occurring in. In America, the founding fathers, well versed in the classics, were at pains to ensure that the United States would not become a democracy. Madison (2001: 46) clearly stated the prevailing view in the *Federalist Papers*: 'democracies have ever been spectacles of turbulence and contention; have ever been found incompatible with personal security, or the rights of property; and have, in general, been as short in their lives, as they have been violent in their deaths'. Nonetheless, the Americans still sought to base the state on popular sovereignty and institute a government that was answerable to the people, but did not see this as being a democracy. In this regard, the founding fathers followed in a long tradition of thought that regarded an unmixed democracy as inappropriate and dangerous. Instead, the Americans established a representative republic, something they identified as separate from democracy. That the modern world's most fabled democracy actively denied this label little over two hundred years ago offers a stark reminder of just how recently the term has come to signify something positive.

Similarly, the French revolutionaries of 1789 largely avoided the idea of democracy. The classical meaning still dominated the imaginaries of those seeking to restore, reform or overthrow the *ancien régime*. Democracy continued to conjure up images of an archaic, unstable form of rule found in city-states; something completely inappropriate and impossible for a large, modern nation like France. Representative is the thought of Abbé de Sieyes, author of the catalysing *What is the Third Estate?*, and a key actor in the first stages of the Revolution. Sieyes still understood democracy as a direct form of rule only possible in a polity of very limited size, leading him to state in unequivocal terms that, 'I always maintain that France is not, and cannot be a *democracy*' (quoted in Forsyth 1987: 138, original emphasis). When the Revolution was further radicalised, it was primarily the language of republicanism, and not that of democracy, which prevailed. During this time, democracy soon became closely associated with the excesses of the Jacobins and the Terror, a reputation which proved difficult to overcome. Reflecting half a century later, Giuseppe Mazzini (2001: 4) observed that people 'no sooner hear the name of democracy than the *phantom* of '93 rises immediately before them. With them democracy is a guillotine surmounted by a red cap.' Events in France were widely taken as unnecessary confirmation that democracy was wholly inappropriate for modern conditions, an anarchic form where the passions of the mob prevailed, until it descended into complete chaos, only for a ruler even more absolute than the monarchs of the *ancien régime* to eventually emerge. Writing to William Wilberforce, John Jay summed up prevailing sentiment: 'The French revolution has so discredited democracy ... that I doubt its giving you much more trouble' (quoted in Morantz 1971: 149).

Jay's prediction proved accurate for much of the nineteenth century: democracy continued to be viewed in largely negative terms, with only a handful of radicals willing to speak of it positively. During the revolutions of 1848, there was a considerable spike in the discussion about democracy, but it was closely linked with more radical positions. In this context Guizot (1849: 35) complained that:

> It is the chaos of our political ideas and our political morality – that chaos disguised sometimes under the word *democracy*, sometimes under that of *equality*, sometimes under that of *people* – which opens all the gates, and throws down all the ramparts of society before it.

Democracy retained the menacing connotations of old – threatening social unrest and turmoil. Notably, in the *Manifesto of the Communist Party*, Marx and Engels (1848) stated that, 'the first step in the revolution by the working class is to raise the proletariat to the position of ruling class to win the battle of democracy'. As discussed above, while democracy was later reconciled with liberalism, at this time it was further stigmatised by being much more closely associated with socialism and communism. The classical interpretation of democracy as a social form of rule was reiterated, only now it was the growing working classes that warned against its institution.

Even when Woodrow Wilson was attempting to 'make the world safe for democracy' (Wilson 1965: 308), it was far from being fully accepted – in either institutional or normative terms – by the very countries supposedly fighting for it. The Entente Powers would only reconcile themselves to Wilson's democratic war aims gradually and incompletely. Nonetheless, the American intervention was fundamental in catalysing democracy's fortunes, effectively transferring the positive connotations of democracy found in the United States into the international sphere (C. Hobson 2009: ch. 6). Crucially, by framing the war in terms of democracy versus autocracy, the victory by the Allied Powers was also a victory for democracy. Reflecting on the ideational climate shortly after the Great War, James Bryce (1921: 4) judged that there was a 'universal acceptance of democracy as the normal and natural form of government'. It was not long before this situation changed drastically, and for much of the twentieth century democracy was strongly challenged and contested by fascism and communism. While recognising this, it was in the opening decades of the century that democracy took on the positive image it has yet to lose. Contestation would no longer be over whether democracy was desirable or possible, but around what exactly it meant.

What this very brief genealogy of democracy illustrates is how recent and unlikely the current normative consensus over democracy is. It was not until the 1840s that democracy had clearly taken on a positive meaning in American domestic politics (C. Hobson 2009: 160–7), and it would take at least another half century for other major Western liberal democracies to start following suit in discursive and institutional terms. It was only with Woodrow Wilson giving democracy pride of place during the First World War that it fully emerged as a positive political concept, even if contestation over its meaning has since continued (C. Hobson 2009: ch. 6). On this point it is worth noting that far from corresponding to Gallie's (1964: ch. 8) now commonplace description of democracy as an 'essentially contested concept', for most of its life democracy was essentially *un*contested. For the greater part of two millennia there was a very high level of consensus, and this was wholly negative: democracy was considered a dangerous, unstable, violent and antiquated form of rule. It was long dismissed and derided as a foolhardy adventure that could only end in disaster. It is only in the last two centuries that the meaning of democracy has been contested, challenged and changed.

Democracy's futures past?

In contrast to the excessive optimism of liberal millenarianism, this has been an attempt to develop a much more reflexive position, whereby consideration of democracy's role in contemporary international politics is influenced by a genuine acknowledgement of the vicissitudes of history. The approach taken here has sought to emphasise 'how brief and slight the impress of democracy upon the course of human history' has been (J.A. Hobson 1934: 1). And through recognising the relatively short historical agreement on democracy as something both possible and desirable, a much more humble and cautious position is promoted. A similar conclusion can be found in Reinhold Niebuhr's classic, *The Children of Light and the Children of Darkness*:

> The excessively optimistic estimates of human nature and of human history with which the democratic credo has been historically associated are a source of peril to democratic society; for contemporary experience is refuting this optimism and there is danger that it will seem to refute the democratic as well.
>
> (Niebuhr 1945: v)

What Niebuhr points towards is that by taking a more reflexive approach to appreciating democracy and its history, a firmer foundation for it can be built.

Through inverting the liberal millenarian account, an important dimension recovered is the unstable and uncertain nature of democracy. While this has historically been used as an argument *against* democracy, it can be the basis for a more reflective case *for* democracy. In the classical interpretation, this form of rule was seen as especially susceptible to collapse, as there was no protection from the whims of the wilful, erratic *dēmos*, liable to change their minds as often as the wind changed. An interesting variation on this perspective surprisingly comes from a number of conservative thinkers in the nineteenth century. Reflecting on Athens, Joseph de Maistre could still admit, 'democracy has one brilliant moment'. This statement was carefully qualified, however: 'but it is one moment, and it is necessary to pay dearly for it.... In general, all democratic governments are only transient meteors, whose brilliance excludes durations' (Maistre 1996: 159–60). Writing half a century later, Henry Sumner Maine (1886: 87–8) echoed these observations, noting that 'of all the forms of government, Democracy is by far the most difficult' and this primarily accounted for its 'ephemeral duration'. Meanwhile, the archconservative Metternich derided its complexity: 'democracy, far from being the oldest and simplest form of government, as it is often maintained, is the last of all to have been invented and the most complicated' (quoted in Sauvigny 1962: 39). These thinkers identified two primary problems. First, not only was the emerging representative form of democracy remarkably complex, it also meant democracy could only be achieved in an incomplete and limited sense, as it was not genuinely possible for the *dēmos* to exercise power in a large society, even indirectly. Second, proponents of democracy did not seriously reflect on the problems and difficulties it entailed. Maine (1886: 20–1) complained, 'convinced partisans of democracy care little for instances which show democratic governments to be unstable. These are merely isolated triumphs of the principle of evil.' Ultimately, for these highly sceptical observers, regardless of any potential benefits democracy may provide, the complexities and difficulties of this form of rule strongly warned against it.

Modern representative democracy has proven these conservative critics wrong, demonstrating that a stable and lasting form of democracy is possible. At the same stage, the people and their will are always approximated, but never fully manifest through the representative system. While one can make strong normative and historical arguments that representation *is* democratic (C. Hobson 2008b; Urbinati 2006), the 'gap' it introduces between the people and those it delegates to creates an ongoing tension, if not antinomy, at modern democracy's heart. The result, as Ankersmit (2002: 230–1) explains, is that 'representative democracy is a far more subtle, sophisticated, and therefore also a far more vulnerable political system than we tend to believe'. Undoubtedly this vulnerability is multiplied by the complexities of (post) modern society. For instance, the grave and extensive challenges posed to current democracies by globalisation have been well detailed. Indeed, many of these changes have further exacerbated problems in regards to questions of representation, accountability, access and the exercise of power in existing democracies. Given the huge array of issues that even the most well-established democracies are now struggling with, the historically longstanding concerns with democracy's fragility and lack of permanence are not completely out of place. Indeed, some notable commentators have suggested that we may already be entering a 'post-democratic' era (e.g. Crouch 2004; Wolin 2008). The linear, teleological conception of history that underwrites the liberal millenarian world-view, however, leaves it poorly equipped for engaging with these kinds of issues. Instead liberals cling vainly to a simplistic narrative of democratic progress and expansion, despite already significant, and still growing, evidence to the contrary.

Conservative sceptics warned against democracy because they thought its complexities meant it was bound to fail. Liberal millenarians, meanwhile, remain overly assured in the permanence of democracy. Neither of these positions is satisfactory: one too pessimistic, the other too confident. What can be taken from the conservatives is the recognition of the difficulties of instituting and sustaining democracy. This suggests humility where democracy exists, and caution if seeking to promote it abroad. Meanwhile, one can benefit from the liberals' faith in democracy, and they are certainly on much stronger ground when pointing to modern democracy's comparative successes at providing basic human goods. Put another way, what is ultimately needed is an account that lies between the extremes of George W. Bush's unchecked faith in democracy's 'good-ness' and universality, and the deceptively corrosive scepticism that lurks in Winston Churchill's famous quip about democracy.

History points towards there being nothing natural or inevitable about the present importance attached to democracy, or the manner in which it is practiced. Things may stay the same, but the past suggests that democracy's meaning will alter again. For instance, in much the same way that the current reconciliation between liberalism and democracy is due to historical circumstances, there is potential that in the future liberals may again separate themselves from democracy, if it is felt that this regime type is no longer the best way of promoting basic liberal rights. In the meantime, the ongoing tensions which arise from the combining of liberalism and democracy in the model now dominant are not ones that can be easily overcome, with the pressures of globalisation and (post) modern society having great potential to further exacerbate these fault lines.

Indeed, how democracies deal with these significant challenges now facing them, combined with how prudently and successfully they seek to promote this form of rule abroad, will help to shape the way democracy is valued in the future. Simply put, by removing the liberal blinkers that limit our view of democracy, we can see that even if a degree of democracy has been achieved in some places, this cannot be taken for granted, or presumed to be something that will continue indefinitely. If anything, history suggests the opposite is more likely. By recognising this, it allows for a perspective better equipped to recognise and respond to the serious challenges democracy now faces.

Conclusions

It has been argued that the contingency and contextuality of democracy has been lost in the liberal reading of its history which dominates our mental horizons. This constructed narrative plays an important role in shaping contemporary practices. Alternative versions of democracy are foreclosed, as the liberal model is seen as applicable to all. Meanwhile, antinomies and tensions within this specific version of democracy are papered over or ignored, as it is regarded as an achieved state and a natural condition in the Western core, bolstered by a presumption that this situation will not drastically change in the future. Universalising democracy in this manner, however, tries to depoliticise its meaning, by removing from consideration such foundational questions as: 'what is democracy?', 'what can it mean?', 'what kind of democracy is best in this specific context?', 'are there democratic alternatives within or beyond liberalism?', and most basically, 'is democracy necessarily the best form of rule?'. Instead, history is seen to provide the answer: liberal democracy. Clearly this move is, in itself, deeply political, by seeking to legitimate a specific vision of democracy, and with it, a certain set of actors and policies, while simultaneously limiting other possibilities.

In the liberal millenarian framework, stable liberal democracies, having reached 'the end of history', are regarded as morally superior, with increasing calls that this self-designated status should give them special rights. To take an important example of this thinking, in the United States there has been wide-ranging support for the formation of a 'league' or 'alliance' of democracies. One of the major proposals of the recent Princeton Report on US National Security was the creation of a 'Concert of Democracies', which would be 'a new global institution dedicated to the principles underpinning liberal democracy, both as a vehicle to spur and support the reform of the United Nations and other global institutions and as a possible alternative to them' (Ikenberry and Slaughter 2006a: 25).[8] In a similar vein, Buchanan and Keohane (2004: 18–20) suggest that if the United Nations Security Council proves unworkable, a 'democratic coalition' should be granted special privileges in determining the use of force because of their 'comparative moral reliability'. In these prominent proposals, liberal democracies are taken as more legitimate due to their comparative or absolute moral 'good-ness'. Underwriting these claims is a particular, linear conception of history: 'post-historical states' that have achieved liberal democracy are more advanced, and thus more entitled to special rights and privileges than those 'still stuck in history' (Fukuyama 1992: 276). One aim of this chapter has been to show how unjustifiable the historical grounds for arguments such as these are.

By moving beyond 'the end of history' and towards a 'radical historicisation' of democracy, an alternative vision is forged, one that is explicitly more open and more political. In looking forward, we do so cognisant of what has come before, aware that democracy is not preordained by History, nature or humankind. Democracy is a fragile, uncertain, fluctuating form, and over the *longue durée*, it has been defined more by its failures and its impermanence, than the opposite. Democracy's meaning is neither determined nor fixed. It has changed over time, and this will undoubtedly continue into the future. Furthermore, the present pairing of democracy and liberalism is a historically specific one, and there are no guarantees this relationship will continue indefinitely. Adopting a historically sensitive position leads to a more pluralist appreciation of contemporary democracy and its future possibilities. It suggests that if we value democracy, we must continue to explore, confront and renovate what it means. This is necessarily an ongoing process, one informed by – but most definitely not limited to – historical reflection. Doing so reminds us that democracy remains an unstable, precarious and incomplete form, with history providing no assurances that the current moment will last. While past and present successes provide us with a degree of hope; the antinomies, limits and shortcomings that mark democracy suggest humility, counselling an awareness of the contingency and potential impermanence of the present normative and political ascendancy of this unique and rare form of rule.

Notes

1 The research leading to these results has received funding from the European Research Council under the European Community's Seventh Framework Programme (FP7/2007–2013), ERC grant agreement no. 202 596. All views expressed here remain those of the author.
2 The return of non-liberal democratic powers, notably China and Russia, suggests this situation may now be changing. Nonetheless, it is notable that there has not been an explicit rejection of the language of democracy. Indeed, both Chinese and Russian leaders define their countries in reference to democracy, albeit a different *kind* to the liberal version.
3 Some of the most notable examples are: Diamond (2008); Franck (1992); McFaul (2010); Plattner (2007); Russett (1993); Slaughter (1995).
4 To take a notable example, in 2004 Larry Diamond went to Iraq as a senior advisor to the Coalition Provisional Authority. In the current Obama administration, Anne-Marie Slaughter and Michael McFaul both occupy senior posts.
5 For a full account, see C. Hobson (2009); Keane (2009).
6 Both rest, to a certain extent, on underspecified ideas of '*fraternité*', where some kind of nation or defined group is largely taken as a given. On this, see Canovan (1996).
7 A parallel argument is made by Nicholas and Peter Onuf in this volume.
8 For an extended discussion on this proposal, see Ian Clark's chapter in this volume.

6 The active making of two foundationally unequal subjects

Liberal democracy's Achilles heel?

Saskia Sassen

My concern in this chapter is with the formation of two foundationally unequal subjects for the articulation of capitalism; critical in the analysis is the fact that these subjects were actively made within the law, and in that process of making the law, liberal democracy, so central to capitalism, began to emerge. These subjects can be identified as the bourgeoisie as owners of productive capital, and the workers as suppliers of labour. As liberal democracy has gone through multiple phases and in many diverse directions since that early industrial phase, but notwithstanding this diversity has democratized society and politics, we might have expected the deep inequality of those foundational subjects to have been neutralized in this evolution. But the current period and its deep socio-economic fractures and injustices show us that the foundational inequality built into the making and legitimating of those two subjects has survived these trans-formations and attempted democratizations. I explain this in terms of some of the specific capabilities through which each of these subjects was constructed in law and that have carried over through the changing organizing logics that mark the evolution of capitalism. Elsewhere (Sassen 2008) I have developed at length this notion of capabilities made in one historical period being able to switch to new organizing logics, a process that is often not particularly legible; this holds, I argue, also for other features of early capitalism and for pre-capitalist political economies in Europe.

The key to this notion of capabilities switching organizing logics is that it helps explain how the many changes in capitalism and in liberal democracy over time could occur *without* a foundational overriding of the sharply unequal cap-abilities marking these two subjects. This overriding did not even happen with the vast extension of property rights to all as a function of the development of markets and the interests of both political and economic actors in this extension. There have been epochs, such as the Keynesian period, when a combination of elements enabled a major expansion of advantages to large sectors of the popu-lation. It was easy to imagine the Keynesian period as the beginning of a whole new kind of capitalism – a kinder and more democratic capitalism.

But the trends that emerged in the 1970s and 1980s made it clear that those original foundational inequalities were indeed systemic, wired into the function-ing of capitalism itself.[1] One open question is whether they are also wired into the functioning of liberal democracy – was liberal democracy ultimately the project of the historic bourgeoisie? This is a subject that no longer exists today in the same form, which perhaps explains the growing incapacities of liberal democracy to address and engage major contemporary challenges to the democratizing of economies and societies, a subject I examine at length elsewhere (Sassen 2008: chs 4 and 5).

This questioning of the future potential of liberal democratic capitalism to evolve into a more distributed and just system is the substantive rationality running through this chapter's examination of the making of the two foundational subjects of capitalism and the symbiosis between liberal democracy and capitalism. Let me clarify promptly that I use both liberal democracy and capitalism to mean an actual trajectory, a living historic process, one that is to be distinguished from normative and theoretical developments in liberal democratic and capitalist thought.

The chapter proceeds with four sections. In the first I discuss the rapidity and national diversity characteristic of the emergence of different bourgeoisies. Second, I deal in detail with the emergence of the legal persona of the national bourgeoisie in England and the United States. Third, I argue that the working class in both countries was also legally constructed as a subject with inferior rights and capabilities. Fourth and in conclusion, I explore the contemporary implications of this foundational inequality for the current state of liberal democracy.

Making capabilities and their consequences

The rich scholarship about the ascendance of capitalism documents the work of making the institutional, legal, discursive, ideational and other capabilities required for implementing the variable and diverse capitalisms that arise in Europe. This work of making, while often highly innovative, was partly shaped by the particular resources, cultures, dispositions and ideational forms of each country and by the key actors whose interests shaped the process. It underlines the national specificities at play in the shaping of each national capitalism and its imperial geography[2] as well as the fact that the development of the world scale was deeply intertwined with the formation of national capitalisms. The bourgeoisie sharply expanded foreign trade, which rose tenfold between 1610 and 1640, and manufacturing, leading to an enormous increase of the workforce. Colonial expansion was a key feature of England's rise from the beginning of the seventeenth century.

The growth in commerce and manufacturing was also the beginning of a new political economy, with its need for specific types of protections and enablements in each country. Though I return to this issue in more detail in the next two sections, for now let me signal that in England the work of making the institutional and ideational infrastructure for the emergence of a national capitalism based in an English-dominated imperial geography followed a rather different path from that of Holland, further contributing to the national specificity of capitalist development. In France, where the absolutist monarchy exercised far more control over the economy than it did in England, the bourgeoisie allied itself with the king against the nobility, and mercantilism was imposed, though it largely served the interests of the state. While France and England both aimed at ensuring the wealth of the prince, from the beginning the bourgeoisie in England also wanted and fought for free trade. In France, the state's major and active role in developing commerce and manufacturing and in promoting mercantilism preempted the emergence of the bourgeoisie as a historic subject with a distinct project. The royal absolutist state strongly supported the development of manufacturing and worldwide trade; the French bourgeoisie was formed under its protection and would bear its imprint for a long time. But notwithstanding the far larger role of the state, English- and Dutch-style mercantilism also took shape in France (which included control of the seas, creation of a company for overseas trading and the protection of monopolies). Mercantilism was at its height in France from 1663 to 1685.

The major transformations taking shape in the seventeenth and early eighteenth centuries were not immediately obvious. Even when the capitalist development of industry was taking over key economic sectors in England in the early nineteenth century, it was still far from prevalent. The industrial bourgeoisie was not yet a distinct social group; nor were wage workers. Older classes, such as the nobility, landowners, farmers, artisans and shopkeepers, were the prevalent presence in the economic landscape. They were also the source of growing criticisms of the new order they sensed was coming, criticism often in the name of values of the past or in the name of an alternative society ruled by norms of equity and reason. But only a few decades later, by the mid-nineteenth century, the bourgeoisie had become the visibly dominant class in England and the working class had become legible as a distinctly disadvantaged social group.

The illegibility of the dominance of industrial capitalism needs to be underscored, especially the fact that it remained so even as it was about to become very legible, or 'explode' on the scene. This supports the argument that in its early phases, a new dominant economic logic may not necessarily be the prevalent social form. By 1870 industrial capitalism was the dominant logic in Great Britain, but it had only changed part of Great Britain and was firmly grounded only in bounded zones of Western Europe and North America. However, it soon spread rapidly through the rise of new techniques and new industries, as well as ever larger and more powerful concentrations of capital whose field of action expanded to the world scale. Further, this expansion took place as the older state-controlled imperialisms declined, which, depending on one's interpretive categories, could easily be chosen to mark the period rather than the features of the new imperialisms. As industrial capitalism erupted on the scene, the enormously exploited national workforce became visible. This was also the moment of the rise and public recognition of a variety of workers' movements, as well as the development and implementation of new modes of domination over workers.

Even as it was reaching its zenith, Britain was already entering a phase of sharpened rivalries with ascendant powers that would challenge its position of dominance. Britain was losing out to Germany and the United States, even though it did not look that way at the time (Beaud 1981). The often problematic legibility of major transformations in the making is underlined by the fact that only in Great Britain had the bourgeoisie become the visible dominant class by the mid-nineteenth century, even as industrial capitalism was developing in what were to become other major powers.[3]

Constructing the legal persona of a national bourgeoisie

There is an interesting tension in the historical development of a national bour-geoisie that needed national political institutions – notably Parliament in the case of the English bourgeoisie – to constitute itself even as its vested interests lay in imperial economic geographies. In this regard, England's development of indus-trial capitalism is a natural experiment for illuminating three sets of issues. The first is the articulation of foreign trade, global pillaging and colonization with the growth and rise of a novel legal persona, the national bourgeoisie. The second is the lack of legibility of the fact that capitalism was dominant in the English economy at a time when it seemed kings and nobility were; elsewhere (Sassen 2008: chs 2 and 3) I examine how this condition recurs in diverse historical phases across time and place. I would see this illegibility of the dominance of industrial capitalism culminating in the early nineteenth century. The third is the political economy that was constructed as the bourgeoisie carved out a legal persona for itself, *a rights-bearing subject that began as a legal non-persona striving against absolutism and the nobility.* The outcome is the construction of a novel subject – a legitimate owner of means of production and a legitimate bearer of the means for powerful controls over the workers it needs and depends on. This process, extended over a century, enacted a major historic switch, which if concentrated over a briefer temporal frame would be akin to what Sewell (1980) has described as 'events' that disrupt existing structurations.

All of this was arising out of an older context where this history in the making was not particularly legible. Wallerstein (1974) notes that the sixteenth century was indecisive. The capitalist strata formed a class that survived politically but did not yet triumph in the political domain. The sectors benefiting from eco-nomic and geographic expansion of the capitalist system, especially in the core areas, tended to operate within the political arena as a group defined primarily by their common role in the economy. This group included farmers, merchants and industrialists with an orientation toward profit making in the world economy. Other actors – the traditional aristocracy, guilds, owners of inherited farms – fought back to maintain their status privileges. But the major historical dynamic was toward novel class formation, even as all these other groups often seemed dominant and even as the 'veneer of culture' led to a sense of unity.

By the seventeenth century the English bourgeoisie was strong enough to defy absolutism and to legitimate a new form of government. Locke gave them some of the instruments with his *Of Civil Government* (1690). It contained a justification for the overthrow of the sovereign in the name of freedom.

Locke's emphasis on the protection of property as key to the social contract leads him to argue that if the sovereign were to take away property it would justify insurrection by the people. Locke's rejection of absolutism (which places the sovereign above the law and thus beyond civil society) pivots on his proposition that what establishes society and government (social contract) is the free consent of the citizens. Yet in Locke's work these principles were in fact confined to the 'proper' classes – those who had won themselves the right to handle their affairs – especially enlightened landowners, commercial and financial bourgeoisies, the landed nobility, clergymen and the gentry. He did not believe the working classes were capable of governing themselves. To cope with the poor he recommended force (Bourne 1969: 378). All in all, the bourgeoisie found in Locke their theoretician. Locke's ideas were also a success among the ruling classes in England and Holland and, in the eighteenth century, among jurists and philosophers in France. They were the ideas for an enlightened bourgeoisie.

Locke offered a substantive rationality for major developments already in motion by the time his work was published. His ideas corresponded to the interests of the sectors of the bourgeoisie that saw in free trade the stimulus for a new expansion of commerce and production, and in Parliament the vehicle for politically legitimating their economic project. Operating at the world scale necessitated innovation in both institutional infrastructure and operational capabilities. The use of Parliament signalled the making of a new political economy, that is to say, more that just an elementary accumulation of capital.[4] In 1694 the Bank of England was created. It raised 1.2 million pounds in twelve days, an indication of the emergent power of capital owners. In return for lending to the government, the bank became the first English joint stock bank and was permitted to discount bills (Carruthers 1996). The government did not have to repay but only serve up interest. The New East India Company was also founded in part to lend the government money (1698). Both the New East India Company and the Bank of England were controlled by Parliament, which increased its control over the Crown (Ashley 1961: 185) and thereby enhanced the political power of the bourgeoisie.

The growing power of Parliament contained a critical political shift that enabled the formation of the bourgeoisie as a rights-bearing subject. This shift was part of a long history of accumulating partial powers and claims in the emergent capitalist class. For instance, the 1624 Statute of Monopolies regularized patent law allowing the developer of an innovation to assert a right to revenues produced by its introduction, i.e. to assert 'property rights over invention' whereas previously the Crown might have awarded prizes for innovation but granted no private returns to the innovator (Hartwell 1971: ch. 11; Douglass C. North 1981: 164ff.).[5] Another indication of accumulating 'rights' was the resolution of a conflict surrounding the wool trade during the Stuart years concerning the extent of taxation; in the terms of the compromise the Crown received revenues, Parliament won the right to set taxation levels and merchants got the monopoly of trade (North and Thomas 1973).

The capabilities developed in this extended and multifaceted politico-economic process of gathering advantages eventually became part of a system of private property protections, enablements for global operations and the formalization of political decisions that began to concentrate advantages in the emerging bourgeoisie. Acts of Parliament, its enhanced taxation powers (Ashley 1961), and the enormous commercial expansion of eighteenth-century England were critical variables in this process.

In the eighteenth century, long-distance trade became crucial to England's rapid development. Colonial domination, pillaging and exploitation of native or imported workers, mostly through slavery, remained fundamental sources of enrichment that contributed to trade and production. The effort included devious tactics, such as the 1700 prohibition on the import of Indian calicoes, a textile superior to anything made in England, which threatened domestic manufacturers. Commerce quintupled and national income quadrupled. Foreign trade was a major factor that enabled the sharp growth of the British port cities – Liverpool, Manchester, Bristol and Glasgow.

However, a sharp difference began to take shape. While state accumulation proceeded in the eighteenth century in the same domains as before (roads, waterways, harbours, fleets, administrative machinery), bourgeois accumulation took a new turn: even as it proceeded through an increase in private fortunes and stocks of merchandise, a growing share of capital became productive capital – raw materials, machines and mills. Turgot (1795), Quesnay (1958 [1757]) and Smith (1976 [1759]) saw this new logic: a net product could be extracted from productive labour that could enlarge or improve production. The principal agent was the bourgeoisie that had come from the merchant and banking sectors, from dealers and manufacturers, and, in England, from a portion of the nobility. This emergent new class articulated its economic and political project around the notion of freedom, something that held across the major powers of the time. In England, this class was involved with affairs of the state through Parliament: it sought and secured freedom of trade and production, freedom to pay labour at its lowest level, and freedom to defend against workers' alliances and revolts.

The emergent notions of a liberal *democracy* gave the bourgeoisie an institutional form that enabled the 'lawful' development of a 'legitimate' system of laws and regulations that privileged the bourgeoisie and property as a criterion for granting rights.[6] It sought authority rather than simply the raw power of capital. This meant a government constituted through a social contract – rather than the divinity of the sovereign – and through political regimes. Where it once had taken shelter in royal authority against the nobility, liberalism now allowed it a variety of alliances in order to advance its own projects, including alliances with artisans and the petty bourgeoisie. Thus, at some point the notion of national unity ceased to be constructed in terms of the monarch and became a vehicle for alliances of the bourgeoisie and others against the monarch. While it remained allied with the monarch through a shared interest in colonial expansion and mercantilism, the English bourgeoisie knew how to use popular discontent in its fight against absolutism, which was also a battle to strengthen its own power. By the end of the eighteenth century, the idea of the nation, connected to mercantilism, was used against the king; the French and American revolutions were the most prominent formulations of this shift.[7]

Consolidating state support

We see at this time the first instantiation of what was to become the liberal state: the development of a 'legitimate' system of laws and regulations that privileged the owners of productive capital. The project of formalizing the rights of capital owners was most developed in England, but the trend was also evident in the other major powers of the time. Holland had long had a sort of embedded regime favouring merchant, banking and manufacturing capitalists. The French Revolution, a far more complex and sudden event than the more extended struggles of the English bourgeoisie, eventually brought enablements to the French bourgeoisie, but these were only rendered fully effective in the 1850s through the alliance with the monarch, Napoleon III.

The losers in this configuration were the nobility, small artisans, and, above all, the workers. The nobility, between the king and the bourgeoisie, saw their relative power and privileges decline. As for small artisans, even as they made claims against the landed nobility, a new mode of value extortion was the indirect domination by intermediaries and traders. Poor artisans did not ask for democracy and freedom but for basic protections by regulation: better prices or wages, a shorter workday and protection from foreign competition. The poorest layers of the peasantry were hurt badly by the new wave of enclosures in the mid-seventeenth century. Agricultural workers became destitute as both the earlier and later waves of enclosures expelled them from land. Various disciplining measures aimed at controlling workers and the poor generally in cities and towns all contributed to much discontent and agitation.

The enclosure movement continued strongly in the eighteenth century, especially after 1760, and increasingly took the form of laws passed by Parliament. The enclosure acts passed by Parliament illuminate the process of developing capabilities that gave the bourgeoisie economic and political instruments. In these acts Parliament formalized specific advantages for the owners of productive capital and enabled the formation of a particularly disadvantaged and vulnerable labour supply. These acts also resolved the tensions between the Crown and the bourgeoisie to the advantage of the latter. Enclosures were not new to the modern period, dating back at least to the Statute of Merton (1236) (North and Thomas 1973: 151). Enclosures were justified in terms of the positive consequences of private ownership rights for agricultural productivity (Thompson 1963: 217). Monarchies had diverse positions on enclosures (Polanyi 2001: 37–8). According to Briggs, 'Between 1761 and 1780 during the first phase of enclosure by Act of Parliament, 4039 Acts were passed: there were a further 900 between 1781 and 1800' (1959: 41).[8] The General Enclosure Act of 1801 rationalized the procedure.[9] The creation of this particular type of working class became a key resource for a dynamic that was expanding in

England: producing more in order to produce more. The implementation of this project brought many changes in the organization of agriculture, mining and processing. In the last third of the eighteenth century and the first third of the nineteenth century, this logic was extended to a growing number of sectors: clothing and textiles, machines, tools and metal domestic utensils, railroads, and armaments.

Perhaps the key analytic import of this type of relationship between workers and the bourgeoisie is that even as it progressed along different paths in the different major European powers of the time, it produced a similar outcome: a proletariat shaped both in terms of a systemic position in the emerging new economy and in terms of a particular type of legal persona through the passing of a variety of laws and regulations in each of the major countries – each with its own specifics. This was the making of a legal subject that *lacked critical rights and enablements*, in contrast to the propertied classes, which had been granted considerable rights. Both of these very different subjects were created as national, and as deeply embedded in and constitutive of a 'national economy'. The progress of this nation-based liberalism across the next centuries never fully overcame that original geometry of 'lawful' inequality, even as it allowed for hard-fought struggles by workers to gain rights. Today's capitalism, with its wider global operational space and neoliberal policy frameworks, has made this brutally clear. This foundational inequality in law had become less evident in the preceding period marked by Keynesian policies and a strengthened social contract in much of the world – both partly a result of workers' struggles and the state's need for soldiers.

The articulation of this industrial project with a particularly disadvantaged working class might suggest the necessity of that disadvantage – the need for such a working class if industrial production was to proceed. While the historical trajectory might further reinforce this notion, the historical record also admits deeper complexity. The Stuarts in England at times sought to resist or at least weaken the enclosure acts as a way of reducing the brutality and velocity through which the rural workforce was made into an urban industrial labour supply. Traditional liberal readings see the Crown as reactionary and impeding progress. But Polanyi (2001: 39) credits king and church with preventing enclosures from completely tearing the social fabric apart; this may have made an extremely destructive process into a somewhat more sustainable system of production and innovation. The king and church were anxious about rural depopulation and sought to impede the process of dislocation of agricultural workers; this brought them into conflict with the local lords and nobles. Parliament, by contrast, tended to favour enclosure. While Parliament seems to have usually been successful legislatively, the Crown did manage to implement the system of Poor Laws, which were aimed at easing the transition and protecting local authority relations.[10] In this effort to slow down enclosures and give some protections to the disadvantaged, the state did also enable the industrial project by making life somewhat more manageable for the workers and the poor even as they were subjected to greater control.

Whatever paternalist protections the state may have provided for weaker groups overall, the state's major role in the process of industrial development was to strengthen the national capitalist project – through protectionist measures, the licences and monopolies of mercantilist policies, and the laws and acts that protected the rights of the propertied classes and sharply weakened the status of workers. On the one hand, the state provided political and military support for commercial and colonial expansion. On the other hand, the state used the police and the law against the poor and to suppress workers' revolts. Parliament frequently aligned with the interests of the bourgeoisie and played a crucial role in this process. For instance, a 1769 law classified the voluntary destruction of machines and the buildings that contained them as a felony, and instituted the death penalty for those found guilty of such destruction and a 1799 law prohibited the formation of workers' associations that wanted wage increases, a shorter workday or any other improvement in working conditions.[11]

The law was used to implement a massive assault on the poor and on workers. In this process the bourgeoisie began to take shape as a privileged legal persona. The new propertied classes mostly benefited from the state's interventions, and in that sense differed from the nobility, which was itself a propertied class but played a far smaller role in stimulating extensive and innovative state work, especially in the legal domain. The emerging bourgeois propertied class included a mix of social groups, both old and new: members of the nobility involved in commercial enterprises, farming or mines; great merchants and financiers who displayed their success by purchasing estates; merchants who became manufacturers and then established mills; and manufacturers and traders who became bankers. Together they handled the country's economy, and the state helped enable this.

We can see here the creation of what we now call the 'rule of law'. In this case, it legitimated private property, protected the rights of the emerging bourgeoisie from abuses of power by the king and the nobility, and sanctioned decisive control over workers as the legitimate right of these specific propertied classes. We see here the making of a rights-bearing subject that represents a contestation of absolutist power, opens up a space for the rights of novel actors and institutionalizes overwhelming power over the workers it employs. It thus emerges as a historic subject in that it sets in motion a variety of processes shaping a new political economy. While this is only part of the formation of capitalism, it helped draw the key alignments in the emerging political economy. The developing practical and legal architecture enabled the formation of national economic projects that could accommodate foreign pillaging and trade, growing rights for the national bourgeoisie and massive social divisions inside that national unit. And yet, the rights discourse was also to become a tool for the claims by the oppressed for expanded formal protections under democracy.

All of this took place against a context of a changing relationship between the bourgeoisie and the nobility. In the second third of the nineteenth century, Britain saw a decisive change in the composition of its national capital: components linked to the development of capitalism (overseas securities, domestic railroads, industrial capital, and commercial and finance capital, including buildings) became dominant compared to traditional landed inheritance (estates and farms).[12] Throughout the nineteenth century the landed aristocracy lost its monopoly over political and local power. Many of the great reforms of this century benefited the rising bourgeoisie, not the old nobility, although they shared interests, were on the same side of the conflicts involving property and were against the 'masses'. In the political arena, confrontation between conservatism (nobility) and liberalism (bourgeoisie) often masked the growing interactions and alliances between them.

But nineteenth-century England is marked by the rise of the bourgeoisie. The landed aristocracy did not necessarily recognize the epochal transformation afoot and its displacement as a powerful political actor by the rising bourgeoisie, whom it could still force into disadvantageous positions through laws and decrees passed in Parliament, a body it could still control. Its displacement was further veiled by the ongoing political and economic weight of traditional economic institutions and activities, even though industrial capitalism was already the dominant political economy.

While the rise of industrial capitalism in England positioned the English bourgeoisie as emblematic of the formation of such a class, the other major powers had their own trajectories in this process. The fact of multiple trajectories is significant because they all eventually fed into the development of imperial geographies and thereby engraved national features and projects in the formation of the world scale. By the late 1800s, the national bourgeoisie in each country pursued the development of imperial geographies for trade and investment.

The United States at this point emerges as an interesting case, separately from the fact of its being on the way to becoming the major power in the world. Its development as an industrial capitalist political economy differed from that of France and Britain. It had no old feudal or agrarian society, as did Britain and France, and was originally a loose confederacy with a weak central state. It also lacked the medieval lineages of the legitimacy of a national sovereign that could become the source of law and authority.

One critical difference with England lies in the origins of the American political economy. While wealth in England had been grounded in land ownership, the abundance of land made this system impractical in the colonies. Land distribution differed across the colonies, but it tended to benefit ordinary people. In New England, the Puritan colonies encouraged social cohesion by granting land to groups of settlers through townships and church congregations, which were then charged with its redistribution. Some of the colonies restricted the transfer of land and maintained common land: overall, however, they preferred individual ownership. Outside New England, a system of 'head right' prevailed – land was awarded to each person immigrating to the colonies; some colonies offered this to indentured servants after their terms expired. Under this system, land could be purchased and sold, and many of the owners were formally required to remit a quitrent to the king or an overlord, although actual collection of these was spotty at best. This system lasted until the late seventeenth century.[13] After 1763, with the French and Indian Wars completed, the British Parliament sought to tighten imperial control over its colonies through stronger enforcement of the Navigation Acts and taxation. The closing of Boston Harbor in the early 1770s, which was seen as an assault on the economic liberty of Bostonians and an appropriation of private property without compensation or representation, shifted the colonies' relationship with England. In 1781 the Articles of Confederation were signed.

A second critical difference was a general disposition toward utility more than privilege. Thus, while generally enacting protections for private property, most colonies also enacted provisions requiring that land be productively used and developed. New England colonies frequently required either settlement or cultivation within a specified period of time. Ely (1992) provides a detailed yet concise overview of specific policies. Before the drafting of the Constitution, each state had a slightly different articulation of property rights – some were embedded in a state's constitution, some in subsequent legislation. Generally, they included some form of protection of private property, some attempt to limit monopoly power, and some trade-off between eminent domain and compensation (Ely 1992: 30–2). A number of diverse conflicts and difficult problems led to growing support for the Constitutional Convention of 1787, which would more consistently protect property rights, regulate commerce and restore public credit.

One of the key dynamics at work in the shaping of industrial capitalism is that its formation entailed the establishment of a working class and the rise of a new ruling class. Each class was a mix of social groups, though eventually some of these became the majority or the marking group. Most, if not all, of the groups within each class were, no matter how heterogeneous internally, on a particular side of the social conflicts of the epoch and the foundational economic relations taking shape. Yet the particular social, political and legal trajectories through which the two groupings were constituted diverged significantly across countries even as key systemic features of the position of each were similar in an abstract sense.

Constructing the legality of a disadvantaged subject

The key analytic issue I want to focus on has received less attention than have the larger social and economic dynamics in the shaping of the working class. It is the active construction of the legal persona of the worker in juxtaposition to that of the owner of productive capital – that is to say, the class that ran the economy. There are rich debates about whether the law generally, particularly in the case of workers, is a derivative factor or can be constitutive (Bok 1971; Rogers 1990; Forbath 1991; Archer 1998; Steinfeld 2001). It is not my purpose here to engage, let alone settle, these debates. Rather, I want to focus on the law as one factor in shaping the disadvantage of workers, a factor sufficiently formalized and explicit as to render legible the work of constructing such a disadvantaged subject. Nor does this particular role of the law preclude the fact that the law was also used by workers and by third parties to claim rights *for* workers. What workers, their organizations and political parties did with these laws varied depending on the conditions in their countries and the institutional channel through which this work proceeded.

British legislation was clearly aimed at controlling workers. Engels (1892) and others at the time observed that the law and the actual conditions of workers had made the proletariat de facto slaves of the property-holding class, with the added advantage that employers could dismiss workers and need not be stuck with them, as was the case with slavery. Workers were subjected to severe regulations, repression by fines, wage reductions or dismissal; unhealthy and unsafe workplaces; harsh work; and long workdays.[14] These conditions were the bases on which British industry developed in the nineteenth century. The relation between the emergent manufacturing working class and the owners of the factories was, at this point, a sort of primitive accumulation, where even minor profit differentials mattered and there were almost none of the intermediary structures that came later with the development of the welfare and regulatory aspects of the state.

By the mid-nineteenth century, the British industrial system was highly diversified and hence engendered a highly diversified working class. The previous system continued to exist through craftwork, homework, manufactories and workhouses, as well as through the mill system, which appeared at the end of the eighteenth century. Handlooms remained dominant for cotton weaving until 1829–31. What did develop was the factory system. The emergence of the factory and putting-out systems signalled the emergence of a new logic. The latter was a new form of work in the home that put workers at a sharp disadvantage and, to variable extents, engaged unpaid family labour; it gave employers full control over wage levels. In 1830, one-third of garments were produced through this system in London.

As had been the case with the Corn Laws, regulating factories became the site for playing out the opposing vested interests of agriculture-linked elites and manufacturing capitalists. A series of laws called the Factory Acts aimed at protecting workers in key manufacturing sectors.[15] In general, Protectionist and Tory MPs were more likely to support factory legislation, while Radicals opposed the 'improper' intrusion of the state (Rubinstein 1998: 80). The Tories' support was tied to their support for maintaining the Corn Laws: noting that most workers remained in agriculture, Tories argued that the best way to protect workers was to maintain agricultural protection, which would prevent the outflow of workers from the countryside to the city and avert high unemployment. There were other conflicts and alliances, often unrelated to concern for the actual conditions of workers, that steered the legislation.[16]

As English industrial capitalism accelerated, manufacturers sharpened their attempts to control workers. A supplementary compromise factory act was passed in August 1850, which lengthened the workday of women and children to ten and a half hours for the first five days of the week, and seven and a half hours on Saturday. Although England in 1848 was not marked by the sharp social uprisings taking place on the Continent, manufacturers used it as an excuse to clamp down on workers by eliminating meals at work, restoring night work for men, dismissing women and children and so forth (Marx 1977: 398). This basically revived the 'relay system' used by employers to evade the regulations by simply shifting young workers to another position in the factory (400–3). English courts had shown themselves to be unwilling to punish manufacturers for such practices; an 1850 decision by the Court of Exchequer ruled that these practices violated the spirit of the law but not its letter, effectively legalizing the practice. Throughout, class antagonism was continually flaring up, and factory conditions now varied widely across the country, depending on the sentiments of factory owners, enforcement of legislation and other variables.

The traditional account about labour in this period identifies legal change as a type of natural, perhaps inevitable, outcome or as a change running parallel to the social and economic forces that shape a market economy.[17] Although English workers were 'free' in the sense that they were not owned or bonded servants, the implementation of a formal apparatus for the control of workers and the possibility of the direct exercise of power by employers over workers make for a far more problematic account. One way into the bundle of issues is a focus on the rules that governed the treatment of British workers who breached their labour contracts in the nineteenth century. Steinfeld (2001) argues that the origins of what we currently call free labour (that is, the right to quit a job without penalty or other forms of pressure such as physical restraint or criminal punishment) did not emerge from market forces and the expansion of contractual social relations in the early nineteenth century, as is commonly assumed. Instead, he finds that 'free waged labor' came out of 'the restrictions placed on freedom of contract by the social and economic legislation adopted during the final quarter of the century' (2001: 10). Steinfeld uses court records, judicial opinions, parliamentary debates and data about criminal and civil prosecutions of labour contract breaches between 1857 and 1873 to demonstrate that for much of the nineteenth century British workers were not free, in the sense of twenty-first-century notions of free labour.[18] If British workers left their employers before they completed their contracts, they faced a variety of non-pecuniary punishments including prison terms with hard labour and whipping.[19] For example, in 1860, 11,938 British workers were prosecuted for breach of contract, among whom many were coal miners and iron workers. A majority of these workers received criminal convictions. Steinfeld writes, 'Of the 7,000-odd convicted, 1,699 served a sentence in the house of correction, 1,971 were fined, 3,380 received other punishments (wages abated and costs assessed, in all likelihood), and one person was ordered whipped' (2001: 80–1). The evidence shows a sharp expansion of penal sanctions in Britain between 1823 and the 1860s, indicating an increase in prosecutions during affluent moments in Britain's trade cycle. When unemployment was high, prosecutions tailed off, as happened between 1857 and 1873 though they stayed above 7,000 a year. Further penal sanctions also reached British workers indirectly through the threat of prosecution should the worker quit or refuse to comply with orders.

The timing of various repressive measures captures the accelerated and massive drive toward capital accumulation. For instance, trade unions and Jacobin associations were organizations with the potential to gain rights and become a stronger subject of liberal democratic capitalism. The 1799 Combination Act outlawed them, a move that coincided with the beginnings of the sharp expansion in the English economy (Rubinstein 1998: 20). Yet, in character with the contradictions of the struggle by the bourgeoisie, their outlawing unintentionally brought these two groups into association (Thompson 1963: 500). The Combination Act that prohibited unions was repealed in 1824 but partly reinstated in 1825. The campaign in the 1820s to abolish the Combination Act found some support in Parliament (in Francis Place and Joseph Hume, though Thompson qualifies this by arguing [517–18] that Place and Hume crushed more radical proposals) among those who argued that the act prevented the cooperation of workers and owners. The act's repeal in 1824 engendered a wave of strikes and riots, and a new parliamentary committee was set up to investigate the repeal. The new act in 1825 allowed 'combination' only to discuss demands concerning wages and hours. Unionization was then not illegal as such, but it was still tightly regulated (Rubinstein 1998: 20ff.; Thompson 1963: 516ff.). Nevertheless, Thompson argues it was during these years (1799–1820) that union organization made its greatest advances (503–4). He further notes that sufficient legislation already existed to make any particular union activity illegal; the legislation was passed mainly to intimidate by sweepingly prohibiting all combination. He suggests that it was used much less against artisans than factory workers, although the threat of its use was probably common. Even in factories, however, the Combination Act was not often used to effect prosecution; rather, an older piece of legislation was often cited (504–7; Briggs 1959: 136). A 'semi-legal' informal world of 'combinations' (mutual benefit societies, trade clubs and so on) was tolerated and created organizational infrastructure for the working class (Thompson 1963: 505, 508).

With the 1825 act, British workers had to give their employers one-month's notice of their intention to strike; if they failed to do so, they faced penal sanctions. The British historian D.C. Woods (1982) finds that 38 per cent of criminal prosecutions in coal-mining districts between 1858 and 1875 were for unlawful strike actions rather than for unlawful quitting. If an employer signed a contract with a worker and then fired her, technically she could still collect wages on a 'minimum' number of days of employment. Yet the Master and Servant Acts were rarely enforced against employers. For example, judges rarely forced employers to hire particular employees when trade was slow (Woods 1982: 165). Employers had 'it both ways, criminally enforcing long agreements while at the same time disclaiming any responsibility for finding work during the term of the contract if fired or not hired' (107). Here again we can see how the laws of the early liberal democracy instituted legally unequal subjects, a possibility both premised on and enabled by differentiated relationships to property.

The developments in England launched a massive phase in the capitalist transformation of production. Production increased sharply, the system of wages was extended, the workforce grew and workers' struggles multiplied. At the heart of this new type of economic logic were the mills and multiple technical inventions to promote increased production. Mills, typically housed in four-storey brick buildings, employed hundreds of workers and were controlled like prisons. The exploited workers, many of whom were women and children, came from many different places and social groups, from farmers driven out of the countryside by enclosures to small artisans driven out of business by merchants. The working class that was taking shape was enormously diverse, but most workers were equally desperate.[20] This wide diversity of origins in the working class was constituted as the raw matter for the work process: this diversity was being reshaped by a particular type of logic.

Just as the formation of the national state in the United States followed a distinct trajectory, so did the shaping of workers' disadvantage and the ensuing struggles by workers. In addition, there was no strong class-based political movement that could fight for workers' rights. As in England, employers used the state to formalize their advantage over workers, but instead of Parliament the United States had the courts. US laws provided, as they continue to do, far fewer protections against abuse, injury, illness and unemployment (e.g. Forbath 1991: chs 1 and 5; Rogers 1990) than did European laws in response to workers' mobilization in the late 1800s and on. They covered, and continue to do so, a small share of all workers and fail to stipulate terms of employment that ensure basic protections (Bok 1971). While Europe's major powers saw the growth of labour organizations that took on broad class-based programmes of reform and redistribution by the end of the nineteenth century, in the United States the American Federation of Labor rejected or avoided such broad programmes (Forbath 1991; Bok 1971). Most of the scholarship explains this American difference or 'exceptionalism' in terms of the conservatism and individualism of US workers.[21] However, some scholars (Bok 1971) have seen the law and the courts, rather than workers' individualism, as critical in explaining US workers' disadvantage. A few have consistently rejected the notion of American workers' 'exceptionalism' (Gutman 1976; Katznelson and Zolberg 1986; Montgomery 1980; Sassen 1988, 1999), and lower rates of workers' organization than in European countries, notably France (Katznelson and Zolberg 1986).

Without reducing the weight of these diverse explanations, I want to isolate the one centred on the role of the law and its institutional orders to see how the law has fed the construction of the disadvantage of workers (Perlman 1928). For example, the US government attacked the labour movement so aggressively that by the end of the 1890s it had been seriously weakened and, with few exceptions, opted for more moderate tactics. In Europe, by contrast, state attacks on workers had radicalized the large labour unions. It was through the courts, including their policy-making, that the US state exercised this function, much more so than through legislative or executive action (Bok 1971). Forbath (1991: ch. 3) documents how one union was destroyed through the courts' outlawing sympathy strikes, ordering mass imprisonments and putting armed force behind court decrees.[22] Judges and courts played a critical role not just in judiciary action but also in policy development, since the US government throughout the nineteenth century lacked a professional civil service, that is to say, a class of state workers that had tenure in the state bureaucracies and agencies, a key feature of the major European states. The legal personae of the worker and of the owner of productive capital were in good part established through a series of major court decisions.

There is a specific American prehistory to these nineteenth-century developments. Employment law in colonial America varied by location. But it was based on that of the Old World (Ray *et al.* 1999). The prevalence of slavery meant that in the eighteenth century much of the labour force was not free; employers could be owners or masters who used slaves, apprentices and/or indentured servants.[23] Unlike British workers, roughly after 1830 they generally experienced no civil or criminal penalties for labour breaches.[24] This was due to the existence of chattel slavery in the United States and the vigorous efforts of Northern wage earners to abolish slavery – and any penal sanctions that evoked it – in Northern states where wages became common after 1820. The particular freedoms of American workers were not a result of capitalist market forces but reflected strong political and moral forces (such as the abolitionist movements of the North). Other legal historians discuss the persistence of coercion in the United States when free labour relations were supposed to be the rule of law. Writing about labour relations after the Civil War, Amy Dru Stanley (1998) notes that local laws against the poor worked to coerce transient individuals into the workforce, even though the Thirteenth Amendment to the Constitution abolished slavery. While American workers were free from penal sanctions (unlike British workers), they were coerced and regulated through a process called wage forfeiture. Under this practice, a worker who left a job before its completion would lose any unpaid wages to the employer. British judiciaries outlawed this practice, but in the United States employers used this practice as a method of controlling workers.[25]

The pertinent laws in the 1800s and early 1900s stated that the relationship between the American worker and her/his employer was simply a matter of contract. This permeated the American legal landscape. Courts conceptualized labour largely in terms of the right to contract, making it difficult for American workers to bargain for better work conditions. For example, in a landmark case (*Lochner v. New York*), the US Supreme Court ruled that a New York state labour law – which regulated the number of hours a baker could work – was unconstitutional because it violated an individual's fundamental right to engage in contracts.[26] The freedom to exchange labour was also part of the common law under the doctrine known as employment-at-will (Feinman 1976).

Because of the employment-at-will doctrine, many American workers did not receive remedy for workplace injuries. Many employers used defences based on contract liberty to escape liability, including contributory negligence (the worker's actions contributed to the injury), assumption of risk (the worker assumed the risk of the danger he/she was engaged in) and the fellow-servant rule (Finkin *et al.* 1989). The freedom to enter contracts also largely protected corporate employers to the detriment of American workers who assembled or organized to improve worker conditions (Forbath 1991).

Employers' use of labour injunctions as legal weapons was well established at the turn of the century. A court-issued labour injunction banned union activities (that is, picketing) during labour disputes. Injunctions also forbade individuals and groups from boycotting an employer. The injunction was an effective weapon through which those who violated the court order could be fined or sentenced to prison. In the 1870s, employers used the labour injunction to fight strike activity when it became prominent once again (particularly on the railways). Courts recognized that individuals could withhold their own labour from employers, but they did not believe that individuals and groups could protest and intimidate other workers and customers. Courts used a theory that, no matter how peaceful, moral intimidation by workers and/or appealing to customers created hostile environments that interfered with employers' businesses. Conspiracy charges were becoming a less effective tool for employers as juries became more sympathetic to unions (both because there was more public support for unions and because workers were increasingly represented on juries). Employers began leaning more on injunctions against labour. The Debs (1895) case ruled this constitutional (Taylor and Witney 1992: 19ff.). This case originated in a dispute between the Pullman Car Company and the American Railway Union in 1894 over a wage cut and the dismissal of union leaders. When the strike failed, the union appealed to railway companies to boycott Pullman cars; when the railways refused, the strikes spread throughout the railway industry. Since the railways were involved in interstate commerce, an injunction was filed against the union.[27]

Employers also used antitrust laws to appeal to the courts to control the activity of labour unions. In *Loewe v. Lawlor*, the Supreme Court allowed the Sherman Antitrust Act of 1890 to be enforced against unions that maintained unfair employer lists.[28] In an attempt to allow unions to organize without fear of antitrust suits, Congress passed the Clayton Act of 1914.[29] But while under the Sherman Act only the government could file to obtain an injunction in an antitrust case, Clayton wound up being interpreted as extending this capacity to employers (Taylor and Witney 1992: 47).

However, as industrial capitalism became an increasingly massive process, the workforce of citizens and immigrants became a force to be reckoned with as well. Both in the major European powers and in the United States, notwithstanding their different trajectories of labour organizing and of employers' uses of the state to control workers, the 1900s saw significant victories for workers' causes. In the United States, the New Deal and its accompanying legislation created a revolution in American labour law. Many of the legal tools from the nineteenth century discussed above were changed. Eventually, employers' widespread use of labour injunctions resulted in the 1932 Norris-LaGuardia Anti-Injunction Act – an attempt to give workers more protections. Congress intended for the act to strengthen workers' rights to assemble and stop courts from prohibiting union organization, strikes and assembly. Some courts remained hostile to workers' activities and continued issuing injunctions during labour disputes (Cox *et al.* 2001: 17–51). But in 1935, Congress passed the Wagner Act (currently known as the National Labor Relations Act [NLRA]), which gave workers the right to organize and engage in collective bargaining or other orchestrated activities; it also formed the National Labor Relations Board (NLRB) to prohibit employers' unfair labour practices and to require workers' compensation.

These hard-won rights for workers were further enabled by the ascendance of a type of economy that needed people as workers and as consumers. This is clearest in the expansion of mass manufacturing, mass consumption, mass construction of suburbs and so on. The associated growth of a prosperous working class and a rising middle class signalled the beginning of a fully realized liberal democratic system. But the crises of the 1970s and the rise of a new global neoliberalism made visible the exceptionalism of that expanded prosperity of workers. Despite the gains of the twentieth century, the political situation and power of workers is precarious, as is evident in the loss of workplace rights and the sharp increase in the rights of employers. Does this show us that that original making of two foundationally unequal subjects cannot be overridden through liberal democratic regimes by themselves?

Conclusion: continuities in contemporary liberal democratic capitalism

The histories discussed in this chapter point to the limits of the rule of law and rights-based legal proceduralism in securing equality in the law. While not the subject of this chapter, elsewhere I have extended this argument to the limits of electoral rights and electoral proceduralism in securing types of equality that go beyond partial formalisms, e.g. the right to vote, and are actually substantive, e.g. making one's vote count to launch new agendas. As I indicate throughout the chapter, these histories are charged with contradictions. The extreme inequality led to vigorous class conflict and struggles by the disadvantaged to gain (some) rights and protections. The regulatory state and the Keynesian social contract are products of these struggles. They illuminate how powerlessness can be complex; in that complexity lies the possibility that the powerless also make history.

At the heart of liberal democracy, both as practice and as doctrine, there is a tension between the privileging of property rights and a more substantive understanding of equality, including today, human rights. That tension has never been resolved. The Keynesian period produced the conditions for a prosperous and growing middle class in many countries and for an active working class. Conceivably this could have been a step in a liberal democratic trajectory that was an advance over the past and was to continue and bring only more equality. But today's phase of global neoliberalism shows us otherwise – an impoverishment of the traditional modest middle classes and working classes in the older liberal democracies – even as some of the newer liberal democracies have entered the process of expanded middle classes, evident in India.

The potential of liberal democracy to enable struggles by the disadvantaged – both in the past and today in emergent democracies – showed its promise in the regulatory state and in the Keynesian social contract. But it may also be showing its limits in the current phase of global neoliberalism, with a return to often extreme inequalities and extreme poverty of a sort that liberals considered part of the past during the Keynesian phase. Today's phase shows us liberal democracy's limits to ensure ongoing progress for the disadvantaged and ongoing curtailment of extreme power and wealth. Instead, the change concerns the composition, rather than the existence, of each extreme. The disadvantaged today include not only impoverished middle classes but also a growing range of capitalist firms that dominated national capitalisms. And the privileged include global elites with thinning national interests and increasingly dominant sovereign wealth-funds which are reshaping the logics of capitalism. Many of the economic, organizational and ideational capabilities historically made by the rising bourgeoisie still exist today, but they have jumped organizing logics.

Ultimately, liberal democracy has not succeeded in overcoming the foundational inequality of its two historic subjects. This does not preclude that, imperfect as it is, it might still be the best option. I could have agreed with this had I not have witnessed the current era of global neoliberalism, and its disastrous social and economic outcomes.

Notes

1 This can be partly explained, I posit, because a given capability is not only specific to a formation but also relational vis-à-vis other capabilities in that formation; the differential capabilities of each the worker and the factory owner are clearly a relational condition that can carry over even as each subject undergoes significant transformation.

2 The question of periodization is always subject to debate and revision. I chose Beaud's (1981: 115ff.) identification of three phases in capitalist industrialization on a world scale: 1780–1880, 1880–1950 and 1950 onward. Each of these phases is marked by specific sectoral and geographic dimensions. What follows owes much to Beaud.

3 Among the other major powers in Europe at the time, Holland had stabilized, Portugal and Spain were declining, and Russia continued its expansion toward Asia. During the Restoration France took possession again of its colonies, which had been neglected during the revolution and the empire. This neglect may partly have been connected to the fact that industrial capitalism was moving slowly, further signalling the importance of colonialism for capitalism. French colonial expansion was mostly military.

4 Sir Dudley North wrote in his 'Discourse upon Trade' (1856 [1691]) in defence of free trade, which was clearly different from mercantilism. There is a strong correspondence between the ideas of political freedom (Locke) and the necessity for economic liberalism (North).

5 Previously patents had been caught up in a system of monarchial privilege and favours, dating back at least to 1331, whereby the Crown used the issuing of a patent or trade monopoly to expand its coffers. This came under attack during the second half of the sixteenth century (North and Thomas 1973: 147ff.).

6 It was the rich peasants, the dealers, the rich gentry and locally important men, the banking and trading bourgeoisie, the jurists and the liberal professions who asked for parliamentary democracy (not necessarily in those words), freedom and property. These groups represented an important new social force, underestimated by the monarchy re-established after Cromwell's death. In a compromise the monarch agreed to

respect a 'Declaration of Rights' (1689), which asserted that the king could not suspend the application of the laws, collect taxes or raise and maintain an army in times of peace without the consent of Parliament.

7　Wallerstein (1974) notes that the bourgeoisie identified with the nation-state, but it could have identified with other entities, notably other bourgeois classes in other nation-states. The bourgeoisie became conscious of its position in a system but did so within the frame of the nation-state. There were other choices: they could have become conscious of themselves as a world class, and many groups pushed for such a definition. There were also capitalist farmers in the peripheral areas. At the height of Charles V's reign, many in the Low Countries, southern Germany, northern Italy and elsewhere tied their hopes to the imperial aspirations of the Hapsburgs: these groups were a social stratum but could have become a class. The failure of the empire made the bourgeoisie in Europe realize that their fate was tied to nation-states. This points to the existence of possible alternative trajectories and thereby de-essentializes the historical record, and, more specifically, it points to contestations of the nation-state and thereby de-essentializes the latter.

8　Briggs (1984) gives 1,300 acts from 1760 to 1801, and another 1,000 from 1800 to 1820.

9　After 1801, 'The procedure used was usually enclosure by act of parliament rather than by voluntary agreement or pressure. A successful Enclosure Act did not require local unanimity but it did require enough money to pay for the lawyers' and survey-ors' fees and for fences, hedges, roads, and drainage after the bill had been passed. This was largely a formality since the Enclosure Commissioners appointed to survey the land invariably favoured the parties wishing to enclose and so, too did Parliament' (Briggs 1984: 172).

10　The reasons for intervention varied, but at the heart was a concern about the rising population (especially in the urban working population). In the late eighteenth century this increased the demand for cheap food, creating further pressure for agricultural improvement.

11　Thus troops were sent to break up the riots in 1779 in Lancaster and in 1796 in Yorkshire.

12　In 1819 there was what we might describe as a return to sound money (Briggs 1984: 201). The 1825 Bank Charter Act liberalized country banks; the 1826 Banking Act had deflationary effects; and so on. The 1844 Bank Charter Act established that only the Bank of England could issue paper bank notes. The 1844–61 corporation laws (McNeill 1986: 507) allowed all companies, except banks, to become limited liability concerns; banks were allowed in 1858.

13　It was most successful in Virginia, Maryland and Pennsylvania; it was *completely* absent in New England, as residents resisted its feudal overtones (Ely 1992: 11ff.).

14　Women and children were a large part of the workforce. In 1834 children under thir-teen made up 13 per cent of the workforce in the English cotton industry; 5 per cent by 1850; and 14 per cent in 1874 (Beaud 1981: 39).

15　The manufacturing sector was quite diverse and included wool, silk, cotton and flax spun or woven by steam or waterpower. Other sectors were knitwear, lace, printed fabric, bleachers, dyes, metal wares, pottery and glass manufacture. And there was an agricultural and mining proletariat. The Factory Acts were passed to protect women and children, the more vulnerable workers, though this in turn engendered efforts among employers to limit these protections. The 1819 Cotton Factory Act prohibited child labour (under nine years old) in cotton factories and limited hours of work for ages nine to eighteen. The 1833 Factory Act required some schooling for children. The 1842 Mines Act prohibited girls, women and boys under ten from working under-ground. The 1844 Factory Act limited the hours of work for children aged eight to thirteen and women in factories; a related bill mandated that the workday should begin at the same time every day (this was the first time Parliament regulated hours of work for adult males) and that clocks should be publicly visible, and it lowered the minimum working age from nine to eight (Marx 1977: 394; Rubinstein 1998: 80). In 1845, calico printing works were subjected to safety legislation (Rubinstein 1998: 80). The 1847 Factory Act–Ten Hours' Bill limited work for women and children to ten hours, and it de facto applied to men, since most factory work also required some child labour (McNeill 1986: 508).

16 During this period the 1833 Emancipation Act was also passed, which abolished slavery or, rather, 'administered freedom drop by drop' (Marx 1977: 392).

17 In this account, workers were not free in the medieval period but gained legal freedoms in the late fourteenth and fifteenth centuries when Englishmen were allowed to work for wages. The law of the employer-employee was known as the law of 'master and servant' for everyone except house servants and apprentices.

18 This is similar to arguments made by Steinfeld in his earlier work on the United States, in which he writes that the replacement of the unfree labour with free labour was not an inevitable by-product of eighteenth- or nineteenth-century capitalism. He argues instead that free labour resulted from struggles in which republicanism, the American Revolution and the persistence of the increasingly odious institution of black slavery (1991: 137–46) impelled average American working men and women to act (123–7, 181).

19 The ability of magistrates to penalize growing numbers of British workers derived from revisions of the Master and Servant Acts, which regulated the interactions between employers and employees.

20 Periods of major social transformation contain the possibility of major upheavals in people's lives and livelihoods, as well as a sharp increase in the level of desperation. The elimination of serfdom had a similar effect in Prussia. And, as I will argue later, the current formation of a highly mixed class of needed workers in major developed economies evinces similar patterns. One could use these features of the formation of a new workforce as an indicator of major transformations.

21 There were other factors, such as the ethnic fragmentation of the American working class, that are often used to explain the failure to organize. For a critique of this factor, see Wilentz (1984). Further, the working classes in all the major European powers had immigrant workers in the 1800s (Sassen 1999), a fact that is not quite made part of 'official' European history.

22 Forbath observes (1991: 27) that the framers of the Constitution, concerned about factionalisms, particularly the possibility of a factionalism of the poor that might lead to political moves to forcefully redistribute wealth, placed matters of property and markets in a suprapolitical realm of private right: these were then constituted as matters of law and not politics. From the perspective of contestation during the period of industrialization, the fact of a diffuse federation made organization difficult, even if early on (by the 1830s) white men had the right to vote: but 'there was no unitary state to defend or transform' (Katznelson 1985: 273).

23 In 1740 South Carolina declared slaves 'to be chattels personal, in the hands of their owners and possessors', and hence could be purchased, sold, inherited, taxed or seized to pay a master's debts (Ely 1992: 15).

24 Steinfeld (1991) also points out that while criminal penalties for employment breaches were not the norm in the United States, some American workers faced the same 'unfree' labour environments as their British counterparts. Not all US workers were free from penal sanctions after 1830. Steinfeld examines groups of workers who continued to face penal sanctions after 1830: sailors who were jailed if they quit; and Southern sharecroppers who faced punishments if they breached work agreements. He uses these (and other) examples to suggest that even in the comparatively free labour context of the United States, workers' actual freedoms were frequently at risk.

25 Early labour organizers were typically attacked by employers through the courts under conspiracy charges drawn from English common law. The first such case was *Commonwealth v. Pullis* (1806, Philadelphia). The place of common law in the

republic was already controversial; republicans wanted only legislatively enacted law to be binding and believed that the power of the police (administration of law) rested exclusively with the legislature and that just outcomes would emerge from a free market. Using the common law, the journeymen combinations (organizations) were seen as a conspiracy. From 1806 to 1842, there were seventeen such trials. Judges typically handed down small fines, with threats of higher fines for repeat offenders; juries were typically composed of merchants and employers (Taylor and Witney 1992: 6–7; Tomlins 1993: 134). These cases tended to invoke the public welfare as a criterion for judging combinations: judges advocated common law as the source of this welfare; radicals advocated the market. Through the 1820s and into the 1830s, the emphasis shifted from forbidding combination as such to the lawfulness of the means used and ends pursued (Tomlins 1993: 144–7).

26 In *Lochner v. New York* (1905) the Court threw out a statute restricting work in bakeries to ten hours a day or sixty hours per week because it violated the liberty of contract embodied in the Fourteenth Amendment. The Court argued that long hours did not endanger the *health* of workers; therefore, the New York legislation was intended to regulate labour relations, not protect health. This decision embodied the laissez-faire libertarian outlook and provided the foundation for stifling Progressive attempts at reforms in the states for the next thirty years (until the depression) (Ely 1992: 103). The Court remained open to cases where health and safety were obviously at stake, for example, in mining and industrial accidents. Further, some restrictions in working hours were allowed. For example, *Muller v. Oregon* (1908) allowed the limitation of working hours for women in factories and laundries to ten hours per day, on the grounds of 'special health needs' (104). The Court struck down prohibitions of 'yellow dog contracts', which stipulated that employees could not belong to a union, since these prohibitions would interfere in contracts (formal equality as a screen for maintenance of inequality). Labour unsurprisingly saw this as confirmation of anti-union bias in the courts (105). The courts were also reluctant to set minimum wages: *Adkins v. Children's Hospital* (1923) overruled a DC statute establishing a minimum wage for women. Similarly, it struck down a Kansas compulsory wage arbitration system in *Charles Wolff Packing Company v. Court of Industrial Relations of Kansas* (1923). Most of these decisions relied on contract logic.

27 By 1931, 1,845 injunctions were issued (Witte 1932: 234, as reported in Taylor and Witney 1992: 20). The *Debs* decision also upheld injunctions against people who might have aided workers in a labour dispute, that is to say, it applied to 'all other people whomsoever' who were 'interfering in any way whatsoever'.

28 The Sherman Antitrust Act declared illegal every contract or combination in restraint of trade among the states. Sherman was applied to unions as well: the clauses in the act outlawing combination and targeting monopolists did not specifically *exclude* labour, so the Court applied the act to unions (Taylor and Witney 1992: 37). The first application to a union came in Louisiana in 1893; the Court found that the interruption of trade resulting from a strike constituted a restraint of trade, forbidden under the act (38). The Supreme Court declined to determine whether the act applied to unions in 1895 (*In Re Debs*), but found that it applied to unions in the *Danbury Hatters* case (*Loewe v. Lawlor* 1908). In this case, the United Hatters brought pressure on Loewe & Company by organizing a successful nationwide boycott; a circuit court found for the union, but the Supreme Court reversed the decision. A second case in 1915 – *Lawlor v. Loewe* – ruled that damages could be recovered from the union and its membership.

29 The Clayton Act (1914) was an attempt to outlaw specific types of competitive behaviour that were thought to result in monopoly conditions (Fligstein 1990: 25).

Part II

Conceptual interrogations

7 Restructuring global governance

Cosmopolitanism, democracy and the global order

David Held

Cosmopolitanism is concerned with disclosing the ethical, cultural and legal basis of political order in a world where political communities and states matter, but not only and exclusively. In circumstances where the trajectories of each and every country are tightly entwined, the partiality of 'reasons of state' needs to be recognised. While states are hugely important vehicles to aid the delivery of effective public recognition, equal liberty and social justice, they should not be thought of as ontologically privileged. They can be judged by how far they deliver these public goods and how far they fail; for the history of states is marked, of course, not just by phases of bad leadership and corruption but also by the most brutal episodes. A cosmopolitanism relevant to our global age must take this as a starting point, and build an ethically sound and politically robust conception of the proper basis of political community, and of the relations among communities.

This chapter examines why cosmopolitanism remains a compelling political philosophy and approach to global challenges. The first section sets out the context of cosmopolitanism; that is, an explanation of why cosmopolitanism is relevant to global political and social problems. It focuses on cosmopolitan values rooted in leading international regimes and organisations. The section that follows explores the structure and meaning of cosmopolitanism in more detail, and sets out how I understand this important concept. It also responds to several criticisms of cosmopolitanism that are repeatedly raised in the literature. The third section discusses the relation between cosmopolitan values and principles and the idea of a cosmopolitan legal community. The final two sections examine the significance of these notions in meeting many of today's global challenges. The argument is that the multilateral order is inadequate, and the principles that underpin it are inappropriate, to the global issues faced in the twenty-first century. Cosmopolitanism, it is contended, discloses a more suitable and productive approach.

The context of cosmopolitanism

Thinking about the future of humankind on the basis of the early years of the twenty-first century does not give grounds for optimism. From 9/11 to the 2006 war in the Middle East, terrorism, conflict, territorial struggle and the clash of identities appear to define the moment. The wars in Afghanistan, Iraq, Israel/Lebanon, Israel/Gaza and elsewhere suggest that political violence is an irreducible feature of our age. Perversely, globalisation seems to have dramatised the significance of differences between peoples; far from the globalisation of communications easing understanding and the translation of ideas, it seems to have highlighted what it is that people do not have in common and find dislikeable about each other (Bull 1977: 127). Moreover, the contemporary drivers of political nationalism – self-determination, secure borders, geo-political and geo-economic advantage – place an emphasis on the pursuit of the national interest above concerns with what it is that humans might have in common.

Yet, it is easy to overstate the moment and exaggerate from one set of historical experiences. While each of the elements mentioned poses a challenge to a rule-based global order, it is a profound mistake to forget that the twentieth century established a series of cosmopolitan steps toward the delimitation of the nature and form of political community, sovereignty and 'reasons of state'. These steps were laid down after the First and Second World Wars which brought humanity to the edge of the abyss – not once, but twice. At a time as difficult as the start of the twenty-first century, it is important to recall why these steps were taken and remind oneself of their significance.

From the foundation of the UN system to the EU, from changes to the laws of war to the entrenchment of human rights, from the emergence of international environmental regimes to the establishment of the International Criminal Court, people have sought to reframe human activity and embed it in law, rights and responsibilities. Many of these developments were initiated against the background of formidable threats to humankind – above all, Nazism, fascism and Stalinism. Those involved in them affirmed the importance of universal principles, human rights and the rule of law in the face of strong temptations to simply put up the shutters and defend the position of only some countries, nations and peoples. They rejected the view of national and moral particularists that belonging to a given community limits and determines the moral worth of individuals and the nature of their freedom, and they defended the irreducible moral status of each and every person. At the centre of such thinking is the cosmopolitan view that human well-being is not defined by geographical or cultural locations, that national or ethnic or gendered boundaries should not determine the limits of rights or responsibilities for the satisfaction of basic human needs, and that all human beings require equal moral respect and concern. The principles of equal respect, equal concern, and the priority of the vital needs of all human beings are not principles for some remote utopia; for they are at the centre of significant post-Second World War legal and political developments.

What does 'cosmopolitan' mean in this context (see Held 2002)? In the first instance, cosmopolitanism refers to those basic values that set down standards or boundaries which no agent, whether a representative of a global body, state or civil association, should be able to violate. Focused on the claims of each person as an individual, these values espouse the idea that human beings are in a fundamental sense equal, and that they deserve equal political treatment; that is, treatment based upon the equal care and consideration of their agency, irrespective of the community in which they were born or brought up. After over two hundred years of nationalism, sustained nation-state formation and seemingly endless conflicts over territory and resources, such values could be thought of as out of place. But such values are already enshrined in the law of war, human rights law, the statute of the ICC, among many other international rules and legal arrangements.

Thus, second, cosmopolitanism can be taken to refer to those forms of political regulation and law-making that create powers, rights and constraints that go beyond the claims of nation-states and that have far-reaching consequences, in principle, for the nature and form of political power. These regulatory forms can be found in the domain between national and international law and regulation – the space between domestic law which regulates the relations between a state and its citizens, and traditional international law which applies primarily to states and interstate relations. This space is already filled by a host of legal regulation, from the legal instruments of the EU, and the international human rights regime as a global framework for promoting rights, to the diverse agreements of the arms control system and environmental regimes. Within Europe, the European Convention for the Protection of Human Rights and Fundamental Freedoms and the EU create new institutions and layers of law and governance that have divided political authority; any assumption that sovereignty is an indivisible, illimitable, exclusive and perpetual form of public power – entrenched within an individual state – is now defunct (Held 1995: 107–13). Within the wider international community, rules governing war, weapons systems, war crimes, human rights and the environment, among other areas, have transformed and delimited the order of states, embedding national polities in new forms and layers of accountability and governance. Accordingly, the boundaries between states, nations and societies can no longer claim the deep legal and moral significance they once had in the era of classic sovereignty. Cosmopolitanism is not made up of political ideals for another age, but embedded in rule systems and institutions that have already altered state sovereignty in distinct ways, and in societies of diverse faiths.

The structure of cosmopolitanism

However, the precise sense in which these developments constitute a form of 'cosmopolitanism' remains to be clarified, especially given that the ideas of cosmopolitanism have a long and complex history. For my purposes here, cosmopolitanism can be taken as the moral and political outlook that builds upon the strengths of the post-1945 multilateral order, particularly its commitment to universal standards, human rights and democratic values, and that seeks to specify general principles upon which all could act. These are principles that can be widely shared, and form the basis for the protection and nurturing of each person's equal interest in the determination of the forces and institutions that govern their lives.

Cosmopolitan values can be expressed formally, and in the interests of brevity, in terms of a set of principles (Held 2002). Eight principles are paramount. They are the principles of: 1. equal worth and dignity; 2. active agency; 3. personal responsibility and accountability; 4. consent; 5. collective decision-making about public issues through voting procedures; 6. inclusiveness and subsidiarity; 7. avoidance of serious harm; and 8. sustainability. While eight principles may seem like a daunting number, they are interrelated and together form the basis of a compelling ethical and political orientation – an orientation that helps illuminate what it is that humankind can have in common.

The eight principles can best be thought of as falling into three clusters. The first cluster (principles 1–3) sets down the fundamental organisational features of the cosmopolitan moral universe. Its crux is that each person is a subject of equal moral concern; that each person is capable of acting autonomously with respect to the range of choices before them; and that, in deciding how to act or which institutions to create, the claims of each person affected should be taken equally into account. Personal responsibility means in this context that actors and agents have to be aware of, and accountable for, the consequences of their actions, direct or indirect, intended or unintended, which may substantially restrict and delimit the choices of others. The second cluster (principles 4–6) forms the basis of translating individually initiated activity, or privately determined activities more broadly, into collectively agreed or collectively sanctioned frameworks of action or regulatory regimes. Public power can be conceived as legitimate to the degree to which principles 4, 5 and 6 are upheld. The final principles (7 and 8) lay down a framework for prioritising urgent need and resource conservation. By distinguishing vital from non-vital needs, principle 7 creates an unambiguous starting point and guiding orientation for public decisions. While this 'prioritising commitment' does not, of course, create a decision procedure to resolve all clashes of priority in politics, it clearly creates a moral framework for focusing public policy on those who are most vulnerable, and who would be unable to act autonomously without certain material capacities. By contrast, principle 8 seeks to set down a prudential orientation to help ensure that public policy is consistent with global ecological balances and that it does not destroy irreplaceable and non-substitutable resources.

It could be objected at this point that, given the plurality of interpretive positions in the contemporary world (social, cultural, religious and so on), it is unwise to construct a political standpoint that depends upon overarching principles. For it is doubtful, the objection could continue, that a bridge can be built between 'the many particular wills' and 'the general will' (see McCarthy 1991: 181–99). Daniel Bray, for instance, makes this argument from a Deweyian ethical perspective, while also continuing to advocate what he terms 'pragmatic cosmopolitanism'. He contends that it is impossible to answer questions such as 'what are the proper boundaries of a democratic community?' using cosmopolitan principles like my 'all-affected principle' (Bray this volume; Held 1995). According to Bray, such questions can only be answered through interconnected communities engaging in collective problem-solving – in the 'conduct of politics itself' (ibid). 'Democratic reconstruction' he suggests, 'and any extension of moral and political boundaries, must grow from the values shared by existing democratic communities' (Bray 2009: 699). Kimberly Hutchings also makes an analogous argument against the use of cosmopolitan principles, but from a quite different perspective (Hutchings 2008). Specifically, she maintains that cosmopolitan arguments similar to mine rest on an interpretation of world affairs that springs from a temporal experience not shared by all.

In a world marked by a diversity of value orientations, on what grounds, if any, can we suppose that all groups or parties could be argumentatively convinced about fundamentally ethical and political principles? I would argue that the principles of cosmopolitanism are the conditions that must be met for taking cultural diversity seriously, and of building a democratic culture to mediate clashes of the cultural good. They are, in short, about the conditions of just difference and democratic dialogue. The aim of modern cosmopolitanism is the conceptualisation and generation of the necessary background conditions for a 'common' or 'basic' structure of individual action and social activity (cf. Rawls 1985: 254ff.).

Thus, while a modern cosmopolitanism acknowledges a plurality of values and a diversity of moral conceptions of the good (how would it be otherwise?), it entails, as one commentator aptly put it, 'a particular type of political arrangement, one which, for one, allows the pursuit of different conceptions of good' (Tan 1998: 283). Only polities that acknowledge the equal status of all persons, that seek neutrality or impartiality with respect to a wide range of personal ends, hopes and aspirations, and that pursue the public justification of social, economic and political arrangements can ensure a basic or common structure of political action that allows individuals to pursue their projects – both individual and collective – as free and equal agents. Hence, cosmopolitan principles are the principles of democratic public life, stripped of one crucial assumption – never fully justified in any case in liberal democratic thought, classic or contemporary – that these principles can only be enacted effectively within a single circumscribed, territorially based political community.

A distinction can be made between 'thick' and 'thin' cosmopolitanism (see Held 2005, for a discussion). There are those for whom membership of humanity at large means that special relationships (including particular moral responsibilities) to family, kin, nation, or religious grouping can never be justified because the people involved have some intrinsic quality that suffices alone to compel special moral attention, or because they are allegedly worth more than other people, or because such affiliations provide sufficient reason for pursuing particular commitments or actions. Against this, there are those who recognise that while each person stands in 'an ethically significant relation' to all other people, this is only one important 'source of reasons and responsibilities among others' (Scheffler 1999: 260). Cosmopolitan principles are, in this context, quite compatible with the recognition of different 'spheres' or 'layers' of moral reasoning (Walzer 1983). As I understand cosmopolitanism, it should be thought of as closer to the second position than the first; cosmopolitanism lays down regulative principles that delimit and govern the range of diversity and difference that ought to be found in public life. It discloses the proper framework for the pursuit of argument, discussion and negotiation about particular spheres of value. Cosmopolitanism thus sets down a set of procedural principles for political life. Of course, the principles of autonomy, dialogue and tolerance are open to objection; they have been contested throughout the modern period. But if they are rejected, it is important to be clear that what is being cast aside is the willingness to test the generalisability of political claims and interests, to pursue the deliberative justification of these, and to ensure the accountability of power in all its forms.

From cosmopolitan principles to cosmopolitan law

The idea of cosmopolitan law invokes the notion of a domain of law different in kind from the law of states and the law made between one state and another for the mutual enhancement of their geopolitical interests. Kant, the leading interpreter of the idea of such a law, interpreted it as the basis for articulating the equal moral status of persons in the 'universal community' (1970: 108). For him, cosmopolitan law is neither a fantastic nor a utopian way of conceiving law, but a 'necessary complement' to the codes of national and international law, and a means to transform them into a public law of humanity (see Held 1995: ch. 10). While Kant limited the form and scope of cosmopolitan law to the conditions of universal hospitality – the right to present oneself and be heard within and across communities – it is understood here more broadly as the appropriate mode of representing the equal moral standing of all human beings, their entitlement to equal liberty and to forms of governance founded on deliberation and consent. In other words, cosmopolitan law should be thought of as the form of law that best articulates and entrenches the eight principles of cosmopolitan order. If these principles were to be systematically entrenched as the foundation of law, the conditions of the cosmopolitan regulation of public life could initially be set down.

In this conception, the nation-state 'withers away'. But this is not to suggest that states and national democratic polities become redundant. Rather, states would no longer be regarded as the sole centres of legitimate power within their borders, as is already the case in many places (Held *et al.* 1999). Rightful authority or sovereignty can be stripped away from the idea of fixed borders and territories and thought of as, in principle, an attribute of basic cosmopolitan democratic law that can be drawn upon and enacted in diverse realms, from local associations and cities to states and wider global networks.

At the heart of a cosmopolitan conception of global order is the idea that citizenship can be based not on an exclusive membership of a territorial community but on general rules and principles which can be entrenched and drawn upon in different settings. The meaning of citizenship thus shifts from membership in a community which bestows, for those who qualify, particular rights and duties to an alternative principle of world order in which all persons have equivalent rights and duties in the cross-cutting spheres of decision-making which can affect their vital needs and interests. As Habermas has written, 'only a democratic citizenship that does not close itself off in a particularistic fashion can pave the way for a world citizenship ... State citizenship and world citizenship form a continuum whose contours, at least, are already becoming visible' (1996: 514–15). There is only a historically contingent connection between the principles underpinning citizenship and the national community; as this connection weakens in a world of overlapping communities and fate, the principles of citizenship must be rearticulated and re-entrenched. Moreover, in the light of this development, the connection between patriotism and nationalism becomes easier to call into question, and a case built to bind patriotism to the defence of core civic and political principles – not to the nation or country for their own sake (Heater 2002). Only national identities open to diverse solidarities, and shaped by respect for general rules and principles, can accommodate themselves successfully to the challenges of the global age. Ultimately, diversity and difference, accountability and political capacity, can flourish only in a cosmopolitan legal community (see Brunkhorst 2005; Held 2002). The global challenges we face are better met in a cosmopolitan legal framework.

The key reasons for this should be highlighted for clarity. First, cosmopolitan values have played, as previously noted, a constitutive role in the development of important aspects of the international and global political realm, and these continue to be of great relevance in the framing of core general civic and political principles. Second, the world of 'overlapping communities of fate', of interlocking and interdependent relations across borders and sectors of society, generated by globalisation, binds the fortunes of people together across countries in dense networks and processes. Third, if the complex and demanding political issues that this gives rise to are to be resolved, not by markets or geopolitical might, but by mechanisms of deliberation, accountability and democracy, then a cosmopolitan legal order can be seen to set down a fair and inclusive political framework to address them, internationally and globally.

Global challenges

Global challenges today can be thought of as divided into three types – those concerned with sharing our planet (global warming, biodiversity and ecosystem losses, water deficits), those concerned with sustaining our life chances (poverty, conflict prevention, global infectious diseases) and those concerned with managing our rulebooks (nuclear proliferation, toxic waste disposal, intellectual property rights, genetic research rules, trade rules, finance and tax rules) (cf. Rischard 2002). In our increasingly interconnected world, these global problems cannot be solved by any one nation-state acting alone. They call for collective and collaborative action – something that the nations of the world have not been good at, and that they need to be better at if these pressing issues are to be adequately tackled.

While complex global processes, from the financial to the ecological, connect the fate of communities to each other across the world, global governance capacity is under pressure. Problem-solving capacities at the global and regional level are weak because of a number of structural difficulties, which compound the problems of generating and implementing urgent policy with respect to global goods and bads. These difficulties are rooted in the post-war settlement and the subsequent development of the multilateral order itself.

The problems faced by international agencies and organisations stem from many sources, including the tension between universal values and state sovereignty built into them from their beginning. For many global political and legal developments since 1945 do not just curtail sovereignty, but support it in distinctive ways. From the UN Charter to the Kyoto protocol, international agreements often serve to entrench the international power structure. The division of the globe into powerful nation-states, with distinctive sets of geopolitical interests, was embedded in the articles and statutes of leading IGOs (see Held 1995: chs 5 and 6). Thus, the sovereign rights of states are frequently affirmed alongside more universal principles. Moreover, while the case can be made that universal principles are part of 'the working creed' of officials in some UN agencies such as the United Nations Children's Fund (UNICEF), UNESCO and the World Health Organization (WHO), and NGOs such as Amnesty International, Save the Children and Oxfam, they can scarcely be said to be constitutive of the conceptual world and working practices of many politicians, national or international (Barry 1999: 34–5).

In addition, the reach of contemporary regional and international law rarely comes with a commitment to establish institutions with the resources and clout to make declared universal rules, values and objectives effective. The susceptibility of the UN to the agendas of the most powerful states, the partiality of many of its enforcement operations (or lack of them altogether), the underfunding of its organisations, the continued dependency of its programmes on financial support from a few major states, the weaknesses of the policing of many environmental regimes (regional and global) are all indicative of the disjuncture between universal principles (and aspirations) and their partial and one-sided application. Four deep-rooted problems need highlighting (see Held 2004: 6).

A first set of problems emerges as a result of the development of globalisation itself, which generates public policy problems that span the 'domestic' and the 'foreign', and the interstate order with its clear political boundaries and lines of responsibility. These problems are often insufficiently understood or acted upon. There is a fundamental lack of ownership of many of them at the global level. A second set of difficulties relates to the inertia found in the system of international agencies, or the inability of these agencies to mount collective problem-solving solutions faced with uncertainty about lines of responsibility and frequent disagreement over objectives, means and costs. This often leads to the situation where the cost of inaction is greater than the cost of taking action. A third set of problems arises because there is no clear division of labour among the myriad of international governmental agencies; functions often overlap, mandates frequently conflict, and aims and objectives too often get blurred. A fourth set of difficulties relates to an accountability deficit, itself linked to two interrelated problems: the power imbalances among states and those between state and non-state actors in the shaping and making of global public policy. Multilateral bodies need to be fully representative of the states involved in them, and they rarely are.

Underlying these four difficulties is the breakdown of symmetry and congruence between decision-makers and decision-takers. The point has been well articulated recently by Kaul and her associates in their work on global public goods. They speak about the forgotten equivalence principle; that is, the span of a good's benefits and costs should be matched with the span of the jurisdiction in which decisions are taken about that good (see Kaul *et al.* 2003). At its root, such a principle suggests that those who are significantly affected by a global public good or bad should have a say in its provision or regulation. Such a principle of equivalence could be circumscribed by a concept of the right to protection from grievous harm. In this way, 'all-inclusiveness' would entail deliberation and engagement in policies that seriously affect life expectations and life chances (Held 2004: ch. 6; cf. Keohane 2004).

Yet, all too often, there is a breakdown of 'equivalence' between decision-makers and decision-takers, between decision-makers and stakeholders, and between the inputs and outputs of the decision-making process. Pressing examples include climate change, financial market regulation, the impact of trade subsidies, AIDS management and the question of intellectual property rights. Thus, the challenge is to find ways to align the circles of those to be involved in decision-making with the spillover range of the good under negotiation, i.e. to address the issue of accountability gaps; to create new organisational mechanisms for policy innovation across borders; and to find new ways of financing urgent global public goods. Legitimate political authority at the global level cannot be entrenched adequately without addressing the representative, organisational and financial gaps in governance arrangements. Cosmopolitan principles point the way forward.

To restore symmetry and congruence between decision-makers and decision-takers requires a reframing of global governance and a resolve to address those challenges generated by cross-border processes and forces. This project must take as its starting point, in other words, a world of overlapping communities of fate. Recognising the complex processes of an interconnected world, it ought to view certain issues – such as industrial and commercial strategy, housing and education – as appropriate for spatially delimited political spheres (the city, region or state), while seeing others – such as the environment, pandemics and global financial regulation – as requiring new, more extensive institutions to address them. Deliberative and decision-making centres beyond national territories are appropriately situated when the principle of all-inclusiveness can only be properly upheld in a transnational context; when those whose life expectancy and life chances are significantly affected by public matters constitute a transnational grouping; and when 'lower' levels decision-making cannot manage satisfactorily transnational or global policy questions. Of course, the boundaries demarcating different levels of governance will always be contested, as they are, for instance, in many local, sub-national regional and national polities. Disputes about the appropriate jurisdiction for handling particular public issues will be complex and intensive; but better complex and intensive in a clear cosmopolitan framework (in which cosmopolitan law frames political power) than abandoned simply to powerful geopolitical interests (dominant states) or market-based organisations to resolve them alone (see Held 2004: ch. 6).

Accordingly, to return to where this chapter began, states are hugely important vehicles to aid the delivery of effective public regulation, equal liberty and social justice, but they should not be thought of as ontologically privileged. They can be judged by how far they deliver these public goods and how far they fail. The same can be said about political agents operating beyond the level of the nation-state. They are by no means necessarily noble or wise, and their wisdom and nobility depend on recognising necessary limits on their action, limits which mark out legitimate spaces for others to pursue their vital needs and interests. IGOs and INGOs, like states, need to be bound by a rule-based order which articulates and entrenches cosmopolitan principles. Only such an order can underwrite a political system which upholds the equal moral standing of all human beings, and their entitlement to equal liberty and to forms of governance founded on deliberation and consent. Here is the foundation on which to build a politically robust and ethically sound conception of the proper basis of political community, and of the relations among communities in a global age. We need to build on the cosmopolitan steps of the twentieth century and deepen the institutional hold of this agenda.

Political openings

Surprisingly perhaps, it is an opportune moment to rethink the nature and form of contemporary global governance and the dominant policies of the last decade or so. The policy packages that have largely set the global agenda – in economics and security – are failing. The Washington Consensus and Washington security doctrines – or market fundamentalism and unilateralism – have dug their own graves. The most successful developing countries in the world (China, India, Vietnam, Uganda, among them) are successful because they have not followed the Washington Consensus agenda, and the conflicts that have most successfully been diffused (the Balkans, Sierra Leone, Liberia, among others) are ones that have benefited from concentrated multilateral support and a human security agenda. Here are clues as to how to proceed in the future. We need to learn to follow these clues and learn from the mistakes of the past if the rule of law, accountability and the effectiveness of the multilateral order are to be advanced.

In addition, the political tectonic plates appear to be shifting. With the faltering of unilateralism in US foreign policy, uncertainty over the role of the EU in global affairs, the crisis of global trade talks, the growing confidence of leading emerging countries in the world economic fora (China, India, Brazil), and the unsettled relations between elements of Islam and the West, business as usual seems unlikely at the global level in the decades ahead. It is highly improbable that the multilateral order can survive for very much longer in its current form; a new political space is being opened up.

Of course, cosmopolitanism has its enemies that may exploit this space (see Archibugi 2008). But I have argued that cosmopolitanism constitutes the political basis and political philosophy of living in a global age. In a world of overlapping communities of fate, individuals need to be not just citizens of their immediate political communities, but of the wider regional and global networks that impact upon their lives. Under such conditions, people would come, in principle, to enjoy multiple citizenships – political membership, that is, in the diverse communities that significantly affect them. This overlapping cosmopolitan polity would be one that in form and substance reflected and embraced the diverse forms of power and authority that operate within and across borders.

8   Democracy in a multipolar world

Chantal Mouffe

I have decided that the best way to address the theme of this volume, *Interrogating Democracy in World Politics*, is to examine the implications of my agonistic approach for envisaging what democracy could mean in a multipolar world.

I will begin by presenting the basic tenets of the theoretical framework that informs my reflection on the political. It has been elaborated in *Hegemony and Socialist Strategy*, co-written with Ernesto Laclau (2001). In this book we argue that the two concepts needed to grasp the nature of the political are 'antagonism' and 'hegemony'. Both point to the need for acknowledging the dimension of radical negativity and the ever present possibility of antagonism that impede the full totalisation of society and foreclose the possibility of a society beyond division and power. They require coming to terms with the lack of a final ground and the undecidability that pervades every order; this means, in our vocabulary, recognising the hegemonic nature of every kind of social order and envisaging society as the product of a series of practices whose aim is to establish order in a context of contingency. The practices of articulation through which a given order is created and the meaning of social institutions is fixed are what we call 'hegemonic practices'. Every order is the temporary and precarious articulation of contingent practices. Things could always have been otherwise and every order is predicated on the exclusion of other possibilities. It is always the expression of a particular configuration of power relations. What is at a given moment accepted as the 'natural' order, jointly with the common sense that accompanies it, is the result of sedimented hegemonic practices; it is never the manifestation of a deeper objectivity that would be exterior to the practices that brought it into being. Every order is therefore susceptible to being challenged by counter-hegemonic practices that attempt to disarticulate it in order to install another form of hegemony.

In *The Return of the Political* (1993), *The Democratic Paradox* (2000) and *On the Political* (2005) I have developed this reflection on 'the political', understood as the antagonistic dimension that is inherent in all human societies. I have proposed to distinguish between 'the political' and 'politics'; 'the political' refers to the dimension of antagonism that can take many forms and can emerge in diverse social relations, a dimension that can never be eradicated; 'politics' refers to the ensemble of practices, discourses and institutions that seek to establish a certain order and to organise human coexistence in conditions that are always potentially conflicting because they are affected by the dimension of 'the political'.

The denial of 'the political' in its antagonistic dimension is, I have argued, what impedes liberal theory's ability to grasp the roots of violence and to envisage politics in an adequate way. Indeed 'the political' in its antagonistic dimension cannot be made to disappear by simply denying or wishing it away, which is the typical liberal gesture; such negation only leads to impotence, an impotence that characterises liberal thought when confronted with the emergence of antagonisms and forms of violence that, according to its theory, belong to a bygone age when reason had not yet managed to control the supposedly archaic passions.

The main problem with liberal rationalism is that it deploys a logic of the social based on an essentialist conception of 'being as presence' and that it conceives objectivity as being inherent to things themselves. This is why it cannot apprehend the process of construction of political identities. It cannot recognise that there can only be an identity when it is constructed as difference and that any social objectivity is constituted through acts of power. What it refuses to admit is that any form of social objectivity is ultimately political and that it must bear the traces of the acts of exclusion that govern its constitution.

The notion of 'constitutive outside' can be helpful here to make this argument more explicit. This term has been proposed by Henry Staten (1985) to refer to a number of themes developed by Jacques Derrida through notions like 'supplement', 'trace' and 'différance'. Its aim is to highlight the fact that the creation of an identity implies the establishment of a difference. When dealing with political identities, which are always collective identities, we are dealing with the creation of an 'us' that can only exist by its demarcation from a 'them'. This does not mean of course that such a relation is by necessity an antagonistic one. But it means that there is always the possibility of this relation us/them becoming one of friend/enemy. This happens when the others, who up to now had been considered as simply different, start to be perceived as putting into question our identity and threatening our existence. From that moment on, any form of us/them relation, be it religious, ethnic or economic, becomes the locus of an antagonism. What is important here is to acknowledge that the very condition of possibility for the formation of political identities is at the same time the condition of impossibility of a society from which antagonism would have been eliminated. Antagonism is therefore an ever-present possibility.

An agonistic model

An important part of my reflection has been dedicated to the elaboration of what I call an 'agonistic' model of democracy. My objective is to provide what Richard Rorty would call a 'metaphoric redescription' of liberal democratic institutions, which, I claim, is better able to grasp what is at stake in pluralist democratic politics than the two main models of democracy currently on offer, the aggregative and the deliberative ones. In a nutshell, my argument goes as follows. Once we acknowledge the dimension of 'the political', we begin to realise that one of the main challenges for pluralist liberal democratic politics consists in trying to defuse the potential antagonism that exists in human relations. Indeed, the fundamental question is not: how to arrive at a consensus reached without exclusion, because this would require the construction of an 'us' that would not have a corresponding 'them'. Yet this is impossible because, as I have just argued, the very condition for the constitution of an 'us' is the demarcation of a 'them'. The crucial issue for democracy then is how to establish this us/them distinction that is constitutive of politics in a way that is compatible with the recognition of pluralism. Conflict in liberal democratic societies cannot and should not be eradicated since the specificity of 'modern democracy' is precisely the recognition and the legitimation of conflict. What modern liberal democratic politics requires is that the others are not seen as enemies to be destroyed but as adversaries whose ideas would be fought against, even fiercely, but whose right to defend those ideas will never be put into question. To put it another way, what is important is that conflict does not take the form of an 'antagonism' (struggle between enemies) but the form of an 'agonism' (struggle between adversaries).

A well-functioning democracy calls for a confrontation of democratic political positions. If this is missing there is always the danger that this democratic confrontation will be replaced by a confrontation between non-negotiable moral values or essentialist forms of identifications. Too much emphasis on consensus, together with aversion towards confrontations leads to apathy and to disaffection with political participation. This is why a liberal democratic society requires a debate about possible alternatives. It must provide political forms of identifications around clearly differentiated democratic positions, or to put it in Niklas Luhmann's terms there must be a clear 'splitting of the summit,' a real choice between the policies put forward by the government and those of the opposition (1990). While consensus is no doubt necessary, it must be accompanied by dissent. Consensus is needed on the institutions that are constitutive of liberal democracy and on the ethico-political values that should inform the political association, but there will always be disagreement concerning the meaning of those values and the way they should be implemented. In a pluralist democracy such disagreements are not only legitimate but also necessary. They allow for different forms of citizenship identification and are the stuff of democratic politics. When the agonistic dynamics of pluralism is hindered because of a lack of democratic forms of identifications, passions cannot be given a democratic outlet and the ground is laid for various forms of politics articulated around essentialist identities of nationalist, religious or ethnic type and for the multiplication of confrontations over non-negotiable moral values, with all the manifestations of violence that such confrontations entail.

Towards a multipolar world

My agonistic model has been elaborated to provide a proper understanding of the nature of a specific political regime: liberal pluralist democracy. However I think that some of its insights, for example the importance of offering the possibility for legitimate, 'agonistic' forms of conflict in order to avoid the explosion of antagonistic ones, can be useful in the field of international relations. Indeed the situation in the international arena is today in many respects similar to the one found in domestic politics, with its lack of an agonistic debate about possible alternatives. Since the end of the Cold War we have been living in a unipolar world and the absence of legitimate alternatives to the dominant hegemonic order means that resistances against this hegemonic order cannot find legitimate forms of expression. This is why those resistances breed conflicts, which when they explode, take antagonistic forms, putting into question the very basis of the existing order. As I have suggested in *On the Political* (2005), it is the lack of political channels for challenging the hegemony of the neo-liberal model of globalisation that is at the origin of the proliferation of discourses and practices of radical negation of the established order.

Contrary to some currently fashionable views, I do not believe that the solution to our current predicament lies in the establishment of a cosmopolitan democracy. The problem, in my view, with the cosmopolitan approach is that, whatever its formulation, it postulates the availability of a world beyond hegemony and beyond sovereignty, therefore negating the dimension of the political. Moreover it is predicated on the universalisation of the western model and therefore does not make room for a plurality of legitimate alternatives. All those who assert that the aim of politics – be it at the national or the international level – should be to establish consensus on one single model, end up foreclosing the possibility of legitimate dissent and creating the terrain for the emergence of violent forms of antagonisms.

In my view, the challenge that we are facing is the following: if on one side we acknowledge that every order is a hegemonic order and that there is no possible order 'beyond hegemony', but on the other side we also acknowledge the negative consequences of a unipolar world, organised around the hegemony of an hyper-power, what is the alternative? My suggestion is that the only solution lies in the pluralisation of hegemonies. Abandoning the illusory hope for a political unification of the world, we should advocate the establishment of a multipolar, agonistic world organised around several big regional units with their different cultures and values. I am not pretending, of course, that this would bring about the end of conflicts but I am convinced that those conflicts are less likely to take an antagonistic form than in a world where a single economic and political model is presented as the only legitimate one and is imposed on all parties in the name of its supposedly superior rationality and morality.

Let me clarify here an important point. By speaking of an 'agonistic' world order, I am not trying to 'apply', strictly speaking, my agonistic domestic model to the field of international relations. What I am doing is bringing to the fore some similarities between those two very different realms. My objective is to stress that what is at stake in both cases is the importance of acknowledging the dimension of 'the political'. We need to realise that, instead of trying to bring about a consensus that would eliminate the very possibility of antagonism, the crucial task is to find ways to deal with conflicts so as to minimise the risks of them taking an antagonistic form. But of course the conditions are very different in the domestic and the international domains. The kind of 'conflictual consensus' based on divergent interpretations of shared ethico-political principles that is necessary for the implementation of an agonistic model of liberal democracy cannot be expected at the global level because such a consensus supposes the existence of a political community, which is not available at the international level. Indeed, to envisage the world order in terms of a plurality of hegemonic blocks requires relinquishing the idea that they need to be parts of an encompassing moral and political unit. The illusions of a global ethics, global civil society and other cosmopolitan dreams impede our ability to recognise that in the field of international relations one can only reach prudential agreements and that all attempts to definitively overcome the 'state of nature' between states, by the establishment of a global covenant, run into insurmountable difficulties.

I refer to Norberto Bobbio's model of 'institutional pacifism' to illustrate this point because it provides a good example of those difficulties. Bobbio's (1995) cosmopolitan approach consists in applying Hobbes's contractualism to the relations between states. Utilising the Hobbesian distinction between *pactum societatis* and *pactum subjectionis*, he argues that what is needed to create a peaceful international order is, in a first move, that states establish among themselves a permanent association through a treaty of non-aggression, in conjunction with a series of rules in order to resolve their disputes. This stage of *pactum societatis* should be followed by their submission to a common power that would ensure their effective adherence to the agreed treaties, using force if necessary (*pactum subjectionis*). Bobbio distinguishes three stages: first, the polemical stage, reflecting the situation in the state of nature in which conflicts are resolved only by force; second, the agonistic stage that corresponds to the *pactum societatis*, which excludes the use of reciprocal force to resolve conflicts and settle them by negotiation; and finally the pacific stage, which is when a *pactum subjectionis* is established with the existence of a Third Party able to enforce the agreements established in the agonistic stage. The pacific stage would see the overcoming of the state of nature in international relations and Bobbio believes that, although we have not yet reached the stage of a *pactum subjectionis*, the creation of the United Nations was an enormous step forward in that direction. He proposes to make a distinction between two different judicial figures:

> one who, despite his superior authority, does not have the coercive power to enforce his decisions (as still happens in international law today) and another whose superior authority grants him this power insofar as the pact of obedience has entrusted the use of legitimate force to it and to it alone. Only when the Judge has coercive power is the pacific stage wholly achieved.
>
> (Bobbio 1995: 25)

The current situation is one in which the United Nations finds itself in the position of a powerless Third Party Judge. This is due to the fact that states remain sovereign and have not yet abandoned their monopoly on the legitimate use of force to a common authority endowed with exclusive rights of coercive power. For Bobbio, a peaceful international system requires the completion of the transition from the agonistic to the pacific stage by the concentration of military force in the hands of a supreme international authority.

Although inspired by Hobbes, Bobbio's project parts from him in two significant aspects. Hobbes of course asserted that the passage from a state of nature to a civil union was not possible in the field on international relations and he repeatedly denied the possibility of both a *pactum societatis* and a *pactum subjectionis* among states. The pact of submission of which his Leviathan offers a model could only exist within a state. Moreover, it was of an autocratic nature. Bobbio intends to go further. Not only does he want to apply this model to the relations among states, he also wants the Third Party to acquire a democratic form. This is why he insists that this entrusting of coercive power to a superior entity should be the result of a universal agreement founded on democratic procedures. He asserts that peace and democracy are inextricably linked and that, for the power of the international Leviathan not to be oppressive, it is important that the states, which originate the contract through which the 'superstate' holding a legal monopoly on the use of international force is established, are democracies constitutionally committed to the protection of the fundamental rights of their citizens. The problem of course is that not all existing states are democratic and this leads him to difficulties that he openly acknowledges:

> I am well aware that my whole argument is based on conjecture inspired by the Kantian idea that perpetual peace is feasible only among states with the same form of republican government (the form in which collective decisions are made by the people) – supplemented by the ideas that the union of states must also be republican in form ... Like any conjecture, my thesis may be expressed only as an 'if-then' hypothetic proposition: 'If all the states were republican, if the society of all states were republican, then...' 'If' is the stumbling block.

> (Bobbio 1995: 38)

Bobbio is clearly caught in a vicious circle that he formulates in the following way: 'states can become democratic only in a fully democratised international society, but a fully democratised international society presupposes that all the states that compose it are democratic. The completion of one process is hindered by the non-completion of the other' (Bobbio 1995: 39). Bobbio is nevertheless hopeful for the future because, in his view, the number of democratic states is increasing and he believes that the process of the democratisation of international society is therefore truly under way.

There are of course many people today who would disagree with such optimism, among them Robert Kagan, who in his recent book *The Return of*

History and the End of Dreams, argues that the global competition between liberal and autocratic governments is likely to intensify in coming years. Kagan is of course a neo-conservative concerned with the maintenance of American hegemony, but many people on the left are also sceptical about the optimistic, 'smooth' view of globalisation.

The question however is not a matter of pessimism versus optimism and it should be addressed in a different way. If, as I have argued, every order is by necessity a hegemonic one, it is clear that the political unification of the world advocated by Bobbio, if it was ever to happen, could only take place under the hegemony of a central power. Bobbio's figure of a democratic international Leviathan, created through a pact of submission by which all states agree through democratic procedures that a Third Party Judge will have the coercive power to resolve their conflicts, could only be a global hegemon. His hoped for democratic world order would in fact be a unipolar world where, in the name of universalism, the western model of democracy would have been imposed worldwide. This would have dire consequences and, as I have already indicated, we are currently witnessing how current attempts to homogenise the world are provoking violent adverse reactions from those societies whose specific values and cultures are rendered illegitimate by the enforced universalisation of the Western model.

It is time, I submit, to relinquish the very idea of a *pactum subjectionis* among states and acknowledge that peace in a pluralist world can only be reached through the establishment of a variety of *pactum societatis*, i.e. a multiplicity of pragmatic multilateral agreements which will always remain precarious and contingent. Against Bobbio's illusion that a pacific stage could ever be reached in the field of international relations, it is necessary to accept that the agonistic stage is the only alternative to the state of nature. To envisage what are, under the current conditions of globalisation, the most adequate forms of constructing such an agonistic order is the challenge that we face.

Which democracy for a multipolar 'agonistic' world?

What could be the place of democracy in such a multipolar order? This is the question that I want to address in the last part of this chapter. It is evident that a multipolar world will not necessarily be a democratic one and that several of its poles might be organised around different political principles. Since we have discarded the presence of an impartial Third Party Judge, able to impose what would be deemed the only legitimate order, a coexistence of political regimes is unavoidable. This is of course the situation that we are beginning to witness, with the first signs of the advent of a multipolar world in which China, certainly not a democracy, will no doubt play an important role. My position on this question is that, a multipolar world composed of a variety of regimes would certainly be better than the current unipolar one because it is less likely to foster the emergence of extreme forms of antagonism.

But I do not think that we need to discard the possibility that democracy might become established worldwide. However, this question would have to be envisaged in a different way, abandoning the claim that this process of democratisation should consist in the global implementation of the Western liberal democratic model. Democracy in a multipolar world could take a variety of forms, according to the different modes of inscription of the democratic ideal in a variety of contexts.

As I have argued in *The Democratic Paradox* (Mouffe 2000), liberal democracy is the articulation between two different traditions: liberalism, with its emphasis on individual liberty and universal rights; and democracy, which privileges the idea of equality and 'rule by the people', i.e. popular sovereignty. Such an articulation is not a necessary but a contingent one; it is the product of a specific history. Indeed, the liberal democratic model, with its particular conception of human rights, is the expression of a particular cultural and historical context, in which, as it has often been noted, the Judeo-Christian tradition has played a central role. Such a model of democracy is constitutive of our form of life and it is certainly worthy of our allegiance, but there is no reason to present it as the only legitimate way of organising human coexistence and to try to impose it on the rest of the world. The kind of individualism dominant in Western societies is alien to many other cultures, whose traditions are informed by different values, and democracy understood as 'rule by the people' can therefore take other forms, in which for instance the value of community is more pregnant than the idea of individual liberty.

The dominant view, found in many different currents of political theory, asserts that moral progress requires the acceptance of the Western model of liberal democracy because it is the only possible shell for the implementation of human rights. This thesis has to be rejected but that does not necessarily mean discarding the idea of human rights. It might in fact continue to play a role but on condition that it is reformulated in a way that permits a pluralism of interpretations. To elucidate this issue we find important insights in the work of Raimundo Panikkar, who in an article entitled 'Is the Notion of Human Rights a Western Concept?' (1982: 81–2), asserts that, in order to understand the meaning of human rights, it is necessary to scrutinise the function played by this notion in our culture. This will allow us, he says, to examine later if this function is not fulfilled in different ways in other cultures. Panikkar urges us to enquire about the possibility of what he calls 'homeomorphic', i.e. functional, equivalents of the notion of human rights. Looking at Western culture, we ascertain that human rights are presented as providing the basic criteria for the recognition of human dignity and as being the necessary condition for a just social and political order. Therefore the question we need to ask is whether other cultures do not give different answers to the same question.

Once it is acknowledged that what is at stake in human rights is the dignity of the person, the possibility of different manners of envisaging this question becomes evident, as well as the different ways in which it can be answered. What Western culture calls 'human rights' is in fact a culturally specific form of asserting the dignity of the person and it would be very presumptuous to declare that it is the only legitimate one. Many theorists have pointed out how the very formulation in terms of 'rights' depends on a way of moral theorising that, while appropriate for modern liberal individualism, can be inappropriate for grasping the question of the dignity of the person in other cultures. According to François Jullien, for instance, the idea of 'rights' privileges the freeing of the subject from its vital context and devalues its integration in a multiplicity of spheres of belonging. It corresponds to a defensive approach that relinquishes the religious dimension and presents the individual as absolute. Jullien notes that the concept of the 'rights of man' does not find any echo in the thought of classical India that does not envisage man as being isolated from the rest of the natural world. While 'liberty' is the final word in European culture, for the Far East, from India to China, the final word is 'harmony' (2008: 24).

In the same line of thought Panikkar illustrates how the concept of human rights relies on a well-known set of presuppositions, all of which are distinctively Western, namely: there is a universal human nature that can be known by rational means; human nature is essentially different from and higher than the rest of reality; the individual has an absolute and irreducible dignity that must be defended against society and the state; the autonomy of that individual requires that society be organised in a non-hierarchical way, as a sum of free individuals. All those presuppositions, claims Panikkar, are definitively Western and liberal and are distinguishable from other conceptions of human dignity in other cultures. For instance, there is no necessary overlap between the idea of the 'person' and the idea of the 'individual'. The 'individual' is the specific way in which Western liberal discourse formulates the concept of the self. Other cultures, however, envisage the self in different ways (Panikkar 1982: 81–2).

Many consequences stem from these considerations. One of the most important is that we have to recognise that the idea of 'autonomy', which is so central in Western liberal discourse and which is at the centre of our understanding of human rights, cannot have such a priority in other cultures where decision-making is less individualistic and more cooperative than in Western societies. This in no way signifies that those cultures are not concerned with the dignity of the person and the conditions for a just social order. What it means is that they deal with those questions in a different way. This is why the search for homeomorphic equivalents is a necessary one. Societies that envisage human dignity in a way that differs from the Western understanding of human rights would also have a different way of envisaging the nature and role of democratic institutions. To take seriously 'value pluralism' in its multiple dimensions therefore requires making room for the pluralism of cultures, forms of life and political regimes. This means that in addition to the recognition of a plurality of understandings of 'human rights', we should recognise a plurality of forms of democracy.

Next to human rights another crucial issue for democracy is the question of secularisation. In fact, even in the West, there is a long-standing debate about the relation between democracy and the mode of existence of a secular society. As Jose Casanova has convincingly shown (2006), an impasse has been reached in that debate between the European and the American approaches and the different ways in which they envisage the nature of a secular society and the link between secularism and modernity. On one side, there are the European sociologists who believe that the decline in the societal power of religious institutions and in religious beliefs and practices among individuals are necessary components of the process of modernisation; on the other side, there are American sociologists of religion who reject the theory of secularisation because they do not see any decline in the religious beliefs and practices of the American people. What is really at stake in this debate is the following question: should secularisation be seen as a necessary feature of modernity and should it be seen as a precondition for modern liberal democratic politics? I am going to leave this question aside because the issue that I want to tackle is another one: even if we give an affirmative answer to this question in the context of Western democracy, does it mean that secularisation is a normative condition for all forms of democracy? Or should we not envisage the possibility of democratic societies where such a process did not take place? Casanova asks 'Can the theory of secularisation as a particular theory of historical development be dissociated from general theories of global modernisation? Can there be a non-Western, non-secular modernity?' (Casanova 2006: 10). I would like to make this question even more precise and ask: can there be a non-Western, non-secular modernity with a non-secular form of democracy? If, as many people assert, the European concept of secularisation is not particularly relevant for the United States, it is clear that it is even less relevant for other civilisations with very different modes of social structuration. What could be its relevance for instance for worldly religions like Confucianism or Taoism? As Casanova notes, their model of transcendence can hardly be called 'religious' and they do not have ecclesiastical organisation. In a sense they have always been 'worldly' and do not need to undergo a process of secularisation. One could say, for instance, that China and the Confucian civilisational area have been secular 'avant la lettre' (Casanova 2006: 13).

The best way to avoid those pitfalls is to acknowledge the possibility of multiple modernities and to accept that the path followed by the West is not the only possible and legitimate one and that non-Western societies can follow different trajectories according to the specificity of their cultural traditions and of their religions. Once it is granted that the set of institutions constitutive of liberal democracy – with their vocabulary of human rights and their form of secularisation – are the result of a contingent historical articulation in a specific cultural context, there is no reason to see their adoption worldwide as the criteria of political modernity and as a necessary component of democracy. A pluralist approach should therefore envisage the possibility of other forms of articulation of the democratic ideal of government by the people, articulations in which religion would have a different type of relation with politics and in which human rights (provided we want to keep this term) would be conceived in ways that depart from their formulation in the individualistic liberal culture.

To be sure, in many parts of the world we find intellectuals and activists who are engaged in precisely that kind of reflection, working to elaborate a vernacular conception of democracy inscribed in their respective cultural and religious traditions. In the case of Islam for instance, Noah Feldman (2008) has shown that what is at stake is how to envisage a constitutional order grounded in the sharia and devoted to the rule of law. He examines different attempts to visualise how a democratic Islamic state, a state governed through Islamic law and Islamic values, could reconcile divine sovereignty with the democratic principle of popular sovereignty. Mainstream Islamism, he notes, has accepted the compatibility of the sharia and democracy but differences exist concerning the mechanisms of reconciliation. The most prominent solution is

> for the constitution of the Islamic state to acknowledge divine sovereignty rather than establish popular sovereignty and then use it to enact Islamic law. On this theoretical model, the people function somewhat as the ruler did in the classical constitutional order: they accept the responsibility for implementing what God has commanded.
>
> (Feldman 2008: 119)

According to some interpretations, this democratically elected legislature responsible for enacting the provisions of the sharia would need to be supervised by a constitutionalised process of Islamic judicial review. Feldman is aware of the difficulties that the establishment of such a democratic Islamic state will encounter but he insists that it would be an error for the West to see it as a threat to democracy and to try to destroy those who are advocating it.

The situation is no doubt different in other parts of the world and in each case the solution will have to take account of specific circumstances and cultural traditions. But all those who want to develop vernacular models of democracy face the same problem with respect to the West: its refusal to acknowledge forms of democracy different from the liberal democratic one. Western powers are adamant that the only legitimate democracy is their current interpretation: multi-party electoral democracy, accompanied by an individualistic conception of human rights, and of course by free market policies. This is the model that they claim to have a moral duty to promote, or impose if necessary. The disastrous consequences of the imposition of such a model can be seen worldwide. To take the case of Africa, for instance, several authors have pointed out that the catastrophic conditions existing in many African countries are the consequence of the inadequate political systems that were bequeathed to them by their former colonisers. Independence often left them, not as stable national states but as a patchwork of ethnic fiefdoms, burdened with parliaments based on those of the former colonial power. In countries with so many ethnicities with their own language, customs and culture, multi-party democracy has led to political fragmentation and bitterly divided politics. Many specialists recognise that forms of democracy more adapted to African customs are needed and that governments of national unity might be better suited for holding those countries together and fostering their development.

As far as Asia is concerned, the situation is again different. There one of the challenges might be to reconcile the democratic principle of popular sovereignty with Confucianism and Taoism. The idea of 'Asian values' is often rejected on the grounds that it is used as an excuse by authoritarian rulers to justify their domination. In some cases there might indeed be some truth in this claim, but this should not lead to the dismissal of the legitimacy of such a notion. In the end the people concerned should decide those issues and it is not up to us Westerners to tell them how to organise their own societies. The thought that I will conclude with is that we should acknowledge that the world is a pluriverse and realise that to accept a diversity of political forms of organisation will be more conducive to peace and stability than the enforcement of a universal model.

9 Critiquing global democracy

David Chandler

Introduction

The attenuation or hollowing out of territorial politics – that posit a fixed relationship between a demos and sovereign decision-making power – reflects a crisis of traditional frameworks of political community. Territorially defined and constructed political communities are suffering from a generic lack of cohering values and sentiments, expressed in regular discussions of the meaning and relevance of different national values, symbols and traditions. Governments have great difficulty in legitimating themselves in traditional ways. With the decline in party membership and voting, even holding elections every five years does little to legitimate governing elites or to cohere political programmes for which they can be held to account. Traditional framings of foreign policy in terms of the national interest appear problematic and are often buttressed with claims of ethical or values-based foreign policy that seek to secure the interests of people elsewhere rather than collectively expressing the interests of their citizens. In the face of this crisis in, and transformation of, traditional ways of understanding and participating in politics it is of little surprise that the discussion of alternative democratic possibilities of post-territorial political community has taken centre stage.

There is a growing consensus that expressing political community in territorially bounded terms is inherently problematic because of its narrow, self-interested and divisive framework, in which radical democratic politics are sidelined. For many critics, territorial political allegiances are held to be the product of uncritical and unreflective understandings of the role of state-based political communities in interpellating subjects that are submissive and uncritical. As the theoretical engagement with the problems or the failure of territorial politics develops, increasingly contraposed to this hollowed out, exclusivist and hierarchical framework are the possibilities of being political and of doing and participating in politics, held to be opening up with global interconnectedness and new forms of media and communications. The traditional state arena, in which modern liberal democratic frameworks of political community first appeared, is now considered to be much less relevant and, in its stead, it seems that the possibilities of post-territorial political community are now about to be realised.

Critical theorists seemingly agree that post-territorial political community is the only possibility for the reconstruction of meaningful political practice in today's globalised world. The possibilities of post-territorial politics became increasingly articulated in the 1990s, mainly by theorists who argued that liberal democratic politics could no longer be meaningful practiced within the confines of the nation state. Liberal cosmopolitan theorists, such as Mary Kaldor, David Held, Andrew Linklater, Richard Falk and Daniele Archibugi, argued for the need for a new cosmopolitan political order, based on the extension of political community beyond the nation state (for overview, see Held, this volume; and Archibugi *et al.* 1998). These theorists assert that democracy and political community can no longer be equated with the territorial limits of nation states: 'democracy must transcend the borders of single states and assert itself on a global level' (Archibugi 2000: 144). Without this shift, cosmopolitans allege the dominant relations of power and inequality will be perpetuated. For Falk, Western states 'do not even purport to represent the great majority of women and men on the planet. Moreover such states represent only the dominant class, gender, and race within their own territorial space' (1995: 50). To meet the needs of cosmopolitan or global citizens, it is necessary to extend democracy beyond the nation state. As Linklater states:

> Transcending state sovereignty which remains the constitutive principle of modern political life is understood as essential to promoting narratives of increasing cosmopolitanism. Expanding the realm of dialogic commitments is regarded as necessitating measures to reduce or eradicate the asymmetries of power and wealth which exist within sovereign states and in the global economic and political system.
>
> (1998: 109; see also 192)

David Beetham argues that in a world of nation states 'the demos that is democracy's subject has come to be defined almost exclusively in national terms, and the scope of democratic rights has been limited to the bounds of the nation state' (1999: 137). He suggests that in the same way that democracy was extended from the level of the town to that of the state in the eighteenth century it should, in the twenty-first century, be extended from the nation to humankind as a whole. Similarly, Jan Aart Scholte suggests that globalisation has generated the 'growth of cosmopolitan bonds, where people identify the demos in terms of humanity as a whole' while conventional 'mechanisms of democracy tend to define "the people" only in territorial-state-nation terms' (2002: 290).

The reason for this new and more expansive institutionalisation of democracy is held to be the impact of globalising processes, which have created a 'democratic deficit' at the national level. As Anthony McGrew notes:

> ...democratic thinkers, from J. S. Mill to Robert Dahl, have assumed a direct symmetry between the institutions of representative democracy and the political community which they serve ... but this presumes a direct

correspondence between rulers and ruled, a correspondence which is disrupted by the existence of global and regional networks of power.

(1997: 237)

For liberal cosmopolitans, the state-based international architecture has been undermined both from above and below: from above, it has been weakened by globalisation and the alleged transformation of capitalist social relations, which has challenged the 'modern system of territorial rule' (Ruggie 1993: 151), creating a much less rigid 'spatial context in which power operates' (Agnew 1999: 501) weakening the consolidation of sovereign rule within fixed territorial boundaries (for a challenge to this argument, see Rosenberg 2000); from below, it has been politically challenged by new expressions of post-territorial political community, organising and communicating in post-territorialised global space; this new arising political subject was global civil society (Kaldor 1999; Baker 2002; Keane 2003; Chandler 2004a; Baker and Chandler 2005).

The 1990s was the high point for liberal cosmopolitanism as a radical critique of traditional territorially bound political community that suggested that we were witnessing a progressive transformation of both domestic and international relations. There was an assumption that the forces of immanent cosmopolitan change would be able to challenge the reactionary, exclusivist and divisive domination of the international agenda by nation-states, creating a new cosmopolitical era. For many of these advocates, the war over Kosovo in 1999 was held to mark the birth of the new cosmopolitan order (Habermas 1999a), however for others the resort to militarism – and the connection between humanitarianism and human rights and a war not sanctioned by the UN Security Council and fought in such as way as to minimise Western casualties – signalled problems in the cosmopolitan agenda being used to legitimise the exercise of Western power and a new interventionist order (Booth 2001). However, it was 9/11 and the birth of the 'Global War on Terror' that saw a shift towards the critical affirmation of an immanent post-territorial community in opposition to the claims of a new cosmopolitan global order.

The development of academic perspectives of post-territorial political community in opposition to those of liberal cosmopolitanism pre-dated 9/11 and was shaped by the development of anti-globalisation campaigns and environmental protests. A radical alternative vision of post-territorial community was formulated by Michael Hardt and Antonio Negri, first in *Empire* (2001, first published 2000) and later in *Multitude* (2006). For Hardt and Negri, post-territorial political community is derived from the shared desires of the 'multitude', the universal people united in democratic struggle against domination:

The virtuality of world space constitutes the first determination of the movements of the multitude ... [which] must achieve a global citizenship. The multitude's resistance to bondage – the struggle against the slavery of belonging to a nation, an identity, and a people, and thus the desertion from sovereignty and the limits it places on subjectivity – is entirely positive.

(2001: 361–2)

Since 2000, the radical critique of liberal cosmopolitan frameworks has been enhanced by the translations into English of Michel Foucault's lectures at the Collège de France (2003; 2007; 2008) and the critical work of post-Foucaultian theorists such as Giorgio Agamben (for example, 1998; 2005). For these critics, the Westphalian or UN-based international order based on the sovereign equality of nation-states has been challenged both from above and below: above from the shifting needs of post-material or biopolitical processes of production (Hardt and Negri 2006; Virno 2004) cohered through the networked power of *Empire* (Hardt and Negri 2001); and below from the resistance to neoliberal biopolitical global governance, through the multitude.

This chapter seeks to draw out the similarities in approach to post-territorial democratic political community, as expressed by both the 1990s liberal cosmopolitans and the 2000s radical poststructuralists. First, that both approaches derive their strengths from their rejection of state-based political community rather than from their capacity to demonstrate the existence or strength of alternative post-territorial political community. Second, that key to both approaches is the degradation of the modern liberal conception of the rights-bearing subject: once the connection between citizenship and democracy is broken then political community lacks any clear conceptual grounding. Third, the article seeks to highlight that discussions about post-territorial political community fail to recognise that particular individuals or struggles appear to directly confront power – either in the form of elite advocacy or oppositional protest – precisely because the mediating links of political community are so attenuated.

More demos, less democracy

The debates around the constitution of post-territorial political community, in the 1990s and 2000s, revolve around different understandings of the emergence of an immanent universalising political subject, capable of constituting a new demos and thereby overcoming exclusion and hierarchy in international relations. For the 1990s critics, this universalising power – which sought to undermine the power of state sovereignty and privilege the rights of cosmopolitan individuals – was often termed global civil society. This universal was grounded in a view of an emerging cosmopolitan, universalist or global consciousness in the wake of the ending of the Cold War (for example, Shaw 1994). The discourse of universal human rights challenged the prerogatives of state sovereignty; therefore it was assumed that states were not capable of originating and bearing this discourse. The leading agents of cosmopolitan political approaches were assumed to be non-state actors, primarily NGOs, often described as 'norm entrepreneurs' (Finnemore and Sikkink 1998). The rise of this universalist discourse was often understood in a social constructivist framework, based on the 'power of ideas' and the importance of global information networks (Risse *et al.* 1999). For liberal cosmopolitans, such as Kaldor, since the end of the Cold War, we have been witnessing a fundamental political struggle between global civil society and state-based approaches (Kaldor 2003; 2007).

For the 1990s critics, the universal discourse was driven by progressive agency 'from below' and therefore was a challenge to power. In our more disillusioned 2000s, particularly since 9/11, there has arisen an alternative critical reading of the discourse of cosmopolitan universality and the nature of post-territorial political community. Often a starting point for these critics is the work of German legal theorist Carl Schmitt, who, writing in the mid twentieth century, was highly critical of US claims to uphold universal cosmopolitan rights in opposition to what he saw as the European view of international law that privileged sovereign rights (see Schmitt 2003). Schmitt claimed famously that 'whoever invokes humanity wants to cheat' (Schmitt 1996: 54). Rather than a new progressive liberal universal subject arising from below, critical theorists in the 2000s saw the dangers of the liberal discourse as one which uncritically legitimated new totalising mechanisms of sovereign powers of intervention and regulation from above.

In a direct challenge to the advocates of liberal cosmopolitan approaches, these critical approaches have been primarily constructed within poststructuralist frameworks, suggesting that a new universal subject may be emerging from below but in opposition to the cosmopolitan discourse of power promoted by the liberal advocates of the 1990s. In the recent work of Mark Duffield (2007) Vivienne Jabri (2007a) and Costas Douzinas (2007) this framework is melded with post-Foucaultian Agambenite readings of cosmopolitan rights as an exclusionary and hierarchical exercise of biopower and the constitution of an alternative political community in the struggle against the universalising power of biopolitical global governance.

In this framework, new global governmental practices are highlighted that are legitimised through the privileging of declarations of the rights of the human over and above the formal rights framework of sovereignty and non-intervention. For Duffield, the focus on cosmopolitan human rights, expressed in the discourses of state failure and the merging of security and development, creates a biopolitical blank cheque to override the formal rights of sovereignty on the basis of the needs of securing the human. For Jabri, the recasting of military intervention in terms of the human undermines the state-based order and the line between domestic and global politics constituting a new global biopolitical order. For Douzinas, human rights discourses undermine territorial forms of sovereignty but enable the emergence of a new 'super-sovereign' of global hegemonic power.

Here, the universalism of liberal cosmopolitan theorists is 'stood on its head' to argue that it is the universalising interests of power, understood in vague terms of biopolitical, neoliberal, global governance, rather than the genuinely cosmopolitan ethics of empowerment, which drives the discursive practices of regimes of regulation and intervention in the international sphere. As the 1990s liberal discourse has been challenged by the 2000s poststructuralist discourse, we seem to be caught up in a contestation over which academics have the most progressive or radical understandings: of hierarchies of power – as a product of 'statist' exercises of national self-interest or as a product of new global governmentalities; and of post-territorial political community – as a response and opposition to these hierarchies, either in the form of global civil society or multitude.

However, it is not clear whether the contestation – in terms of the ontological framings of the relations and dynamics of power or of alternative political subjects of post-territorial political community – reflects much more than the starting positions of the critical academic theorists concerned. It seems that the radical differences between those who claim to espouse and those who claim to critique global liberal ontologies – and thereby read post-territorial community in liberal or poststructuralist framings – are derived less from empirical investigations than from their own normative aspirations. For cosmopolitan theorists, their normative aspirations for a more ethical and engaged foreign policy agenda were given added legitimacy through linking their demands with those of activist NGOs and assertions of global civil society's immanent existence. As Kaldor asserts, the concept of global or transnational civil society is used on the one hand as an analytical device, but on the other hand, it is also used to express 'a political project' (1999: 195).

Similarly, for poststructuralist critics, the struggle against 'empire' is alleged to be more than mere philosophical idealism precisely because it is founded upon the immanent existence of the 'multitude'. Just as with the concept of global civil society, Hardt and Negri's multitude is partly framed as an abstract heuristic device (2006: 221). But more importantly it is also a normative project: 'The multitude needs a political project to bring it into existence' (2006: 212). As they state: 'The proletariat is not what it used to be' (2001: 53). Their, task, therefore, is to discover a new form of global democratic agency. They describe this mixture of academic investigation and normative aspiration as illustrating that multitude 'has a strange double temporality: always-already and not-yet' (2006: 222). It appears that the new post-territorial political communities, held to be coming into existence, conflate empirical and normative aspirations in the critique of the perceived hierarchies of power: either being seen as constituted against the narrow state-interests dominating international politics or against the biopolitics of global 'empire'.

At the level of discursive analysis (as we shall see) the choice between these two approaches can easily appear to be a purely subjective one. Neither one appears to satisfactorily ground the existence of a new emerging universal subject capable of constituting post-territorial political community – as the agent of cosmopolitical regimes or of post-cosmopolitical resistance to these regimes. In both, the democratic subject – that is alleged to demonstrate both the lack *and* the presence of post-territorial political community – is grounded in a way that confuses normative political critique with empirical analysis. Both approaches suggest that traditional territorial political communities have been fundamentally undermined by the changing nature of social relations – by globalisation or by biopolitical production processes. These changing social relations are held to have undermined territorial political community through the deconstruction of the unitary assumptions involved in modern liberal democratic political theory. However, they have been much less successful in demonstrating that new post-territorial forms of political community have been constructed in their stead.

What is clear is that, in the name of post-territorial political community, liberal and radical critics have sought to represent the crisis of legitimacy of representative political bodies as a product of political contestation emerging from post-territorial democratic agency. In these frameworks of understanding global politics, the shift towards post-territorial community is seen as indicative of new lines of political struggle that have replaced those of the territorialised framework of Left and Right. For liberal and critical theorists, this is the struggle for cosmopolitan and human rights and for emancipation against the sovereign power of states. For poststructuralist theorists, this is seen as the struggle for autonomy and difference against the universalising war waged 'over ways of life itself' by neoliberal biopolitical governance (Reid 2006). However, these struggles remain imminent ones, in which global political social forces of progress are intimated but are yet to fully develop. There is a problem of the social agency, the collective political subject, which can give democratic content to the theorising of global struggle articulated by academic theorists. It seems that neither liberal nor poststructuralist theorists are able to envisage the possibility that we could live in a world where politics appears to have become deterritorialised, not as a result of the expanded nature of collective political engagement, but precisely because of the absence of political struggle (see further Chandler 2009).

Political community without political subjects

Neither the liberal nor the poststructuralist visions of post-territorial community contain modern liberal rights-bearing subjects. For neither is there a universalising sphere of legal or political equality constituted by autonomous rights-bearing subjects. The liberal cosmopolitical critique of liberal democratic frameworks of political community is precisely that they are not able to empower and protect minorities and the marginal or excluded and that, therefore, there needs to be an external level of regulatory rights enforcement of cosmopolitan rights. As Falk argues:

> It is now evident that democracy, at least as constituted in liberal democratic societies, is not by itself a sufficient precondition for a peaceful and just world. Democracy as an operative political form seems quite compatible with certain types of militarism and racism, perhaps resting in turn on patriarchal practices and hidden assumptions.
>
> (1995: 24)

The cosmopolitan project seeks to legitimise liberal policy-frameworks without engaging with the electorate, increasingly seen to be too 'egoistic' or 'apathetic' and distanced from liberal policy elites, and, under 'reflexive modernity', lacking commonality (for example, Beck 1998). The challenge to the liberal democratic rights framework is based on the belief that progressive ends – such as the protection of human rights, international peace or sustainable development – would be more easily achieved without the institutional constraints of democratic accountability. In Falk's words, the problem is: 'the reluctance of national citizenries for emotive and self-interested reasons to endorse globalizing initiatives' (1995: 216).

The cosmopolitan, or post-territorial, democratic subject is defined through being freed from any political framework that institutionalises liberal democratic norms of formal accountability. The bearer of human rights or rights of global citizenship, by definition, has no fixed territorial identity and thereby no place within any institutionalised framework of legal and political equality from which to hold policy actors to formal account. Because they are freed from any such framework, the 'rights' of the cosmopolitan citizen are dependent on the advocacy of an external agency. By default, the cosmopolitan subject becomes concrete only through 'representation' on a particular issue through the agency of global civil society advocates who also have an existence 'free' from the institutionalised political framework of the nation-state.

Without the institutionalisation of mechanisms of accountability, global civil society claims to 'represent the people' remain unsubstantiated (Edwards 1999: 180). Whereas the claim for representation is inevitably contested, global civil society actors and movements often assert that the crucial role they perform is that of 'articulation' of the needs of global citizens. Because the global citizen cannot directly hold policy-makers to account, the role of global civil society interlocutors becomes central to give content to claims of democracy without formal representation. Kaldor, for example, argues that 'the role of NGOs is not to be representative but to raise awareness', adding that the 'appeal is to moral conscience' not to political majorities (2001). Johan Galtung, similarly, gives support to this form of 'empowerment', which he terms 'democracy by articulation, not by representation' (2000: 155).

Cosmopolitan frameworks inverse the grounding liberal relationship between rights and their subjects in their construction of rights independently of their subjects (see Chandler 2003). These rights are fictitious – in the same way as animal rights or the rights of the environment or of future generations would be – because there is a separation between the subjects of these rights and the political or social agency giving content to them. The proposed framework of cosmopolitan regulation is based on the fictitious rights of the 'global citizen' or of the 'human' not the expression of rights through the formal democratic framework of political and legal equality of citizen-subjects. This framework recognises neither the democratic rights of citizens nor the collective expression of these rights in state sovereignty. It is important to stress the qualitative difference between the liberal-democratic approach, which derives rights from self-governing human subjects, and the cosmopolitan approach of claiming rights on the behalf of others, who can only be constituted as non-subjects (see further, Chandler 2002: 103–5).

In reinterpreting 'rights' as moral or discursive claims, a contradiction appears between the enforcement and guarantee of cosmopolitan rights and the formal equality of the liberal democratic legal and political framework.

Within the normative framework of cosmopolitan theory, vital areas of formal accountability, at both the domestic and international level, are questioned while new and increasingly ad hoc frameworks of decision-making are seen to be positive and 'emancipatory'. First, the formal right of sovereign equality under international law would be a conditional or residual right under the cosmopolitan framework. As Held notes: 'sovereignty per se is no longer a straightforward guarantee of international legitimacy' (2000: 24). Archibugi argues that it is a matter of urgency that 'democratic procedures should somehow be assessed by external agents' (1998: 210) effectively transferring sovereign power elsewhere. In this framing, states that failed these external assessments of their legitimacy would no longer have equal standing or full sovereign rights and could be legitimately acted against in the international arena.

More fundamentally, the domestic rights of citizens to democratic self-government would be removed. Cosmopolitans assert that, despite adherence to all internationally accepted formal democratic procedures, a state's government may not be truly democratic. In the cosmopolitan framework the formal demos is no longer necessarily the final arbiter of democratic outcomes because:

> ... the choices of a people, even when made democratically, might be biased by self-interest. It may, for example, be in the interests of the French public to obtain cheap nuclear energy if they manage to dispose of radioactive waste in a Pacific isle under their control, but this will obviously be against the interests of the public living there.
>
> (Archibugi 1998: 211)

For cosmopolitan theorists the ethical ends for which they advocate are privileged above the sphere of democracy. As Linklater argues, this means a 'break with the supposition that national populations have the sovereign right to withhold their consent' if cosmopolitan demands 'clash with their conception of national interests' (1998: 192). In this framework, a small minority may be more 'democratic' than a large majority, if they have an outlook attuned to cosmopolitan aspirations. Kaldor draws out the implications of the argument when she suggests that the international community should not necessarily consult elected local representatives but seek 'to identify local advocates of cosmopolitanism' where there are 'islands of civility' (1999: 120). Just as states cannot be equally trusted with cosmopolitan rights, neither can people. Instead of the 'limited' but fixed and formally equal demos of the nation-state, there is a highly selective 'demos' identified by international institutions guided by the cosmopolitan impulse.

The biopolitical critique of the discourse of cosmopolitan rights is that rather than a mechanism of empowerment it is an exercise of power. So far, so good. But, rather than critique cosmopolitan rights for the fictional nature of the rights claimed, many of these poststructuralist critics, reading Foucault through Agamben, wish to portray all rights constructions – whether posed in terms of the territorialised 'citizen' or the deterritorialised 'human' – as equally oppressive and hierarchical. The poststructuralist critique, in fact, reflects a very similar view of citizen rights as the liberal cosmopolitan vision: expressing a similar aspiration to evade the problematic question of political representation and the formal constitution of political community. For cosmopolitan human rights advocates, there is no distinct difference between global, deterritorialised, human rights and territorial, sovereignty-bounded, democratic and civil rights. All rights claims are seen to be equally empowering and able to tame power in the name of ethics and equality. Here, the extension of cosmopolitan frameworks of global governance is read to be the extension of the realm of freedom and a restriction on state sovereign power. For many poststructuralist critics, the response is to argue that the liberal discourse reveals the truth in its blurring of rights claims: the hidden relationship between democracy and dictatorship; law as ad hoc and arbitrary power is therefore the inner truth of the appearance that law is a reflection of the autonomy and agency of legally constituted subjects (Agamben 1998: 10).

For the critics of cosmopolitan rights regimes, the extension of a discourse of rights and law merely enhances the power of liberal governance. Indeed, Giorgio Agamben has captured well the ethico-juridical blurring of human rights regimes as a 'state of exception', by which he means not a dictatorship but a hollowing out or emptying of the content of law:

> ...the state of exception has today reached its maximum worldwide deployment. The normative aspect of law can thus be obliterated and contradicted with impunity by a governmental violence that – while ignoring international law externally and producing a permanent state of exception internally – nevertheless still claims to be applying the law.
>
> (2005: 87)

Cosmopolitan claims do, in fact, advocate for a 'permanent state of exception'. However, in reading the state of exception as the essential nature of the sovereign state and law, Agamben argues that the lesson is that progressive politics can never operate within the modern state form: 'Politics has suffered a lasting eclipse because it has been contaminated by law, seeing itself, at best, as constituent power (that is violence that makes law), when it is not reduced to merely the power to negotiate with the law' (2005: 88). In his earlier work, *Homo Sacer*, he argued:

> It is almost as if ... every decisive political event were double-sided: the spaces, the liberties, and the rights won by individuals in their conflicts with central powers always simultaneously prepared a tacit but increasing inscription of the individual's lives within the state order, thus offering a new and more dreadful foundation for the very sovereign power from which they wanted to liberate themselves.
>
> (1998: 121)

For both the liberal cosmopolitan advocates of human rights and these radical poststructuralist critics, there is no specific understanding of the problem of cosmopolitan rights as based on non-socially constituted legal subjects (Lewis 1998). For both liberal cosmopolitan theorists and poststructuralists, rights regimes are understood to be constituted independently of and prior to the rights subjects. For cosmopolitan advocates, it is precisely because the poor and excluded cannot autonomously enforce their rights that an external agency needs to step in to empower them and constitute them as rights holders. For many post-structuralists, rights are also constituted independently and prior to their subjects: it is the declaration of rights that constitutes the subject; rights therefore are understood as preceding and interpolating their subject (Douzinas 2007: 92). Douzinas therefore stresses the darker side of rights: 'the inexorable rise of registration, classification and control of individuals and populations' (2007: 129). Poststructuralist critics tend to exaggerate the cosmopolitan claim that rights are independent from subjects in order to view all rights claims as fictions and all rights-subjects as non-subjects (Agamben's 'bare life').

For these radical poststructuralists, the ambiguity of cosmopolitan frameworks of political community – which can only empower those who decide on the content and ad hoc implementation – are read to be, not an attack on modern liberal demo-cratic frameworks of rights and law, but instead essentialised as the key to under-standing the modern state as a biopolitical power. These radical critics critique the claims of the liberal cosmopolitans by essentialising them as modern liberal rights claims per se. This one-sided understanding of rights, through breaking their con-nection to rights-subjects, produces in an exaggerated form the cosmopolitan cri-tique of the political sphere of representation. For liberal advocates of cosmopolitan rights, representational claims are problematic because they may undermine rights protections and therefore regulatory power needs to exist above the nation-state; for many poststructuralists, any participation in the political sphere of the territorial state is inherently disempowering, necessitating a 'flight from sovereignty' and the formal sphere of representation (Hardt and Negri 2006: 341).

The flight from the sphere of the democratic rights-bearing subject of liberal modernity, in both cosmopolitan and poststructuralist frameworks, is crucial to enable the move to post-territorial constructions of political community. For modern liberal political theory, it was the rights framework that reflected and institutionalised the existence of a political community of equal rights-bearing subjects. The liberal political ontology has the autonomous rights-bearing indi-vidual as the foundational subject of legal and political spheres of formal equal-ity. The rule of law and the legitimacy of government were derived from the consent and accountability of rights-holding citizens.

In the frameworks of cosmopolitan and biopolitical theorists of post-territorial political community, political community is no longer constituted on the basis of a rights framework of autonomous subjects. Formal frameworks of politics and law are held to be independent of the political subject (which is reinterpreted as the object of administration and regulation rather than as a rights subject). For liberal cosmopolitans, the existence of rights (law) prior to and independently of political subjects is held to legitimise regimes of international intervention and regulation, while for many poststructuralists the autonomy of law is read as the autonomy of power to interpellate and create the ruled subject. In both frameworks, by theoretical construction, there is no longer a distinction between the citizen and the non-citizen as rights claims are merely a reflection of the claims of rule made by (benign or oppressive) power.

Once the construction of political community is freed from political and legal frameworks of liberal democratic rights, both cosmopolitan and post-structural approaches are free to establish the existence of democratic political community at the global level, as a post-territorial construction. The only problem with this construction is the question of how political community can be constituted without the rights and duties of citizenship. The approaches to this problem will be briefly addressed below.

Individuals and the 'community'

In modern liberal theorising, it is the rights and duties of citizenship that constitute the shared bonds of democratic political community. The political sphere is clearly distinct as the public sphere of law and politics from the private sphere of particularist identities, hobbies and interests. Political community is therefore distinct from the bonds of family, friendship or groupings of special interests. What makes political community distinct is its public nature, which forces people to engage with others, whom they do not necessarily know or agree with in order to contest representational alternatives. It seems clear that the attenuation of political contestation, of the struggle between Left and Right, has meant that political community has less meaning for many of us than other (non-political) communities with which we may participate or identify.

The advocates of post-territorial political community dismiss the bonds of citizenship, constituted by modern liberal rights frameworks; this means that the bonds that constitute post-territorial community are much more difficult to locate. For cosmopolitan theorist, John Keane, global civil society, constituted by networked actors, constitutes a form of political community, albeit a 'paradoxical' one:

> It refers to a vast, sprawling non-governmental constellation of many institutionalised structures, associations and networks within which individual and group actors are interrelated and functionally interdependent. As a society of societies, it is 'bigger' and 'weightier' than any individual actor or organisation or combined sum of its thousands of constituent parts – most of whom, paradoxically, neither 'know' each other nor have any chance of ever meeting each other face-to-face.
>
> (2003: 11)

The idealised view of global civil society relies on claims about the communicative interaction of global civic actors that have little connection to reality.

Similarly, William Connolly has to go through some contortions to substantiate his claim that 'network pluralism sustains a *thick* political culture', as he adds by way of parenthesis:

> ...but this is a thickness in which the centre devolves into multiple lines of connection across numerous dimensions of difference ... such as ethnicity, religion, language, gender practice and sexuality. These lines of flow slice through the centre as diverse constituencies connect to one another, pulling it from concentric pluralism toward a network pattern of multidimensional connections.
>
> (2001: 352)

The line between a complete lack of social or political interconnection and having a 'thick political culture' seems to be in the eye of the beholder. It is important to highlight the abstract and socially disengaged nature of the post-territorial project. Advocates of global civil society, such as Kaldor, are keen to assert that global civil society is actively engaged in debating global issues, but they are much less specific when it comes to detailing the concrete nature of these 'debates': the content or ideas generated; if a record was kept; or if the debate had any consequences. It appears that, in making these assertions of communicative debates, these advocates repeatedly use the concept of 'public/global/ethical *debate*' in an intellectually dishonest way. The dictionary definition of 'debate' is a formal form of argument in which parties attempt to persuade an audience of their position and there are rules enabling people to discuss and decide on differences. Public debate inside or across national boundaries is, of course, a positive exercise but this does not mean that there is any form of public debate in deterritorialised 'global space'. Debate is a purposive human activity: websites do not talk to themselves – or personal blogs – just as diaries that we keep under our beds do not communicate with each other.

The question of democratic engagement and interconnection between the multitude of networked actors constituting the alternative framework for post-territorial political community is a problematic one, which reveals the lack of mediation between the particular and the ostensible political 'community' or the 'many'. This lack of mediation is highlighted in Hardt and Negri's description of the multitude as neither one nor many. They assert that the multitude 'violates all such numerical distinctions. It is both one and many', thereby allegedly threatening all the principles of order (2006: 139). In fact, it is the lack of social or political connection between the various struggles, from those of Los Angeles rioters to Chiapas rebels, which defines the multitude. This lack of connection is described by Hardt and Negri as 'incommunicability': 'This paradox of incommunicability makes it extremely difficult to grasp and express the new power posed by the struggles that have emerged' (2001: 54).

However, the more isolated and marginal these struggles are then the more transgressive and 'global' they become, in their 'direct' challenge to 'power' or 'empire'. For example, the Los Angeles rioters are held to challenge racial and hierarchical forms of 'post-Fordist' social control, or the Chiapas rebels are seen as challenging the regional construction of world markets. The key assertion is that: 'Perhaps precisely because all these struggles are incommunicable and thus blocked from travelling horizontally in the form of a cycle, they are forced instead to leap vertically and touch immediately on the global level' (2001: 56). These struggles are immediately global because of their lack of inter-connection in the same way that they are 'deterritorialised' because they lack the capacity to strategically or instrumentally challenge power. It is their lack of social or political connection that makes these struggles non-territorial or 'global'.

The multitude no more constitutes a political community than liberal cosmopolitan constructions of global civil society (Chandler 2004b; 2007). In both frameworks, there is no mediation between the particular, at the level of the individual or the particular struggle, and any collective democratic political subject. Post-territorial political community is therefore constructed precisely on the basis of prioritising an abstract universal, which preserves the individual and the particular. Any declaration of 'community' can only be a highly abstract one. As Jabri argues, in expressing the post-territorial alternative of 'political cosmopolitanism': the alternative is 'a conception of solidarity without community'; one which does not assume any shared vision or views and, in fact, seeks to deconstruct universal perspectives as merely the project of hegemony (2007b: 728).

It is not clear what the theorists of post-territorial political community – whether in its liberal cosmopolitan or post-liberal post-cosmopolitan forms – have to offer in terms of any convincing thesis that new forms of political community are in the process of emerging. Political community necessarily takes a territorial form at the level of the organisation for political representation on the basis of the nation-state (in a world without a world government) but has a post- or non-territorial content at the level of ideological and political affiliation, which has meant that support and solidarity could be offered for numerous struggles taking place on an international level (given formal frameworks in the nineteenth and twentieth century internationals of anarchists, workers, women and nationalists) (see, for example, Colas 2002).

For the content of territorial political community to be meaningful does not mean that democratic politics can be confined to territorial boundaries: the contestation of ideologies, ideas and practices has never been a purely national endeavour. However, without a formal focal point of accountability – of government – there can be no political community; no framework binding and subordinating individuals as political subjects. The critique of territorial political community and assertion of the imminent birth of post-territorial political community, in fact, seeks to evade the problem of the implosion of political community in terms of collective engagement in social change. The attenuation of democratic politics and with it the implosion of bonds of political community is thereby over-politicised by both 1990s liberals and 2000s radicals.

With the attenuation of popular engagement in political struggles, any conception of a clear or fixed demos disappears, political power seems to be much more intangible and political conflicts much more free-floating and ephemeral. It is the lack of clear and meaningful political contestation that reduces any distinction between the political and the everyday, dissolving the political into the social. As the political sphere dissolves so does any conception of a fixed demos giving rise to the discussion of the meaning of post-territorial politics. Hardt and Negri highlight this when they counter-pose post-territorial, networked, struggles of the multitude to territorial struggles, revealing that: 'Many of these [territorial] movements, especially when they are defeated, begin to transform and take on [post-territorial] network characteristics' (2006: 83).

To take a concrete example, it was the defeat of the Zapatistas that freed them to take up life as a virtual internet struggle. It was political defeat and marginalisation that meant they could take up an even more radical challenge than confronting the Mexican government, that of the postmodern subject, attempting to 'change the world without taking power' (2006: 85). The failure of modernist political projects based on the collective subject is clear; as Hardt and Negri observe: 'The people is missing' (2006: 191). But unlike Paolo Virno's theorising of the multitude (2004) as reflecting merely the crisis of the state form in terms of the plurality and incommensurabilty of political experiences – i.e. the lack of political community – Hardt and Negri seek to see the multitude as the constitutive agent of the postmodern and post-territorial political world.

Many authors have understood the rejection of territorial politics as the rejection of the ontological privileging of state power, articulated in particularly radical terms by Hardt and Negri as 'a flight, an exodus from sovereignty' (2006: 341). Fewer have understood that this implies the rejection of political engagement itself. Politics without the goal of power would be purely performative or an expression of individual opinions, in which case, democratic engagement could have no meaning. Politics has been considered important because community was constituted not through the private sphere but through the public sphere in which shared interests and perspectives were generated through engagement and debate with the goal of building and creating collective expressions of interests. Without the goal of power, i.e. the capacity to shape decision-making, political engagement would be a personal private expression rather than a public democratic one. There would be no need to attempt to convince another person in an argument or to persuade someone why one policy was better than another. In fact, in rejecting territorial politics it is not power or the state which is problematised – power will still exist and states are still seen as important actors even in post-territorial frameworks.

The essential target of these critical theorists of post-territorial community is democratic political engagement with fellow citizens, i.e. the necessity to legitimise one's views and aspirations through the struggle for representation. As Falk describes:

> ...transnational solidarities, whether between women, lawyers, environmentalists, human rights activists, or other varieties of 'citizen pilgrim' associated with globalisation from below ... [have] already transferred their loyalties to the invisible political community of their hopes and dreams, one

which could exist in future time but is nowhere currently embodied in the life-world of the planet.

(1995: 212)

The interconnectedness which is celebrated is, in fact, the flip-side of a lack of connection domestically: 'Air travel and the Internet create new horizontal communities of people, who perhaps have more in common, than with those who live close by' (Kaldor 2003: 111–12). What these 'citizen pilgrims' have in common is their isolation from and rejection of their own political communities. The transfer of loyalties to an 'invisible political community' is merely a radical re-representation of their rejection of real and visible political communities – the electorate.

For both liberal and radical views of post-territorial political community, democratic political contestation is unnecessary. Political views are considered self-legitimating without the need to engage in politics – i.e. bypassing society or the masses – and directly expressing the claims to power in radical protests at world summits or in the power of NGO lobbying. This evasion of society, this retreat from political community, is expressed in radical terms as the fundamental 'right to difference' (Hardt and Negri 2006: 340) or 'freedom from a singular Universal Ethic' (Keane 2003: 196). Radical approaches became 'globalised' at the same time as their political horizons became more and more parochial and limited and they drew back from seeking to engage instrumentally or strategically with the external world. For Alberto Melucci, these new social movements existed outside of the traditional civil society-state nexus, submerged in everyday life. Without reference to a political community, Melucci argues traditional measurements of efficacy or success miss the point: 'This is because conflict takes place principally on symbolic ground ... The mere existence of a symbolic challenge is in itself a method of unmasking the dominant codes, a different way of perceiving and naming the world' (1988: 248). This, in Melucci's words is the 'democracy of everyday life', where legitimacy and recognition stem from 'mere existence' rather than the power of argument or representation (1988: 259). Rather than the struggle for representation, the post-territorial struggle of 'globalisation from below' is framed as one of autonomy and held to be self-constituting.

The radical self-constitution of the political subject avoids the mediating link of the democratic political process. Political legitimacy is no longer derived from the political process of building support in society but rather from recognition and acceptance of social isolation. This is a logical consequence of the New Left's rejection of any legitimate collective political subject. As Laclau and Mouffe assert in their summation of the essence of 'radical democracy':

Pluralism is *radical* only to the extent that each term of this plurality of identities finds within itself the principle of its own validity ... And this radical pluralism is *democratic* to the extent that the autoconstitutivity of each one of its terms is the result of displacements of the egalitarian imaginary. Hence, the project for a radical and plural democracy, *in a primary sense*, is nothing other than the struggle for a maximum autonomization of spheres on the basis of the generalization of the equivalential-egalitarian logic.

(2001: 167)

The claim is not for equality but for autonomy; for recognition on the basis of self-constituted difference rather than collective or shared support. The focus upon the marginal and the subaltern appears to provide a radical critique of power but, without a transformative alternative, can easily become a critique of modern mass society. Here, the critique of 'power' or 'the state' becomes, in fact, a critique of democratic political engagement. Political community is only constituted on the basis of the potential to agree on the basis of shared, collective, interests. The refusal to subordinate difference to unity is merely another expression for the rejection of democratic political engagement. Political community cannot be constituted on the basis of post-territorial politics in which there is no central authority and no subordination to any agreed programme. For Hardt and Negri: 'The multitude is an irreducible multiplicity; the singular social differences that constitute the multitude must always be expressed and can never be flattened into sameness, unity, identity, or indifference' (2006: 105).

Beyond the territorial boundaries of the nation-state, it is precisely the missing essence of political community (the formal political sphere of sovereignty and citizenship) that becomes constitutive of post-territorial political community. Without the need to worry about the constitutive relationship between government (sovereign) and citizen, political community becomes entirely abstract. There is no longer any need to formulate or win adherence to a political programme and to attempt to challenge or overcome individual sectional or parochial interests. Engagement between individuals no longer has to take a democratic political form: all that is left is networked communication. For Hardt and Negri: 'The common does not refer to traditional notions of either the community or the public; it is based on the communication among singularities' (2006: 204). While communication is important there is little point in communication without purpose; what the multitude lacks is precisely this subjective purpose that could bind them and constitute a democratic political community.

In the absence of popular engagement in politics it could be argued that Jean Baudrillard's warning, *In the Shadow of the Silent Majorities* (1983), of the simulacrum of the contestation over political power, is being fully realised:

[Out of the disengagement of the masses] some would like to make a new source of revolutionary energy ... They would like to give it meaning and to reinstate it in its very banality, as historical negativity ... Final somersault of the intellectuals to exalt insignificance, to promote non-sense into the order of sense. Banality, inertia, apoliticism used to be fascist; they are now in the process of becoming revolutionary – without changing meaning...

(1983: 40)

The demise of political community reflecting the attenuation of political contestation has been reinterpreted by theorists of post-territorial community in ways which over-politicise the attenuation of political contestation and collective engagement by constructing abstract forms of democratic community, alleged to articulate and to legitimise particular theorists' own normative beliefs (whether liberal or poststructuralist). This is done through, first, dismissing the idea of democratic politics as subordinated to the goal of representation, necessitating the engagement of formal equal rights-bearing citizens and thus blurring the meaning of democracy. Then, second, dismissing the idea of political community as one constructed on the basis of engagement in a common political project, thus collapsing the political into the social, as the conception of community becomes separated from any conception of a demos.

Cosmopolitan theorists remove the distinction between the citizen and the non-citizen to constitute a political engagement based on the inequalities of advocacy. However, many poststructuralists argue that even engagement at the level of advocacy is oppressive and that awareness of the Other is all that political engagement can constitute without creating new frameworks of domination. Duffield, for example, suggests that the only alternative to the hierarchies of liberal advocacy is to assert that we are all victims of governmentalism: 'we are all governed and therefore in solidarity' (2007: 232). Apparently we should focus on what we share with postcolonial societies, not offering the hierarchical 'solidarity' of development or political autonomy but instead the solidarity of learning from the poor and being marginalised as equals; once humbled: 'through a practical politics based on the solidarity of the governed we can aspire to opening ourselves to the spontaneity of unpredictable encounters' (2007: 234).

Jabri argues that we need a new cosmopolitanism, but one that reflectively recognises that 'any discourses that view their worth in universal terms, are but expressions of "forces of domination" based upon explicit principles of exclusion' (2007a: 177). Instead, the '*politics* of peace' [emphasis in original] emphasises solidarity that: 'makes no claim to universality, nor is it teleological in outlook ... Rather, the politics of peace expresses local and often rather invisible acts, expressions of solidarity that are neither hierarchically defined nor suggestive of any claim to universality' (2007a: 177).

For Douzinas, political opposition has to take the form of a 'cosmopolitanism to come' of individualised protest:

> Dissatisfaction [–] with nation, state, the international [–] comes from a bond between singularities. What binds me to an Iraqi or a Palestinian is not membership of humanity, citizenship of the world or of a community but a protest against citizenship, against nationality and thick community. This bond cannot be contained in traditional concepts of community and cosmos or of polis and state. What binds my world to that of others is our absolute singularity and total responsibility beyond citizen and human, beyond

national and international. The cosmos to come is the world of each unique one, of whoever or anyone; the polis, the infinite number of encounters of singularities.

(2007: 295)

Poststructuralist constructions of post-territorial political community often celebrate the atomisation and dislocation of the individual with the implosion of political community. But what connects atomised individuals is merely the lack of political community. The cosmopolitanism 'to come' looks rather like the world we are already living in. Post-territorial political community is the world that exists but radically reinterpreted; this is why global civil society is both a descriptive and normative concept and why multitude 'has a strange double temporality: always-already and not-yet' (Hardt and Negri 2006: 222). As Baudrillard presciently noted, once the political subject – the people – is disengaged from politics, the vacuum left can be reinterpreted by radical academics to suit their predilections without reality changing.

Conclusion

The attenuation of politics and hollowing out of the meaningful nature of representation constitutes the collapse of any meaningful democratic political community. In the 1990s, the inability of political elites to create projects of political meaning, which were able to cohere their societies or offer a programme of shared values, led to attempts to evade the problems of legitimising political programmes on the basis of electoral representation alone. The advocates of cosmopolitan political community in the 1990s were the first to distance themselves from state-based politics, finding a freedom in the free-floating rights of global advocacy. It was under this banner of global liberalism and ethical policy-making that political elites sought their own 'exodus from sovereignty' – justified on the basis of a critique of the liberal rights subject – and, in the process, further attenuated the relationship between government and citizen. This was a discourse that sought to respond to the collapse of democratic political community rather than one that reflected the birth of a newer or more expansive one at a global level.

In the 2000s, the hollow nature of liberal cosmopolitan claims appeared to be clearly exposed in the Global War on Terror. The radical discourse of post-structuralist post-territorial political community sought to critique this international order as a product of global liberalism; however, the nature of the critique was in content and form little different from that of 1990s cosmopolitanism. There is little difference between the frameworks of these poststructuralist critics and the liberal cosmopolitans because the groundwork of the critique was already laid by the crisis within liberal thinking. It was the work of the self-proclaimed 'liberal' cosmopolitan theorists that fundamentally challenged the foundational liberal ontology, which established the modern liberal order through deriving political legitimacy from the rights of autonomous individual subjects. The liberal basis of political order and of political community on the basis of shared rights and duties had already corroded from within. The radical critique of the cosmopolitan discourse of global rights offers a critique of sovereign power, representational politics and its grounding liberal ontology, but one that merely echoes, to the point of parody, that of its ostensible subject of critique.

10 Mobilising (global) democracy

A political reading of mobility between universal rights and the mob[1]

Claudia Aradau and Jef Huysmans

At a time when the borders of nation-states appear to have become increasingly porous and democracy is often entangled with imperial and neoliberal projects, there has been a resurgence of interest in the concept. From cosmopolitan democracy that aims at trans-nationalising liberal decision-making to communicative democracy that rethinks the public sphere under global conditions, and from democracy as a mode of governance to radical democracy, the adequacy of the concept of democracy for the international is increasingly under scrutiny.

In particular two developments are at the heart of the resurgence of democracy debates in International Relations. First, the continuing intensification of the contradiction between structures of power, which operate on a global or international scale, and structures of democratic representation, accountability and legitimacy, which operate mainly within and through state institutions (Walker 1993: 143). This contradiction grounds the question of 'what democracy can possibly be given to the structures of world politics' (Walker 1993: 142)? The second development is that democracy functions as a global concept attached to an increasingly wide variety of practices. With the demise of the Cold War, Western notions of democracy lost their 'others', variously named as communism, dictatorship, tyranny or totalitarianism (Rancière 1999). In both democratic theory and politics, this raised the question of what are democracy's functional, territorial and/or temporal limits that facilitate judgements of what counts and does not count as democratic practice. These two problematiques are closely interrelated. The creation of democratic practices in the globalised structures of power implies defining the nature of those political practices as democratic, thus leading to the question of 'what are the nature and limits of democracy?' For the purposes of this chapter, democracy is not considered as a particular political regime or as a 'model' of representation or participation, but a practice that disturbs the status quo, the given political order. Starting from this understanding of democracy, in this chapter we argue that mobility has been historically a democratic practice and that it can also give democracy to global structures of power. Its main question is: *how do practices of mobility constitute a democratic moment?*

To tackle this question, we proceed in three stages. First, we contend that a political reading of mobility is needed to understand its function as a democratic practice working upon power structures. Much of the globalised structuration of power bears a relation to mobility that transgresses national boundaries and the spatial logic through which these are constituted. Nonetheless, the potential of mobility remains underexplored in much of the literature on global democracy. Second, we propose to start from a particular historical development of mobility and theorise it as political and democratic practice. Rather than starting from the opposition of territorialisation/deterritorialisation, bordered/fluid, immobile/ nomadic that informs much of the research on global democracy and mobility today, we draw on Georg Simmel's sociology of money to analyse mobility as a condition of the possibility and practice of democracy. We reconceptualise mobility as a form of sociality with the stranger that leads to the creation of spheres of rights and mass mobilisation. We argue specifically that universal rights and the 'mob' represent two different traditions of democracy. While the former is fairly well developed in studies of post-national citizenship and human rights, the connection between mobility, mass politics and democracy is much less present in studies of global and transnational democracy. Finally, we show that the democratic quality of practices of mobility functions through the inscription of equality, both through the articulation of equal rights and through the egalitarian force of the 'mob' or mass politics. This inscription of equality brought about by mobility through rights and the 'mob' can make mobility do democratic work directly in the global realm.

Global democracy and mobility

The main traditions of thought where we would expect to find a theorisation of the connection between transnational mobility and democracy beyond the nation-state largely ignore the intimate connection between mobility and democracy. Mobility remains a relatively marginal issue in the literature on global democracy. This literature focuses on questions of *institutional* accountability and transparency in a globalising world as well as the question of how to constitute democratic institutions and transnational public spheres on a global scale (for example Archibugi *et al.* 1998; Dryzek 1999; Habermas 2001; Held 1997; Holden 2000). The alternative literature on global mobility and transnational flows seems to largely ignore the political and democratic nature of mobilities. It focuses on the constitution of socio-economic networks and societal flows across states, thereby separating a political democratic reading of mobility from its socio-economic significance (see for example Canzler *et al.* 2008).[2]

The absence of linkage between these two approaches is not simply the result of disciplinary divides (between sociology and political science, between a political and a more socio-economic theorising of the international, etc.). Rather, one of the main reasons is that politics is primarily interpreted as a question of the formation and exercise of democratic authority formulated in terms of representative institutions, political accountability and a public sphere where opinions can circulate and be negotiated. Although the need to renegotiate democratic authority can follow changes in transnational socio-economic mobility, mobility itself is not seen as a political practice, let alone a democratic one. For example, migrants crossing the Mediterranean – the figure *par excellence* of the globalised world – are not understood as making a political claim but are represented as destitute and frustrated people driven by economic and/or humanitarian needs in an increasingly globalised 'society'.

> Waves of Would-Be Immigrants Target EU Shores
> Spiegel Online 24 June 2008
>
> ...
>
> The immigrants arrive in Libya from central Africa and from there are ferried to European shores, often by organized crime groups, in rickety, overcrowded boats. Most are trying to escape dire poverty at home. Many give up everything for the journey ... in the hopes that, once they arrive in Europe, they will be able to support their families from afar.
>
> (*Der Spiegel* 2008)

Their mobility seems to remain largely apolitical in the sense that they do not intentionally seek to renegotiate the structures of power and authority through their mobility. Migrants are represented as simply driven by individual desires and economic needs. In addition, they are often rendered as a disorderly mass of people made up of individuals frustrated with living conditions and seeking to cross territory and water. As this quote indicates, the organisational aspect of their mobility is the responsibility of criminal groups, which reinforces the difficulty to read transnational mobility as political. Criminalisation has historically been a key instrument of keeping social problems and developments out of the political realm.

In this reading, mobility is part of global societal and economic developments that cannot be contained by territorial boundaries. They set the socio-economic conditions against which questions of governance and authority beyond the nation-state emerge. In line with functionalist (Mitrany 1948; 1966), regional integration (Deutsch 1957; Haas 1968; Pentland 1973) and transnational politics (Kaiser 1969) approaches, cross-border mobility requires modes of governing that move beyond the nation-state. Migration, for example, interlocks different societies – the society of origin, the societies through which one travels and the society of destination. One of the political responses to this cross-national societal interlocking is to increase cooperation between states and/or to set up either regional or global political authorities. For example, the European integration project is often legitimised in these terms. Further integration in the Area of Freedom, Security and Justice is justified through the increased need for a common migration policy so as to deal more effectively with immigration.

In these accounts, democracy emerges as a problem of the legitimacy of these regional and global governing authorities. The central issues concern the transnational or global constitution of a public sphere, the institutionalisation of representation and accountability mechanisms, and public participation. The questions and the models that drive these debates do not really differ in whether they are applied to state, regional or global authority structures. Global and regional democracy is treated in terms of the questions of whether or not and how it is possible to scale up national institutional mechanisms to transnational, regional and global institutions (Habermas 2001). The two main approaches here are cosmopolitan democracy and communicative democracy.

Cosmopolitan democracy builds upon the structures of global governance with the added requirements of public participation and public accountability. These democratic injunctions can be achieved either by means of reforming international institutions and the processes of global governance to integrate democratic criteria with the technocratic ones of efficiency (Held 1997; Teune 2002) or by the mobilisation of global civil society as a democratic actor (Scholte 2002). In these approaches, cosmopolitan democracy is seen as achievable either in a 'top-down' or 'bottom-up' fashion. David Held's work typifies a top-down reform of the international system, ranging from a more inclusive UN Security Council to ultimately cosmopolitan law, a global legal system and a global parliament. Internationally, democratic practices reiterate the role of civil society in the domestic polity and propose to create new institutions that would reinforce the rights of the global citizen.

Unlike cosmopolitan democracy, communicative democracy considers the discursive sources of governance transnationally and not just the institutional ones (Dryzek 1999). It tries to solve the question of the territorially and nationally bounded nature of democracy by downplaying it – if communication or deliberation are the defining features of democracy, then democratic outcomes can be achieved independently of territorial and national borders. For Habermas (2001), democracy emerges by means of discursive procedures through which individuals attempt to build grounds for the legitimacy of their claims. Nonetheless, communicative democracy also ultimately attempts to 'scale up' processes of discursive legitimation and negotiation that take place within the nation-state and does not solve the problem of borders and boundaries delimiting the public sphere that remain necessary for the possibility of global communicative processes.

In both approaches, mobility, if considered at all, operates in the background as socio-economic flows that create a need for scaling up democratic structures of accountability or discursive legitimation. Therefore, by locking mobility into a socio-economic reading, these debates do not touch on how mobility itself can be a democratic practice. The cosmopolitan and communicative democracy approaches cannot interpret democracy as a modality of the practices of mobility themselves. Rather, they focus on how regional or global governance can move from a community of states and a politics of inter-state bargaining to a community of individuals and a politics of rights. Democracy is fundamentally a question of building an institutional political structure and a regional or global demos. These need to guarantee that mobility can be governed through democratic processes and that the demos does not become the 'mob' or a conflictual crowd, but is an ordered audience, public or electorate. From this perspective, the structures of political power act upon the immigrants' mobility as an issue of security, economics or humanitarianism. But their mobility itself is not read politically: the immigrants crossing the Mediterranean remain destitute, abused, needy individuals constituting a flow that needs to be administered, preferably through democratic institutions.

Similarly, the other body of literature that theorises mobility, the 'mobility turn' in sociology and geography, does not consider democracy in relation to mobility. The lack of engagement with democracy is, first, underpinned by a similar socio-economic reading of mobility. The literature on mobility is mainly concerned with the governance of mobility, the increase in flows and the acceleration of mobility rather than its political (or democratic) nature (for example Canzler *et al.* 2008; Hannam *et al.* 2006). Even when mobility is directly considered in relation to the constitution of mobile and immobile subjects, social exclusion and citizenship, mobility as a condition of possibility of democracy and democratic practice is not analysed (Urry 2000, 2007).

Thus, the literatures that we would expect to engage with the relationship between mobility and democracy mostly ignore how mobility has historically created a condition of possibility for democracy by both enlarging the possibility for universalising freedoms and making practices of mass movement politically forceful. The remainder of the chapter seeks to recover this specific political reading of mobility for the purpose of demonstrating that practices of mobility are not just flows or networks upon which democratic institutions act but that they are an immanent part of democratic politics; in other words, mobility can function as a political democratic practice which disrupts the status quo.

Mobility, money and strangers

Rather than a new development brought about by globalisation and to which different theories of democracy attempt to find a palliative, a political reading of mobility reveals a more intimate connection between practices of mobility and democracy. We argue that the understanding of democracy as practice, as a particular process, is historically connected with a particular development in modernity.[3] Drawing on Simmel's sociology of money, we show how mobility became entwined with democracy through a double inscription of equality via rights and mass mobilisation.[4]

Simmel connects the role of mobility in modern societies with the circulation of money in the mature money economies and processes of exchange. Circulation, Simmel has argued, was an 'original form and function of social life' (1978: 100). It is the most developed form of social interaction and social interactions generally need to be thought in terms of the model of the exchange. Through exchange, society became an 'inner bond between men [sic]' rather than a 'simple collection of individuals' (Simmel 1978: 265). Money made possible a particular form of social interaction and the transformation of society by rendering everything quantifiable according to a single measure and allows for comparisons among previously incommensurable objects. Money 'commensurates incommensurabilities' and creates a particular form of egalitarianism and equivalence (Maurer 2006: 16). As Simmel (1978: 427) puts it, 'The essence of all money … is its unconditional interchangeability, the internal uniformity that makes each piece exchangeable for another…' This interchangeable and abstract commensurability creates new relationships between elements that would otherwise have no connection. Money, therefore, 'has provided us with the sole possibility for uniting people while excluding everything personal and specific' (Simmel 1978: 345).

Simmel's reading of money takes up a historical materialist analysis according to which capitalist money and exchange entail particular social effects: money creates a form of *sociality* that is based on equivalence, reciprocity and the rejection of traditional family and communitarian values.[5] From this perspective, it is important to understand mobility not simply as a form of disconnectedness, fluidity or nomadism, but as a particular form of sociality and interaction brought about by money and exchange.[6] Money therefore appears as a social force that unmakes traditional social relations and replaces them with new forms of social interactions. As a form of sociality, mobility becomes a threat to entrenched hierarchical social relations and close-knit communities. This is particularly evident in the way societies experience the stranger who, according to Simmel, is the paradigmatic form of interaction brought about by mobility. The stranger is defined by a paradoxical relation to community. It is a form of mobility that fixes people to a specific community – strangers live in a community – but that simultaneously frees them from any specific ties to fixed communities – they do not belong to the community in an organic way. Money makes it possible to be in close-knit contact with other people without being organically or territorially bound to them. It enables being within a community but not of community.

By socialising people as strangers, money places them in different types of relationships where hierarchies, differences between nobility and the lower orders become dangerously unstable. Money, notes Simmel, 'becomes the centre of interest and the proper domain of individuals and classes who, because of their social position, are excluded from many kinds of personal and specific goals' (1978: 221). While the circulation of money unravels traditional community relations, money also threatens to unravel social hierarchies by offering those who had nothing, who were excluded from the possibility of achieving full membership in a community, access to the community and to social status. The 'power of money', concludes Simmel (1978: 223), 'contributes positively to the attainment of positions, influence and enjoyments wherever people are excluded from achieving, by certain direct means, social rank and fulfilment as officials or in professions from which they are barred'. Thus, money becomes in one sense a social equaliser, the means for those who are excluded from social status to attain some form of membership in society. By generalising a means of equivalence, the circulation of money inscribes egalitarian ideals and relations to the stranger at the heart of society. In what follows, we show how these social effects can become political through claims to abstract rights and mass or 'mob' mobilisation.

Political mobility 1: universal rights

Money introduces relations between strangers as relations mediated by abstract principles: '...with the stranger one has only certain more general qualities in common, whereas the relation to more organically connected persons is based on the commonness of specific differences from merely general features' (Simmel 1950: 402–8). The peculiar generality and abstractness of relations to the stranger characterises them not through their individuality but rather through something that they have in common with other strangers. The relation between strangers is one of universals:

> [Strangeness] is rather caused by the fact that similarity, harmony, and near-ness are accompanied by the feeling that they are not really the unique prop-erty of this particular   relationship: they are something more general, something which potentially prevails between the partners and an indetermi-nate number of others, and therefore gives the relation, which alone was realized, no inner and exclusive necessity.
>
> (Simmel 1950: 407)

The connection between money and mobility is central for creating the con-ditions of possibility of a less organic and more abstract form of sociality that is at the same time a condition of possibility for extending freedom and equality beyond the confines of close-knit community relations. Yet, this condition remains enacted through economic and social practices.[7] Although Simmel shows us how mobility as a particular form of sociality opens serious political questions about forms of allegiance, freedom and equality, they remain locked within the socio-economic as a possibility. Mobility remains a social practice that is not necessarily political, but has a capacity to be so.

How does one take these practices of mobility into a democratic political terrain? Through the generalisation of equivalence and exchange, mobility ensured the possibility for excluded social groups to enter the political process and accede to equality. Money created the conditions of possibility for sociality mediated through abstraction and equality of exchange rather than, say, hier-archy. The introduction of an abstract measure in the mediation of things – money and exchange value in the mature money economies – has as its correlate the introduction of an abstract measure – universal rights – in the mediation of conflict among social groups. The equivalence that money introduces between different objects is correlated with the equivalence between subjects. Thus, the central vehicle for the move of mobility from a form of sociality into a demo-cratic practice is universal rights. As Simmel discusses in his analysis of the right of assistance to the poor, rights shifted assistance from the subjective arbi-trariness of charity to an objective claim that the poor can make upon others. Rights did the double work of transforming the poor from an object into a subject who could act upon other subjects, and society more generally, and of connecting their claims to an abstract notion of humanity (Simmel 1971a).

From this perspective, migrants traversing territories and seas to arrive in Europe can at least in principle claim minimal human rights. In doing so, they change a set of social and economic connections into claims that connect them to a political terrain, as long as the political authorities recognise the status of humanity in the form of a legal or quasi-legal system of rights. In contemporary politics, human rights are a central vehicle through which transversal mobilities work themselves into the political field, as noted in the idea of post-national citizenship (Sassen 2006; Soysal 1994). Money-strangers-rights are a continuum made possible by the introduction of an abstract measure within modern societies.

The democratic political terrain that mobility enters by 'mobilising' a rights status is defined through the relation between legally codified rights and public institutions. Mobility can function as a political democratic practice when it activates a legal status that can be mobilised within an institutional structure. In relation to transnational mobilities, this can imply either that mobile people deploy universal rights within democratic states or that mobile people claim rights against national and transnational structures of power.

Therefore, mobile people disrupt structures of power by claiming rights upon public and private authorities. Judicial systems are the institutional sites where these claims take place. In the end, transforming mobility from social into political (democratic) practice through universal rights appears to lead us back to the question posed by the global democracy literature on the nature of political institutions within which these rights can be legitimately claimed. So, are we back where we started? Is the problem ultimately that of scaling up democratic institutions that have been developed within the nation-state? Claiming rights through mobility has actually worked slightly differently.

On the one hand, universal rights are carried by mobile people into national institutional arenas, as argued by the post-national citizenship literature. While the institutional structure is territorially bound to the nation-state, the people making rights claims within them do not belong to the state in the same sense as national citizens. They are strangers drawing on more abstract universal rights. As Soysal (1994: 149) has remarked about the proliferation of transnational arrangements and human rights instruments, 'by setting norms, framing discourses, and engineering legal categories and legitimate models, they enjoin obligations on nation-states to take actions'.

On the other hand, contemporary politics also witnesses the rise of supranational and transnational legal and quasi-legal institutions. Here, the political terrain is defined in terms of a constitutive tension between legal and political authority. However, legal authorities work on a wider scale than political authorities, which remain very much enclosed within the nation-state. This process of legalising transnational and international politics thus consists in a differential scaling up of democracy. Legal and quasi-legal institutions work beyond the nation-state seeking to constrain the national authorities whose democratic legitimacy is constituted within the national states. The European Union and its European Court of Justice are particularly interesting cases here, given the EU's multi-level political nature (Bigo 2005; Guild 2003; 2004).[8]

Nonetheless, the transformation of mobility into a political democratic practice through the mediation of the rights of strangers has important limitations. First, it works through an individualising process turning subjects into rights holders who then also need access to the judicial (and administrative) systems where they can claim their rights. Second, law entails a double process of particularisation (Rancière 2007). In its explicit form, particularising the universal can deny rights to categories of the population, based on racial, gender or class grounds. In its implicit form, it can restrict democracy and citizenship to particular institutions, agents, problems and procedures. The notion of rights therefore reproduces within democratic politics a distinction between masses and citizens (Balibar 1997: 106ff.). The masses refer here to the group of the people whose access to the rights status is severely limited, either by being denied rights or by their limited capacity to effectively claim rights. This distinction not only operates within a state but also in the state system.

The migrants seeking to traverse the Mediterranean fall within the category of the masses rather than of post-national citizens. Their capacity to access institutions in which they can enact their already very limited rights claims is severely curtailed by means of an elaborate detention regime among others. Their access to political institutions is also restricted in terms of agents and procedures. For instance, their access to rights is mediated through the legal field and legal agents. This is particularly problematic as law neutralises the stakes in a conflict by converting a struggle between parties into a dialogue between mediators (Bourdieu 1987: 831). Law publicly represents social conflicts while distancing itself from them and offering an 'impartial' and reasoned solution to social problems. Moreover, the recourse to law can be limited by exceptional decisions in situations of emergency or crisis. Given these limitations of how rights are inscribed politically through the mediation of law, it is important to see universal rights as only one aspect of the political reading of mobility. The other aspect is mass politics, political action by the mob, which challenges both the limitations of law and its possible suspension by exceptional decisions (Huysmans 2004; Scheuerman 1994).

Therefore, it is important to retain the category of the mob as immanent to rather than excluded from democratic practice. In democracy, the people have traditionally been a split category. The reason for recovering the 'mob' as a category of democracy rather than as its outside, is not simply that enacting as well as challenging the split between the mob and the people has been constitutive of democracy (Balibar 1997). Looking more closely into this connection opens up the terrain of democratic politics that mobilities enact in relation to power structures as different from, but not unrelated to the terrain of rights.

Political mobility 2: mobilisation and the political mob

Let us first return to Simmel. Through its power of equalisation, equivalence and reciprocity, money not only threatens hierarchical social relations but creates possibilities of new social relations beyond the limited confines of close-knit associations – especially the guilds and feudal power relations. As Simmel has argued, in modernity groups are no longer formed based on similarity or proximity but through free choice. By making possible new forms of sociality between strangers, money also makes possible the modern constitution of the masses or the 'mob'. The strangers become numbers on the move dislocating and dislocated from the feudal and guild structures. For Simmel, the phenomenon of mass culture and the emergence of large groups coincide with the development of mature money economies, the metropolis and waged labour. The solidarity of wage labour and the solidarity of the mercantile class lead to large group affiliations that are radically different from the medieval concentric groups (Simmel 1955).

In this context, the double etymology of mobility is hardly surprising. Mobility and its truncation, 'the mob', is a seventeenth-century coinage by the Earl of Shaftesbury to refer to the *mobile vulgus*, the citizens-discontents marshalled by the Whigs for political processions and rallies (Seidel 1972). The term was introduced into English language to replace the more passive term 'rabble' and included, according to the novelist Henry Fielding, not just the rioters, but everyone in London's lower classes who was present in the streets (Shoemaker 2004: xi). The mob refers to politically motivated groups who are represented as numerous, mobile and an urban phenomenon. Metropolis, mobility and money are closely entwined, as Simmel has observed: 'The modern city, however, is supplied almost exclusively by production for the market, that is, for entirely unknown purchasers who never appear in the actual field of vision of the producers themselves' (Simmel 1950 [1903]: 411). If rights are the political correlate of abstraction that money brings about, the 'mob' – i.e. mobile masses – can be seen as the political correlate of mass culture. Although Simmel interpreted groups dominantly sociologically rather than politically and did not develop the relationship between masses, movement and democracy, the democratic quality of the masses as 'the mob' is of central importance for recapturing a political reading of mobility.

Although the *mobile vulgus* or the fickle multitude had long been the object of contempt, starting from the seventeenth century the mob is seen to acquire 'a tremendously real and symbolic force in society' (Seidel 1972: 430). Increasingly, the mob is seen as a problem for democracy. The mob appeared as a disorderly force, whose actions were depoliticised either as economically determined – e.g. by hunger – or as socially irrational. While the demos was perceived as the orderly force that democracies needed to foster and to sustain, the mob was its antinomy, the excess and unrest that were threatening for democratic forces.

The 'mob' or the mass has been theorised both as a problem for and as a constitutive force of democracy. Democratic theory has worked this terrain by decomposing and recomposing the notion of people in various ways. Many theories of democracy contain a separation of the mob as *vulgus* from citizens.[9] This 'sanitising' or 'rationalising' of the category of the political people through the notion of citizens left the mob outside of democracy as the undisciplined part of the people (Balibar 1997).

Nonetheless, more recently, the democratic political potential of the 'mob' has been revitalised through an engagement with Spinoza's work. As Etienne Balibar has argued, by taking mass movement seriously as an object of investigation in its own right – that is, without immediately reducing it to the question of the constitution of the state – Spinoza articulated a fundamental paradox in democracy (Balibar 1997: 57–99). Masses can be both destructive and creative of democratic practice. Thus, Spinoza oscillated between a series of terms to name the 'masses', most of which had pejorative meanings. The term that acquires a positive connotation represents numbers most directly – the *multitude*.

In terms of their numbers, the *multitude* has the power to impose limits on the rulers. For Spinoza, there is a political connection that emerges not from an abstract representation of the masses but from their historical reality that consists in the capacity of the masses to turn numbers into a movement. This has different implications for democracy than universal rights. Democracy is grounded in the realisation that the masses needed to be included into the political body through the representation of a double unity: a unity of the masses – as a people – and a unity between the masses and the rulers grounded in the latter representing the unity of all into a single figure of political rule. But how can this be done without turning the existence of the masses and their capacity for political action into an empty category – something that disappears from view as an historical act and becomes an abstract idea of a people represented by the rulers? Spinoza makes clear that the masses as a real political force cannot be historically eliminated from democratic theory through representational politics; they remain a mobile numerical force that can physically move against political order (Balibar 1997: 73–80).

The legal constitution of this unity in contract theory tries to reduce the masses to an individualistic entity and to the problem of rights. Spinoza retains the historical reality of the masses in developing a numerical constitutional construction (Balibar 1997: 82). While for Hobbes the *multitude* is a fragmented and individualistic entity that needs to be overcome to found a political unity, for Spinoza the masses are a historical physical force that *is* political because of its numbers. That means that for Spinoza the relation between ruler and masses is not mediated through distributing rights and obligations but by the management and mobilisation of numbers. The existing *multitude* is decomposed and then rationally recomposed in accordance with certain conditions (e.g. cultural conditions or economic conditions). The recompositions work on the one hand as a form of governing populations through statistical techniques (mapping categories of population and administering them in light of various policy objectives). On the other, masses of individuals are united into various bodies identified by a common idea (e.g. the hungry, the disenfranchised, the proletariat) and capable of moving 'onto the street' to challenge rulers, conditions of life and political order (Balibar 1997).

Important for us here is that the democratic political terrain is opened up differently from the one in which mobility is constituted as a political practice through rights. This terrain is that of the representation of unity of rulers and masses as well as of a balancing of the relation of force between them. This terrain fundamentally depends on the real historical capacity of the masses to mobilise numbers into a political force that can disrupt the ruling state of affairs. This political terrain is not defined by a distribution of rights but by a calculus of force depending on the capacity to physically move in numbers against others. In our understanding, this is what mobility as the mobilisation of the mob does. Mobility as a democratic practice of 'the mob' introduces a numerical calculus of force into a political terrain that tends to be dominated by the primacy of legal reasoning.

The migrants crossing the Mediterranean are then not represented as iterations of the abstract notion of a state of nature made concrete at the territorial border, which justifies the use of violence to protect the EU's already 'contracted' citizens and the differentiation between those who can be part of the contract and those who have to remain outside because they embody the violence or chaos associated with the state of nature. From the perspective of mobility developed here, they present collective acts of mobility that bring a range of claims and projects to bear upon the EU and its citizens. The collective dimension is at first sight purely numerical but it also opens a political terrain at the EU's territorial and citizenry boundaries where mobility as a form of sociality negotiates the globalising economic and social structures of power. On the one hand, the migrants' mobility appears to 'embody' the effects of globalisation. On the other hand, growing numbers of moving people also open a political terrain where the effects of global power structures need to be renegotiated.

This understanding of the political dimensions of mobility leads to a different reading of the metaphors of flood, which are so often used in anti-immigration discourse, for example. In anti-immigration discourse, they are used to summon the spectre of the state of nature and the limit of the political contract, thereby replacing the complexity of claims and projects the immigrants' mobility brings to bear upon the EU with the abstractions of contract theory. But metaphors of flood also bring into play the sheer physical power of numbers of people on the move and the opening of a political terrain that is defined through a calculus of force rather than through institutionalised rights claims.[10] These representations open politics towards violence against immigrants but simultaneously invite the mobilisation of political action that depends not on mobilising a rights status but on a movement that has a capacity to dislodge the state of affairs.

Mobility as mass, mob, multitude or crowd is simultaneously excessive to individual rights and the collectivist people (Montag 2005: 663). This also implies that the limit of democracy is not totalitarianism because the masses can never be reduced to a collective unity, their movement is naturally one of decomposing and recomposing. The question of the limit of democratic mobilisation can also not be thought of in terms of exceptionalism, which would place the mob outside of democratic politics because it destroys the predictability and rationality of the law (Huysmans 2004). The mob is both opposed to law understood as decisionist and to its mediating role in social conflicts. The central question that arises here is what gives this political terrain that is defined through a calculus of force and the movement of numbers of people its democratic quality? As we will argue in the next section, similarly – but not identically – to universal rights the democratic content of mass politics follows from its mobilisation of equality.

Mobility as a democratic practice of equality

Our reading of mobility has started from the conditions of possibility of the circulation of money and has unpacked its political potential as universal rights and mass politics. We have argued that rights claims and the force of the mob are two forms of political practice brought about by the particular constitution of mobility as abstract sociality with the stranger in modernity. Through the emergence of abstraction and sociality with the stranger, the abstract principle of equality enters the political terrain. Yet, equality does not simply inform the particular understanding of mobility in modernity, but also defines its content as democratic practice.[11] The notion of equality makes rights different from the privileging of a particular category of European white male and democratic mobilisation distinct from nationalist anti-immigration mobilisation. Contra the reformulations of rights as those of a suffering and traumatised subject in need for protection, mobility as instantiated in the circulation of money allows us to capture rights as formulas for equality in claim-making rather than being limited to assistance reception.

In its double instantiation as universal rights and mass politics, mobility brings out the content-giving role of equality. As democratic practices, universal rights and mass politics are informed by the principle of equality. On the one hand, equality ensures that law does not become either exceptional, verging onto dictatorship or a form of mediation that reinforces the power of the state or the anthropological assumptions about the 'civilised' subject of human rights. On the other hand, equality is fundamental to ensuring that democracy as expressed in the 'mob' does not amount to chaos and violence but to a reworking of relations between the citizens and the *vulgus* in reference to claims for assistance, redistribution or access to the political field. How does equality give content to mobility as a democratic practice?

In the case of universal rights, equality can be thought of as a point of destination that is institutionally actualised in the foundational principle of formal equality before the law. Law processes social inequalities and discriminations in order to achieve a more just social order in conformity with the universal principles enshrined in it. Nonetheless, the processing of social wrongs in the judicial field is limited inasmuch as law offers to replace a system of institutional power that is found to be oppressive (dictatorship) with another system of institutional power (rule of law) that is less oppressive. Social inequalities are processed in light of this attainable equality. But as argued in the section on universal rights, drawing on law and rights significantly limits the way in which equality can be politically wielded.

The judicial field is both institutionally and sociologically immanent to the system of governance through which the existing stratifications within the people and between the people and the *vulgus* are sanctioned (Unger 1983). Entry in the judicial field takes place as an individual rights holder that often instantiates a double limitation: it reiterates the distinction between those with rights and those without and it individualises and thus tends to particularise collective demands.

While the enactment of equality through rights and law entails limitations, the politics of the mob is the supplement of collective power to the individualising aspect of human rights. Unlike the judicial realm, the politics of the mob takes equality as a maxim of *action* and not as a formal foundational principle or a goal to be achieved.[12] The politics of the mob claims equality through actual mobilisation from outside the law precisely for and by those who are excluded from the formal principle of legal equality because they do not have a status; those who are excluded by the particularisation of universal rights can enter the political field through collective movement. Thus, while some immigrants can have access to law if they can make a claim to asylum, have been victims of trafficking, have joined the country for family reunification or, for example, have been discriminated against, other categories of immigrants fall out of the purview of the law. The judicial system can only minimally address undocumented migrants – even in situations when they are subjected to exploitation and abuse, they are not directly a party in the social conflict, but it is rather the state and the abuser (be those smugglers or employers) whose conflicts are mediated by law. Undocumented migrants in detention camps can, for example, trigger the mechanism of law by starting hunger strikes. Nonetheless, the mechanism of the hunger strike is often responded to in charitable and biopolitical terms rather than from the standpoint of achievable equality. Hence, undocumented migrants have been involved in numerous protests, strikes, demonstrations and solidarity movements with trade unions.[13]

The recourse to rights and law and the recourse to the force of the mob are both democratic practices that supplement each other and supplement their mutual limitations. As Rancière has pointed out in relation to a tailors' strike in 1833, claims of equality are possible given the 'inscription of equality, as it appears in the founding texts, from the Declaration of the Rights of Man to the preamble of the Charter' (Rancière 1995: 48). As equality is enshrined in legal and political texts, it can be subsequently translated, displaced and maximised in everyday life (Rancière 1995). Equality cannot be specified a priori, but *happens* through the mobilisation of the mob against the limits of the judicial system. The politics of the 'mob' functions both as a 'check' upon the democratic practices of rights (by challenging who is a subject of rights and which agents and institutions are allowed to be rights mediators) and an 'invention' of democratic practice.

Conclusion

This chapter has argued for a political reading of mobility to rethink the conditions of possibility of democracy and democratic practice in the contemporary structures of world politics. Realising that the societal and economic dynamics are now seriously beyond the grip of democratic decision-making within a national state has often led to a demand for scaling up democratic institutions to a global scale. Regional scaling up can be seen to be a halfway step because it is meant to increase the leverage political authority can have upon globalising socio-economic practices while nevertheless reproducing the problem that it locks democracy into territorially circumscribed institutions.

Instead of reading mobility as a socio-economic practice, we have tried to rethink mobility as a political democratic practice. How do practices of mobility constitute democratic moments in relation to global structures of power? To answer this, we have started from the historical relationship between mobility and democracy. The circulation of money creates a particular form of sociality with and between strangers, who are present in or move through territorially and organically defined communities but do not specifically belong to them. Universal rights are often taken to be the main vehicle through which the stranger's mobility can be politically articulated in a democratic way. Although universal rights are vital for the political rendition of the abstract relations between strangers that emerge within the money economy, they also have a series of limitations. The individualising focus on rights holders, the often conservative sociological nature of the legal field, and the separation between those deemed worthy of legal status and those not limit the capacity of the mobile to enter a political terrain through rights claims. The democratic line running from mobility to the mobilisation of the mob makes visible an extra-legal tradition of collective democratic practice. This form of mobility contains the possibility of the continuous transformation and recomposition of the people as citizens through the figure of the mob. Therefore, the mob is not outside of the democratic political terrain but is immanent to it.

Starting from this historical reconstruction of mobility as a condition of possibility and form of political (democratic) practice, it is possible to conceive of mobility as acting upon global structures of power. We have illustrated the possibilities of such a democratic reworking of the people and of the distribution of rights that the globalising structures of power constitute through migration. It is at the interstice between the mob and universal rights that transnational mobility can constitute global democratic practices bearing upon the globalised structures of world politics. When mobility as a particular form of sociality leads to claims of equality expressed through rights and the mobilisation of numbers of people, it constitutes a political terrain where power comes within the remit of democracy. In this reading, mobility is not simply a socio-economic flow that sparks questions about how to reconfigure democracy in a globalising world. Rather, it is a democratic political practice that is constitutive of and immanent to the world political terrain.

Notes

1 This chapter is part of the European Commission Framework Programme 7 (FP7-SSH) project ENACT – Enacting European Citizenship (217504). http://enacting-citizenship.eu/.
2 John Urry's (2007) and Saskia Sassen's (2008) work contains discussions of political dimensions through the notion of citizenship. But the question of what makes mobility a democratic political practice remains largely absent.

3 We differ here from Rancière's (1999) reading of democracy that locates its origins in ancient Athens. The democratic practice privileged here is not simply *an-arche* (anarchic disruption of order) but a particular inscription of equality that the circulation of money has made possible in modernity.

4 Although Simmel's sociology of money has inspired a growing literature on mobility, cities and the transformation of money in late modernity, his work has not been linked to political questions of democracy, rights and mass mobilisation. For Simmel's influence on the mobility literature, see Urry (2007); on cities, Jensen (2006); on money, Allen and Pryke (1999).

5 Simmel (1971b: 24) defined sociality as 'the form (realized in innumerably different ways) in which individuals grow together into a unity and within which their interests are realized'.

6 Practices of mobility simultaneously summon mobility and immobility, fixity and fluidity and the dichotomy between fixity and nomadism is not adequate for understanding the ways in which practices of mobility constitute the social. For a pertinent criticism of mobility as nomadism, see Cresswell (2006).

7 In anthropology and sociology, scholars have noted that money does not necessarily abolish close-knit community relations. Mobility has the potential to change social practices, yet it does not mean it abolishes them. Capitalist modernity itself is not reducible to exchange and abstraction, but is also constituted by relations of production and consumption and inscribed upon pre-capitalist social relations. Unpacking this is, however, beyond the scope of this article. See for instance Zelizer (1997) and Maurer (2006).

8 The transnational and international legalisation of politics also seeks to work more directly on the global structures of power, thereby enacting a legal constraint upon the authorities, which can be both public and private, operating within these structures (Sassen 2006). A discussion of these is, however, beyond the scope of this article.

9 This is most apparent with Tocqueville. See Corey Robin's discussion of Tocqueville: (Robin 2004). The literature on crowd psychology in the nineteenth and early twentieth century can also be read in this light. For example, in Gustave Le Bon's widely influential account of the psychology of the crowd, the force of the mob was lying in their unconscious and instinctual make-up. Yet, the crowds that Le Bon fears are actually revealed to be the 'popular classes' that were organising themselves in syndicates and trade unions and whose claims for transforming social order Le Bon associated with that 'primitive communism which was the normal condition of all human groups before the dawn of civilisation' (Le Bon 1995 [1896]). Le Bon's theory of the crowds shared ideas with two other main works on the crowd psychology by Sighele (1901) and Tarde (1901 [1989]).

10 Metaphors of mobs as the sea and the resulting imaginary of storms, floods and fury has been a long-standing topos in the literature on crowds. On the use of the metaphor in Spinoza, see Montag (1999).

11 While agonistic and pluralistic theories of democracy (Connolly 2005; Mouffe 1999) have also integrated the masses in their conceptualisation of democracy, we differ by our conceptualisation of equality as giving content to democratic practice. Mobility, equality and democracy are intrinsically connected.

12 The distinction between these two functions of equality has been made by Rancière *et al.* (2000). For the implications of this distinction for the politics of human trafficking, see Aradau (2008).

13 There is a growing literature that discusses the collective politics and agency of undocumented migrants. For excellent examples, see Mezzadra (2006) and Nyers (2006).

11 Pragmatic cosmopolitanism and the role of leadership in transnational democracy

Daniel Bray

Introduction

One of the most pressing challenges for contemporary democrats is to rethink the theory and practice of democracy in light of intensifying cross-border flows of people, pollution, money, commodities, images and ideas. Everywhere, it seems, democracy fails to keep pace with processes of internationalisation that make political boundaries more porous and multiply the opportunities for collective action beyond nation-states.[1] Alarmingly (for democrats at least), this internationalisation of political life has created 'legitimation gaps' as competencies and jurisdictions have been shifted away from the national level and state actors have become part of broader governance networks that include relations with a variety of non-state and international actors. From this angle, national democratic publics seem like shrinking islands of autonomy in a sea of complex cross-border flows. In this environment, committed democrats are forced to ponder whether the nation-state is the single and most appropriate shell for democracy.

These sorts of reflections have generated an extensive normative literature on global and transnational democracy that largely centres on the claims of two broad camps: the 'liberal cosmopolitans' and the 'deliberative democrats'.[2] Liberal cosmopolitans like David Held (1995) want to create a multi-level system of formal legal and political institutions founded on cosmopolitan principles in order to safeguard individual autonomy from the corrosive effects of contemporary globalisation. Deliberative democrats like John Dryzek (2000), in contrast, highlight the importance of communicative freedom in transnational public spheres and see these critical publics as the primary basis for realising democracy in a globalising world. These two camps share the cosmopolitan goal to democratise contemporary forms of globalisation, but they tend to differ on the trajectory of democratic change: liberal cosmopolitans are usually characterised as 'top-down' architects of global democratic institutions, while deliberative democrats are seen as 'bottom-up' builders of transnational public spheres.

In this chapter, I broadly endorse the underlying case for extending democracy beyond the nation-state but draw on the moral and political resources contained in the work of philosopher John Dewey to offer an alternative perspective that I call 'pragmatic cosmopolitanism'.[3] This approach is 'pragmatic' because it is broadly developed from a Deweyan philosophy that rejects the traditional search for fixed ends, ultimate principles or *a priori* knowledge that exist above and beyond human experience. As such, I do not justify pragmatic cosmopolitanism as a fixed and universal theory of democracy, but rather offer an approach to *democratic reconstruction* that focuses on widening and deepening democratic life in more cosmopolitan directions. My approach is broadly cosmopolitan in the sense that it grounds this movement towards transnational democracy in the growth of individuals through a shared human capacity for intelligent self-transformation – and takes this particular interpretation of human freedom as the normative warrant for transnational democracy at a time when cross-border associations increasingly impact on the capacities of individuals and their communities.

My argument for pragmatic cosmopolitanism consists of two main parts. In the first part, I briefly outline the Deweyan ethical ideas that serve as my grounding for the transnationalisation of democratic life. This grounding is based on an ethic of growth that sees the use of critical intelligence and imaginative representation as the primary basis for generating transnational democratic communities. In the second part, I flesh out this framework by providing normative responses to what I identify as the four main problems in conceiving and realising transnational democracy: namely, problems of constituency, democratic scope, social prerequisites and practical institutionalisation. I develop a perspective that focuses on the necessary roles of leadership and representation in constituting the political agency of transnational publics. My main argument is that without people who can successfully represent certain problematic situations (like democratic deficits) as issues requiring public action, we cannot engender the common consciousnesses required for transnational democratic activity. Taken together, then, my reflections focus on the social preconditions and methodological orientation for democratic politics beyond the nation-state. To this end, I develop a normative framework for democratic reconstruction rather than a fixed model of global democracy that we must all aspire to.

The normative ethics of Deweyan pragmatism

Pragmatism is a philosophical approach that emerged in the work of Charles Peirce, William James and John Dewey in nineteenth-century America. Despite important differences, these early pragmatists shared the view that traditional philosophy was preoccupied with a futile search for fixed and universal absolutes. Dewey, in particular, was frustrated with traditional philosophical endeavours that attempted to ground moral and political norms in transcendental reason or natural rights, and argued for a 'recovery of philosophy' that sought to reconnect it with the concrete concerns of his day. Philosophy recovers itself, he argued, when it 'ceases to be a device for dealing with the problems of philosophers and becomes a *method*, cultivated by philosophers, for dealing with the problems of men' (Dewey 1998a: 68, emphasis added).

Given these philosophical proclivities, pragmatism has long been used as a method for challenging the assumptions of established philosophical traditions. But what can be taken from Deweyan pragmatism for a project of transnational democracy? More particularly, how is the work of John Dewey relevant to contexts that transcend nation-states? In this first part of my argument for pragmatic cosmopolitanism, I briefly outline Deweyan ideas of human growth, justice and democracy that provide the normative underpinnings of my approach.

Human growth

At its core, pragmatic ethics is concerned with the realisation of improved forms of human self-transformation. A Deweyan interpretation of this ethics grounds it in an account of individuality that prioritises: (1) a conception of human capacities that highlights the role and significance of critical-experimental intelligence; and (2) the social embeddedness of individual selves and their growth in and through associations. In highlighting the significance of critical intelligence in everyday life, Dewey argues that 'problematic' circumstances act as stimuli to inquiry that requires us to reflect intelligently on what we ought to do in indeterminate situations. Because such intelligent conduct is a shared human capacity of paramount importance, Dewey enjoins us to respect its existence and encourage its development in all human beings (MacGilvray 1999: 549). And because associated behaviour is the universal attribute of all existences, we must recognise the social basis of individuality. Individuals, according to Dewey (1998b: 27), 'will always be the centre and the consummation of experience, but what an individual actually *is* in his life-experience depends upon the nature and movement of associated life'.

For Dewey, these ontological priorities tie the growth of individuals and their communities to the development and exercise of the human capacity for critical inquiry. In transforming existing experiences, critical-experimental inquiry gains its ethical significance as a method for intentionally directing change characterised by deliberation, foresight, learning, openmindedness, an assumption of fallibility and respect for empirical consequences. In this way, ethical agents use their past experiences to construct new and better ones by reflectively evaluating the consequences of their practical judgements against their given ideals (Dewey 1948). That is, individuals act experimentally in problematic situations on the basis of hypotheses developed in past experience about how one should live; they appraise experiences of living in accordance with these ideals; and *grow* through the development of new values based on these experiments. Human growth in experience thus involves the actualisation of human potentialities that are called out by critical inquiry under conditions of uncertainty and contingency (Dewey 1998c: 224). Dewey's social ethics thus focuses on the institutional arrangements that influence the capacity of people to conduct critical inquiry intelligently, and, specifically, on the ways in which schools and civil society need to be reconstructed in order to promote habits of experimental intelligence and wider sympathies in social life (Anderson 2005: 18).

Justice

The egalitarian basis of pragmatic philosophy thus lies in the claim that the capacity for experimental intelligence is a universal feature of humanity that should be developed by all individuals. Human individuals are morally equal, according to pragmatists, in the sense that they all carry with them the capacity for self-transformation through critical-experimental inquiry. This universal capacity takes on moral weight because it is the basis of each person's irreplaceable individuality:

> In social and moral matters, equality does not mean mathematical equivalence ... It means that no matter how great the quantitative differences of ability, strength, position, wealth, such differences are negligible in comparison with something else – the fact of individuality, the manifestation of something irreplaceable.
>
> (Dewey 1998d: 352–3)

This individuality involves the exercise of a basic capacity for intelligent action that makes critical-experimental inquiry possible and constitutes the ontological basis for human freedom. According to Dewey, the *potential* for freedom is a 'native gift' in the sense that we all have 'the *capacity* for growth and for being actively concerned in the direction it takes'. But 'actual or positive freedom' is not a natural endowment; it is acquired by creating certain habits that allow individuals to grow through intelligent conduct as it leads to 'better choices' and 'better doing' in future interactions with objective conditions (ibid.). For pragmatists, these habits of critical intelligence should be developed by all individuals and applied more widely in social life because of their demonstrable success in securing human goods in activities like the natural sciences, journalism, art and literature.

Importantly, Dewey integrates this idea of free individuality in an account that recognises the central role of sociality in self-development. As Carol Gould (2004: 3) argues, this kind of approach sees self-development as requiring not only the making of choices but also the availability of the means or access to the material and social conditions for making these choices effective. In other words, the power or capacity to develop is framed by a distribution of material means and a complex of social norms that, negatively, constrain people's choices, and, positively, provide capabilities for carrying out certain activities. As such, self-development requires social conditions in which people are empowered to make and effectively act on intelligent choices in bounded but indeterminate contexts. Since this capacity for critical-experimental intelligence is said to be a universal human characteristic, and since the exercise of freedom requires social conditions that allow us to effectively realise this potential, a Deweyan ethic of growth implies an equal 'right' to the social conditions of intelligent self-transformation as its primary principle of justice. From a pragmatist perspective, this principle is not a fixed and universal maxim grounded in natural law; it is an inherited tool that is used in particular situations to consider what is morally relevant and decide what justice requires. Dewey thus recognised that in order for this 'right' to command authority in particular situations it had to be anchored in an intersubjective understanding of equality in which people recognise each other's freedom to develop, which must then be made effective through social and political institutions.

Democracy

The key to understanding Dewey's normative approach to democracy lies in his basic distinction between democracy 'as a social idea' and 'political democracy as a system of government' (Dewey 1991: 143). For Dewey, '[t]he idea of democracy is a wider and fuller idea than can be exemplified in the state even at its best' (ibid.). In this view, the idea of democracy is of unlimited scope; it potentially affects 'all modes of human association, the family, the school, industry, religion. And even so far as political arrangements are concerned, governmental institutions are but a mechanism for securing to an idea channels of effective operation' (ibid.). Furthermore, as an *ideal*, democracy denotes 'a tendency and movement of some thing which exists carried to its final limit, viewed as completed, perfected', but 'since things do not attain such fulfilment but are in actuality distracted and interfered with, democracy is this sense is not a fact and never will be' (ibid.: 148). This means that rather than regarding democracy as a quality that a social site either has or lacks, Dewey asks us to focus on how democratic (or undemocratic) they are, how democratic they might (or ought to) be, and how democracy within them can be enhanced (Cunningham 2002: 144). That is, Dewey argues that democracy is context-sensitive and can only ever be a matter of degree. From these considerations, we can see that Dewey's normative approach to democracy is not concerned with realising a fixed political ideal, but with the social preconditions and methodological orientation for democratic reconstruction.[4]

In this endeavour, Dewey places the notion of a 'public' at the centre of this social idea of democracy. In broad terms, a public is conceived as a discursive medium of cooperative problem-solving that is generated when an effort is made to regulate the enduring and extensive consequences of social transactions that affect the welfare of many others. Crucially, this means that the formation of a 'public' requires a social group to successfully establish that certain consequences are in need of general regulation. That is, a public must be constituted by a group of people who, on the basis of a jointly experienced concern, share the conviction that society must regulate a set of social transactions (Honneth 1998: 774). Here, Dewey casts the problem-solving needs of a cooperating society as the social mechanism upon which democratic will-formation as a normative principle is based (ibid.: 771). In doing so, he grounds the ethical life of a democratic society not in everyday procedures of intersubjective speech (as Habermasians do), or in republican political virtues, but in the consciousness of social cooperation. For Dewey, the main precondition for the development of democratic publics lies in the social division of labour, which must be regulated in such a just manner that each member of society can understand herself as sharing a common consciousness of responsibility and cooperation (ibid.: 777).

From this vantage point, we are able to appreciate the normative significance of political representation in Deweyan notions of justice and democracy. First, given the scale and complexity of modern social life, representation is cognitively required to make sense of the distant and multifarious human interactions that affect our daily lives. As Dewey points out, '[o]nly when there exist signs or symbols of activities and of their outcome can the flux [of human interaction] be viewed as from without, be arrested for consideration and esteem, and be regulated' (Dewey 1991: 152). That is to say, the common consciousness required for democratic action can exist only when the consequences of combined action are translated into shared objects by means of signs and symbols (representations). This is why Dewey was deeply concerned with 'the problem of presentation' and the *aesthetic* capabilities needed to 'break though the crust of conventionalised and routine consciousness' and (re)present certain situations as public problems requiring democratic action (ibid.: 183).

Second, according to Dewey, publics are politically organised and made effective through representatives. Since those who are indirectly affected by consequences of social transactions are not direct participants in the transactions in question, 'it is necessary that certain persons be set apart to represent them, and see to it that their interests are conserved and protected' (ibid.: 16). Abandoning the myth of the omnicompetent citizen,[5] Dewey recognises that in modern societies citizens leave many important aspects of information gathering and specialised judgement to the assessments of others. As James Bohman (1999: 597) points out, this involves the proliferation of principal-agent relationships that create pervasive asymmetries of competence and access to information that 'may actually work to undermine the putative advantages of the division of labour for democracy, creating a passive citizenry of principal/clients to agent/experts who are now responsible for regulatory control of vast areas of social life'. In consequence, Bohman rightly argues that what makes the division of labour democratic and helps to prevent the social tendency toward technocracy is critical interaction between experts and politicians (representatives) mediated through extensive and reciprocal communication with the broader public who make and judge representations of means and ends in light of shared interests, norms and values (ibid.). From this perspective, Dewey's proposals for democratic reconstruction centred on improving the social and epistemic conditions for a common interest to emerge in tackling the shared problems of a widely dispersed people. The key theme of this reconstruction was the expansion of organised social inquiry and the revitalisation of democratic communication through *aesthetic* processes of public dissemination and deliberation.

Pragmatic cosmopolitanism: key normative responses

From the preceding account, it is clear that pragmatic cosmopolitanism is built on a robust and principled interpretation of pragmatism that recognises its deep moral and political attachments to a particular view of ethical social life. What Dewey provides is an ethics tied to the realisation of intelligent self-transformation and an approach to democracy centred on the development of problem-solving 'publics' that are made effective through representative practices.

Turning now to contemporary global politics, it is remarkable to what extent the threats to democracy diagnosed by Dewey in his own time remain salient today. Dewey identified economic inequality, distrust of government, corruption, indifference, absolutism, drudgery, consumerism, control of the public by propaganda, and a system of formal education that does not sufficiently cultivate democratic habits (to name a few) as problems that prevent us from having a better quality of shared experience (Pappas 2008: 218, 249). These general problems remain with us today, but to these we must now add the contemporary challenges raised by the internationalisation and transnationalisation of social and political life, processes that far surpass the nascent international interdependence Dewey observed in his own day. The general problem is that to varying degrees processes that transcend the borders of nation-states increasingly determine the social conditions for the growth of individuality and the quality of shared (democratic) experiences. Individuals and their communities in discrete nation-states are increasingly implicated as generators and bearers of consequences of cross-border transactions. Pragmatic cosmopolitanism thus argues that the democratic reconstruction envisioned by Dewey must have transnational dimensions in order to encompass the contemporary array of social transactions that affect individuals and their communities.

In what follows, I flesh out my pragmatic approach by providing a set of normative responses to the key problems that bedevil the theory and practice of transnational democracy: problems of constituency, democratic scope, social prerequisites and practical institutionalisation. What emerges is a perspective that uses Deweyan pragmatism to justify a particular movement toward democracy beyond the nation-state, but does so in a way that remains aware of the contingency of these foundations, is respectful of empirical consequences, and takes account of the existing contexts from which democracy must emerge.

The problem of constituency

The problem of constituency is one of defining the proper boundaries of the regime within which democracy is to be practiced. Democratic theory struggles to grapple with this problem because the boundaries of a political community cannot be determined by democratic means. That is, the initial formation of a democratic collective cannot be a result of democratic choice because we do not know who the *demos* is to decide what the boundaries of the collective should be. Put simply, the people cannot decide until somebody decides who the people are.

This problem has sharpened in contemporary global politics as increasing transnational activity challenges the appropriateness of territorial borders as the primary basis for delineating political boundaries. In an increasingly interconnected world, the range and importance of cross-border issues has highlighted the lack of symmetry between national decision-makers and those affected by their decisions. In this context, some theorists have offered 'the all-affected principle' as a way of determining the proper boundaries of political community in a globalising world.[6] Given the ongoing importance of territorial borders, however, most advocates of the all-affected principle do not completely abandon territoriality. The debate thus centres on what principle should serve as the *primary* basis for delineating political constituencies.

Liberal cosmopolitans like David Held and Daniele Archibugi advocate the creation of a new constitutional settlement in which the legal jurisdictions of local, national, regional and global political communities are constituted by all those *significantly* affected by an issue (Held 1995: 236). Held retains a role for territorial political communities, but the levels of territorial authority would owe the extent of their power (or domain) to an effort to incorporate the all-affected principle (Saward 2000: 37). Deliberative democrats like John Dryzek, in contrast, do not seek to introduce new system-level democratic institutions. Dryzek instead aims to democratise the discursive sources of governance that are already present in the international system by cultivating transnational public spheres in which there can be genuine dialogue among all those affected by an issue. Central to this project is rethinking democracy along deliberative lines: conceiving democracy in terms of deliberation and communication makes it easier to extend democracy to the international system because it downplays the boundary problem and allows us to cope better with fluid constituencies (Dryzek 2000: 129).

In keeping with my Deweyan approach, pragmatic cosmopolitanism eschews the temptation to lay down one universally fixed principle to which all democratic communities must conform. This kind of methodology can only lead to a dangerous situation where we are compelled to reorganise the entire global political system on the basis of a single principle. In this vein, many scholars have pointed out the serious problems with reorganising political boundaries in complete accordance with the all-affected principle (for example, the difficulties associated with forming a different all-affected constituency for every decision).[7] In contrast, adopting a pragmatic perspective means questions about the proper boundaries of *demoi* are not purely theoretical ones that must be answered prior to engaging in democratic politics; they arise as practical problems in the conduct of such politics itself (Cunningham 2002: 214).

As such, pragmatic cosmopolitanism proceeds from the empirical observation that new constituencies are emerging in global politics through transnational cooperation in addressing shared cross-border problems. Its approach to the question of boundaries is a fluid and contextual one that focuses on the development and democratisation of transnational publics that coexist and overlap with the entrenched system of states. Because, from a Deweyan perspective, democracy emerges from social associations, there is no *a priori* reason to believe that democratic life must stop at the political boundaries of existing nation-states, especially at a time when social interaction in many parts of the world has an increasingly transnational dimension.

In the current context of global politics, I accept that in many situations primary territorial bases are needed to guarantee basic democratic rights and address bundles of common problems that are limited to a particular territorial community. However, I also see a role for the all-affected principle as a critical tool for tackling problematic democratic deficits generated by activities that extend beyond territorial borders. That is, when territorial borders are experienced as problematic in the organisation of democratic life, people *who recognise themselves as affected* must organise themselves as a critical public in order to ameliorate these problems. In these situations, the experience of affectedness is what generates democratic politics and the all-affected principle becomes a moral resource in democratic problem-solving rather than an abstract rule for determining political boundaries that must be applied universally. This approach recognises that in the current environment many citizens of nation-states are unlikely to want to trade their concretely experienced rights in a territorial community for the much more abstract, transient and conditional guarantees of cosmopolitan citizenship in multiple and overlapping constituencies. In terms of identifying *demoi*, then, this perspective seeks the democratic reconstruction of existing territorial entities in conjunction with the creation of transnational democratic communities generated by the need to address shared problems (like global warming or regulating international trade).

At this point, my conception of transnational democracy as involving both territorially based collective self-government and the development of transnational democratic communities raises a critical issue concerning the potential conflicts between these types of publics as wielders of power and authority. That is, this theory of multiple and overlapping *demoi* inevitably raises the question of sovereignty. When overlapping territorial and non-territorial *demoi* clash, which has an overarching claim to democratic legitimacy and how will these competing claims be resolved? David Held (1995) attempts to resolve this problem by using the principle of subsidiarity to allocate decision-making authority for a particular issue. Dewey, however, did not emphasise the role of legal structures in resolving moral conflicts or conflicts of interest. He instead argued that conflicting interests are best tackled through the 'method of democracy', which brings 'these conflicts out into the open where their special claims can be seen and appraised, where they can be discussed and judged in light of more inclusive interests than are represented by either of them separately' (quoted in Festenstein 1997: 79).

The response of pragmatic cosmopolitanism, then, is to see the tensions between territorially based communities and transnational publics not as a call for the wholesale imposition of an abstract principle but as ongoing problems that act as stimuli to critical inquiry and thus open up possibilities for the expansion of moral and political boundaries. In this way, my approach is more sensitive to the contextual conditions that act as constraints in these situations. For example, determining the appropriate level for developing aspects of social policy in the European Union cannot be resolved simply by asserting an incontrovertible maxim like the all-affected principle or subsidiarity. In the case of proposed smoking bans in bars, pubs and restaurants, these principles are invoked in a historical and political context in which EU Commissioners press for an EU-wide ban on behalf of European workers, and national and local communities (particularly in Eastern Europe) fight to retain control over traditions that are important in their daily lives. In this light, we must attempt to resolve these problems through critical inquiry in which the claims of EU officials, national representatives, sectoral experts and local populations are publicly articulated, contested and judged in ongoing engagements. This implies that democratic reconstruction, and any accompanying extension of moral and political boundaries, must grow from the values shared by existing democratic communities. It must harness overlapping beliefs about democratic life that have developed in modern societies.

Thus, in the pragmatist view, addressing the tensions between democratic publics with overlapping boundaries broadly requires a normative structure consisting of open communities in which people are concerned to develop and use their critical faculties and the associated virtues of pragmatic inquiry (including deliberation, foresight, learning and the assumption of fallibility). At a minimum, this must include a level of social engagement and responsibility to others that allows one to look beyond their immediate context and imagine alternative possibilities (Cochran 1999: 251). This mechanism of imaginative representation is central to the 'sympathy' that 'carries thought out beyond the self and which extends its scope till it approaches the universal as its limit' (Dewey 1998e: 333). Additionally, and more demandingly, this normative structure must secure for citizens a normative status sufficient for them to exercise these creative powers in reshaping the terms of their communal relations (Bohman 2007: 28). In this sense, pragmatic inquiry grows out of communal life, but also has the potential to change such life by solving practical problems and reconstituting the basis of communal membership (Dewey 1991: 193). Ultimately, however, these requirements merely open up the possibility of intersocietal value convergence through the imaginative overlap that can be identified in empathetic relationships, dialogic interaction or participation in common activities, but do not guarantee that a consensus about political norms will be reached.

In short, the *normative ideal* here is that problems of sovereignty that emerge among different publics ought to be resolved through critical inquiry focused on the particular problematic boundaries rather than through force or the wholesale adherence to a fixed rule. However, it is important to recognise that this inquiry takes place in a constellation of social forces that constitutes the problematic situation: the formulation of boundary problems and the ways in which they are resolved will be shaped by the power of different actors advocating for existing territorial arrangements or expanded forms of democratic governance. In any process of public problem-solving, some actors will seek to advance interpretations of problems and solutions that accord with their own partial interests; others will attempt to deny that there is a problem at all. In this way, power relations shape the very process of formulating shared problems. And as Matthew Festenstein (2002: 569) argues, what counts as a successful resolution in boundary problems is in part constructed politically. Crucially, this politics of boundaries requires leaders to publicly represent the different visions of constituency relevant to the problem at hand, which generates and directs the broader contestation and deliberation central to reconstituting communal membership across existing boundaries. Without leaders who can successfully construct, mobilise and sustain global or transnational constituencies, existing territorial boundaries will constitute the limits of democratic life.

Democratic scope

The question of boundaries is, of course, closely related to the problem of democratic scope, which I define as one of determining which domains of social life ought to be subject to democratic control. In recent decades, long-standing debates between liberals, socialists and feminists about the separation of public and private spheres have re-emerged at the global level as the scope of international governance has grown. In these debates, defining the proper spheres of democratic governance involves making judgements about what range of actions or institutions should be regulated by democratic norms in a context where the range and intensity of cross-border problems has increased dramatically.

Held's model of 'cosmopolitan democracy' proposes the democratic reconstruction of global governance, including the regulation of the global economy in order to further humanitarian, environmental and traditional social-democratic goals. The rationale for this project lies in a deep commitment to individual autonomy, which must be advanced and protected by deepening democracy within national communities and extending democratic processes across existing nation-states. Many advocates of deliberative democracy would no doubt agree with some of these goals, but want to shift the focus to the promotion of deliberation in transnational public spheres. John Dryzek wants to extend the scope of democracy beyond the nation-state by subjecting existing international discourses to broad deliberative contestation. He cites discursive contests in areas like ozone depletion, whaling, 'bioprospecting' and sustainable development as examples where broad contestation in transnational issue communities led to important political outcomes, some of which involved securing environmental protections in opposition to powerful state actors (Dryzek 1999: 39–43). For Dryzek, then, the primary targets for democratic control are the transnational discourses that sustain and order global politics.

In accordance with the Deweyan view that democracy as a social idea has no fixed limits, my approach to the question of democratic scope does not make *a priori* arguments about the scope of democratic governance beyond the nation-state. I maintain that beyond basic territorial entities, any transnational social activity can be seen as a relevant context for democratic decision; we should not exclude *a priori* any social domains as logically immune from democratic control. Indeed, according to Dewey, the question of what transactions should be left to private initiative and agreement and what should come under the regulation of a public is a question of time, place and concrete conditions: 'there cannot be any universal rule laid down ... regarding the respective role of private and public action' (quoted in Pappas 2008: 242). Specifically, Dewey (1991: 193) argues that the scope of public action will vary depending on the nature of the consequences of social transactions and *the ability of affected people to perceive and act upon them*. This approach is particularly useful for thinking about transnational democracy because it highlights that

> the need for further democracy cannot simply be instituted from above, but should be allowed to rise from below, where it is deemed to be needed by interested parties. There must be a form of collective recognition by the actors involved that a particular democratic deficit represents a particularly problematic situation.
>
> (Cochran 1999: 543)

This understanding of the genesis and limits of public power raises two important problems to which pragmatic cosmopolitanism must respond. First, lacking a set of principles that provide antecedent boundaries to the political realm, pragmatic politics is open to the liberal charge that it is in constant danger of collapsing into the tyranny of the majority (or the stronger) (MacGilvray 1999: 553). In place of these principles, however, pragmatism offers a conception of human freedom that celebrates individual capacities and thus offers prudential support for liberal protections that help to safeguard spheres of intelligent self-transformation. As MacGilvray (ibid.) puts it:

> The celebration of individual capacities is made prior to both the democratic pursuit of the public interest and the liberal protection of private interests, and so pragmatism combines a prudential endorsement of state/society and public/private distinctions with an equally prudential refusal to treat such distinctions as fixed or insurmountable.

Concerned with empirical consequences, pragmatism sees liberal rights as instruments that have been successfully refined through experience in order to remove the obstructions of arbitrary state power, but also highlights the way in which these rights have led to new burdens and new modes of oppression when harnessed to ideas of *laissez faire* economics and the inviolability of the private sphere. In other words, pragmatism recognises the historically unacknowledged suffering created by *a priori* liberal distinctions between public and private realms and the way they serve to depoliticise certain issues. From this perspective, public-private distinctions, and the rights derived from them, can never be beyond criticism.

Similarly, the approach of pragmatic cosmopolitanism offers prudential support for ideas and practices of state sovereignty that contribute to the protection of autonomous spheres of individual and communal development, but also highlights the oppressions and abuses that have been perpetuated under its protections. In terms of pragmatic philosophy, the most important consequence of the system of national sovereignty is the way in which it forecloses human experience and moral imagination by assuming the nation-state is the outer limit of community. With the increasing frequency and intensity of cross-border trans-actions in recent decades, there already exist dense networks of contact and exchange that extend beyond national borders, but due to the 'stickiness' of national affiliations these transactions tend to be interpreted in discrete national frameworks that stifle moral and political engagements with the perspectives of others. Drawing on its conception of human growth, pragmatic cosmopolitanism sees this situation as one that unduly limits and impoverishes the experience of individuals and therefore profoundly narrows the possibilities for transnational cooperation. In terms of democratic scope, then, the underlying presumption of pragmatic cosmopolitanism is that democratic projects must follow social prac-tices that extend beyond national borders in order to keep pace with the expand-ing context of social development.

The second problem relates to my understanding of the 'bottom-up' nature of democratic reconstruction. Specifically, it concerns the practical obstacles to a group of citizens recognising that a particular situation constitutes a problem requiring collective action: what if citizens lack the information, inclination, freedom and skills to rise up from below and constitute themselves as a public motor of change? How can citizens act critically and experimentally in concert with others when their experiences of politics are based on partial and fleeting conceptions of distant, complex and indirect causes and consequences? Here, pragmatic cosmopolitanism highlights the important role of political leadership in publicising the problematic consequences of cross-border transactions. That is, it argues that the ability of people to perceive and act upon problematic con-sequences first requires leaders to represent these consequences as matters of common public concern at critical junctures.

But what precisely does this leadership involve? Dewey, like many demo-cratic theorists, took a sceptical view of political leaders: 'The world', he argued, 'has suffered more from leaders than from the masses' (quoted in Pappas 2008: 243). My conception of political leadership, however, focuses on *leadership acts and their consequences*, rather than linking it with a formal relationship of rule or command between leaders and followers. Specifically, a political leader is someone who participates in initiating, directing or informing public action *in a problematic situation*. That is, leadership is called for at times of uncertainty, change and choice, times when deliberation and decision occur about what course of collective action is desirable for a political community. At other more routine times, the direction of the day-to-day activities of a group is properly called *management*, not leadership (Tucker 1981: 16). Leadership arises when someone defines a set of circumstances as a problematic situation demanding coordinated action, and direction and information is required to formulate group responses. As Robert Tucker (ibid.: 18–19) writes, this can involve three, often interpenetrating functions: (1) defining or diagnosing the situation; (2) prescrib-ing a specific course of action; and (3) mobilising a group by gaining support for diagnoses and prescriptions.

In terms of transnational democracy, the value of these leadership functions lies in the extent to which they foster democratic inquiry in a transnational public. As such, this kind of political leadership need not be associated with governmental officials or elected representatives, but more broadly with any actor that acts to represent different experiences of cross-border transactions in a common frame required for effective public action. Here, the *democratic* roles of NGOs, transnational activists, government agencies, international organisations, journalists, experts, intellectuals or global celebrities should not be conceived as 'representatives' in the traditional liberal understanding, but rather as 'representers' that initiate, direct or inform transnational inquiry. This understanding of leadership shares much with Margaret Keck and Kathryn Sikkink's notion of political entrepreneurship in the way it emphasises the use of 'information' and 'symbolic politics'. Keck and Sikkink (1998) highlight the role of a relatively small number of individuals in transnational advocacy networks who recognise new political opportunities and seek to creatively frame problems in innovative ways in order to bring them to the public agenda and persuade state actors to change their policies. My understanding of leadership, however, goes beyond the tactics employed by transnational activists in influencing state actors. In a more normative sense, it seeks to capture the communicative role of a much wider group of actors (including government agencies) in promoting and participating in transnational democratic inquiry.

The contemporary politics of climate change provides an excellent example here because leadership itself is a central controversy in climate change debates. In the decade following the creation of the Kyoto Protocol, the failure of developed states like Australia and the United States to ratify the Protocol meant that they abandoned a leadership role in the critical inquiries that were taking place within global institutions and broader publics. The claims emanating from some sections of these administrations argued that either human-induced climate change simply did not exist (they disputed the diagnosis), or the Protocol was an inadequate response because it did not include developing countries (they disputed the prescription). This was despite the fact that Article 3.1 of the United Nations Framework Convention on Climate Change (which both governments signed) states that developed countries 'should take the lead in combating climate change and the adverse effects thereof' (United Nations 1992: 4). Perhaps motivated by the US government's lack of leadership, former Vice-President Al Gore subsequently assumed a leadership role in publicising climate change as a global problem and educating publics on the causes and consequences of climate change. In the same period, international organisations, scientists and civil society groups have participated as 'observers' in climate change negotiations, seeking to inform and influence state representatives through their official speeches and in informal 'second track' interactions in meetings and working groups that offer better prospects for deliberation. To the extent that this kind of leadership creates a more inclusive and deliberative inquiry by representing local, transnational and global concerns that transcend state interests, we can see it as contributing to the democratisation of climate change negotiations.

Of course, many questions are raised concerning the democratic credentials of these types of leaders. Indeed, some representative claims in global politics are made by people with little contact with the constituency they invoke, or with astoundingly long chains of delegation. For example, at the UN Climate Change Conference in Poznań, Poland in December 2008, a speech was given by a spokesperson of Direction du Développement Durable Électricité France, who claimed to speak 'on behalf of global business and industry'; and another was given by activists from Nature and Youth Denmark and Indian Youth Climate Network, 'speaking for the world's youth' (United Nations Framework Convention on Climate Change 2008: 13). While not wishing to dismiss important concerns about the representativeness of these kinds of actors, by focusing on leadership acts and their consequences for democracy, pragmatic cosmopolitanism shifts the focus from the democratic credentials of the actors themselves to the purposes and content of their representative claims and the importance of critical scrutiny in judging their validity. In assessing whether leadership is good or bad for democracy, contextual judgements must be made about whether particular leadership acts help or hinder the conduct of democratic inquiry in specific situations. That is, we must ask: does this leadership act support the context of democratic decision-making (by, for example, publicising a problem, representing an excluded group or educating broader publics) (Ackerly 2006: 126)? Ultimately, the best guarantee against the reduction of public discourse to demagoguery and propaganda are the habits of critical intelligence that prompt us to interrogate the representative claims made by political leaders.[8] Indeed, Dewey worked to nurture citizens' critical intelligence not because he naively trusted the people but because he was so suspicious of those who presumed to lead and instruct them (Kloppenberg 1994: 71).

Social prerequisites

Sceptics of global or transnational democracy tend to claim that the social prerequisites for democracy are missing beyond the nation-state. According to many sceptics, it is the concept of the nation that defines the proper boundaries of the political community (solving the boundary problem) and legitimises the exercise of popular sovereignty (see Miller 1995 and Kymlicka 2001). Thus, for sceptics, democracy beyond the nation-state is not possible where corresponding transnational *demoi* with strong senses of collective identity are currently absent. In the absence of strong transnational solidarities, then, global and transnational democrats must clearly articulate what social prerequisites are needed for particular democratic arrangements and how they should be developed where they are lacking.

Liberal cosmopolitans place their emphasis on the development of a sense of cosmopolitan citizenship through the creation of a new institutional architecture. According to Held (2000: 28), if the possibility of cosmopolitan democracy is to be consolidated 'each citizen of a state must *learn* to become a cosmopolitan citizen – a person capable of mediating between national traditions, communities and alternative forms of life'. Ultimately, however, Held is too complacent about how his cosmopolitan institutions would generate the global public sphere and solidaristic communities required for resource redistribution and democratic decision-making. Without an avenue for citizen participation in global institutions beyond electing distant global parliamentarians, how will the cosmopolitan citizen be created when the primary sites of social learning will remain in local and national communities?

Deliberative democrats tackle this question directly and argue that in complex societies it is the democratic opinion- and will-formation of citizens that forms the basis of a legally constructed solidarity that links members in a political community (Habermas 1999b: 118–19). For Dryzek (2000: 113), given that transnational discourses are the primary target of democratic control, the communicative power of civil society takes centre stage in the politics of questioning, criticising and publicising. The possibility of democratic action in global politics thus rests on the networks of transnational civil society and their reflexive control of discourses. These kinds of deliberative processes obviously require informed and active citizens that are empowered by basic democratic rights.

The general response of pragmatic cosmopolitanism to the question of social prerequisites is that the creation of transnational democratic publics must emerge from leadership in fostering a consciousness of shared responsibility and cooperation. Only the experience of social conditions in which citizens recognise themselves as members of a common enterprise will see democratic procedures as a legitimate means of joint problem-solving. In examining the specific implications of this approach for the project of transnational democracy, I follow Michael Zürn (2000) in adopting a disaggregated conception of the *demos* in order to establish in practical terms what kind of democratic processes can be generated on the basis of its partially given components.

Against the view that *demoi* are systematically related to national identity, Zürn (ibid.: 195–200) argues that this all-embracing conception of the *demos* can be disaggregated into five analytically separable elements: rights, trust, public spirit, public discourse and solidarity. Based on the notion of justice I developed above, pragmatic cosmopolitanism clearly asserts that certain rights need to be recognised as *human rights*. Dewey did not speak in a rights language, but since his time (he died in 1952 aged 92) human rights have been deeply entrenched in international institutions and now constitute a powerful discourse for legitimising moral and political claims all over the world. In this context, projects of global or transnational democracy must build on existing human rights frameworks because they provide the most promising paths for promoting conditions of equal social status and life-opportunity for peoples and individuals. As Hauke Brunkhorst (2002: 690) points out, the moral language of human rights can enable the mobilisation of public interest and communicative pressure, and as a legal language it is one the political class and its administrative adjuncts can understand and take into account in decision-making. In the perspective of pragmatic cosmopolitanism, these rights are normatively conceived as universal and equal claims to social conditions of individual self-transformation that individuals make on all others as humans. As Bohman (2007: 109) points out, these rights involve a *standing* by which the claimant is recognised as someone who may make such an appeal and to whom others may address a similar appeal; that is, it involves a basic normative power to make claims to others that may obligate them. Without this basic standing, grounded in an intersubjective understanding of human rights, people will have no capacity to initiate deliberation about claims to justice that extend beyond the borders of their national communities. They will be unable to claim a right to participate in cross-border activities in which their interests are implicated. Ultimately, transnational democracy must be fundamentally anchored in cross-border understandings of human rights in which distant others come to be viewed as legitimate claimants in common social frameworks.

In terms of trust and public spirit, Zürn (2000: 196–8) points out that the increased compliance pull of international regulations when societal participation is possible indicates that political trust is today not restricted to the national and intergovernmental sphere; and when transnational sectoral publics in fields like environmental politics deliberate on the 'right' policies they show signs of public spirit beyond nations. Trust and public spirit are no doubt important elements of a democratic mode of cooperative problem-solving, but they only take on central importance if we conceive of *demoi* as completely harmonious entities. In the context of representative authority and asymmetrical information, a harmonious view of politics requires us to build in idealisations of complete mutual trust or denial of self-interest in order to render the democratic division of labour practically feasible (Bohman 1999: 595). Under the conflictual conditions of global politics, however, trust and public spirit cannot bear the primary burden of explaining how a division of labour incorporating complex principal-agent relationships can be democratic. Rather, that burden is borne by the quality of public communication among critical agents and the openness of norms of inquiry to democratic challenge (ibid.: 596). The problem of cooperation here is one of maintaining the credibility of expert authority and legitimacy of existing norms more than trust or public spirit. In the pragmatic view, expert knowledge enters into public discourse in addressing problematic situations and its authority is tested and judged in relation to its consequences. This reliance on critical scrutiny suggests that there is no pragmatic reason to develop a *generalised* trust in the epistemic authority of experts (ibid.: 598). From this angle, we must build on the *leading* roles of civil society in publicising and scrutinising the claims of experts and politicians and distributing social knowledge to broader publics.

Public discourse and solidarity are clearly the weakest features of emerging transnational *demoi*. Despite the seeming public-spiritedness and dense communication of transnational issue networks, the absence of a common language and common media impedes the development of broader public discourses. Beyond this, broadening transnational discourse requires *institutional* solutions that provide a wider range of actors with the capacity to communicate publicly on issues of mutual concern. Indeed, it has been demonstrated in contexts like EU environmental policy that incorporating NGOs and epistemic communities has improved the democratic quality of policy-making by upgrading issue networks into sectoral publics that represent widespread interests (Zürn 2000: 206). In the same way, representing the concerns of transnational publics in formal global institutions has the potential to transform intergovernmental bargaining into more inclusive and transparent transnational negotiations. This kind of democratic politics does not require the development of a unitary global discourse, only the development of multiple transnational publics where they are deemed necessary (Cochran 2002: 538).

In terms of solidarity, pragmatic cosmopolitanism suggests that rather than placing one's faith in a particular type of rational communication (as Habermas does), cross-border relationships developed through the recognition of shared problems is a less demanding basis for fostering senses of community in contexts of cultural diversity. This view holds out the possibility that the recognition of shared problems '*can lead* to persons learning the value of social cooperation and the creation of community through repeated interaction in relation to those problems' (ibid., original emphasis). Solidarities might be fostered based on a concern for the suffering or oppression of distant others, for example, that may be quite removed from participation in rational discourse. These kinds of solidarities are already evident in transnational civil society groups that act on shared concerns like gender inequality, environmental degradation and labour rights. By experimenting with innovative democratic processes that build on these existing components, we might facilitate the development of the broader discourses and stronger solidarities required for further democratisation. As Zürn (2000: 212) points out, 'democratic institutions are not only dependent on social prerequisites, they are also a generative source of them'.

Practical institutionalisation

In thinking about these possibilities for democratic change, we are obviously faced with serious practical constraints. These relate to the ways in which geography, time constraints and the limitations of human capabilities impose practical limits on the institutionalisation of democratic principles in political life. Obviously, when thinking about democracy at a global or transnational level the problem of practicality is magnified severely. The expanded geographical scale and diversity of a global or transnational political community presents considerable challenges when democratic debate and decision-making must stretch across many continents and time zones. The increased range and complexity of global issues also increases demands on the time, knowledge and interest of socially distant citizens. Furthermore, there are also extreme differences in power, wealth and education that shape an individual or group's ability to participate in a global or transnational democratic process.

In addressing these problems, liberal cosmopolitans make political representation the key institutional feature of global democracy. In general, cosmopolitan democracy is seen as a multi-level system of overlapping communities with progressively 'higher' levels of political representation. In the (likely) event that there are disputes about the appropriate level of decision-making for a particular issue, Held relies on the principle of subsidiarity to aid in adjudicating political boundaries; he argues that collective decision-making is best located closest to those whose life chances are determined by significant social processes and forces (Held 2003: 471).

Given their emphasis on participatory politics, deliberative democrats face more serious practical challenges when extending democracy to the global level. As Andrew Kuper (2004: 59) points out, attempts to identify procedures and institutions that enable ideal deliberation face constraints on numbers, time and distance in any remotely large-scale and pluralistic society. Moreover, practical challenges confront deliberative democrats when they must provide an account of the institutional linkages between the public sphere and formal institutions. For Dryzek (1999: 30), globalisation means that important issues increasingly elude the control of states and so transnational democracy may mean *bypassing* the state and relying on decentralised networks of actors acting across state boundaries. He wishes to maintain a strict separation between transnational civil society and formal global institutions, but due to the bottom-up nature of his approach, he is not specific about the *institutional* conditions under which democratic deliberation can be achieved, and the representative basis upon which affected individuals and communities will be included in deliberative forums.[9]

In keeping with pragmatist tenets, my approach to the problem of practical institutionalisation is a context-sensitive one that does not impose an *a priori* 'direct' or 'representative' template for the political institutionalisation of democracy, which may require more or less degrees of mediation and delegation depending on the particular problematic situation. As Saward (2000) points out, different democratic mechanisms may be called for depending on whether they require permanent structures or temporary measures and on whether they are undertaken by governments or by non-governmental actors.[10] Thus, one may have a normative preference for minimising the degree of mediation and delegation in any democratic regime, but these features of democratic practice should not be viewed as inherently bad. Indeed, given the scale and complexity of modern politics, transnational democratic publics are likely to require significant levels of mediation and delegation if they are to be effective actors in global politics.

The key response of pragmatic cosmopolitanism here is to see transnational publics as *institutions of critical inquiry* that are formed when associated individuals work collectively to address transnational problems. As Molly Cochran (2002: 531) points out, in Deweyan terms these publics exist on a continuum from 'weak' publics that are understood to involve associated activity that is only informally organised (like a neighbourhood group) or narrowly focused on a single issue (like the control and prevention of HIV/AIDS[11]), to stronger publics that have political agencies invested with public authority that are capable of issuing binding decisions for a societal group (an international regime, say, or a more densely articulated public we commonly regard as a political 'state').[12] Today, in the absence of adequately responsive global institutions, most transnational associations take contestation rather than popular control as their fundamental political purpose (Bohman 2007: 62). When they seek to provide alternative sites for deliberation where dominators are not present they form what Nancy Fraser (1992: 123) calls 'subaltern counterpublics' that attempt to influence formal organisations by mobilising broader public opinion. These oppositional networks and movements can only be conceived as transnational public institutions, however, when their efforts are directed at shifting authority away from states and their agents by making their own concerns *authoritative* in the decision-making that takes place where international public authority exists in global politics – international law, regimes, the United Nations and in the broader bilateral and multilateral relations between states (Cochran 1999: 532). In the view of pragmatic cosmopolitanism, this process constitutes the core dynamic of democratic reconstruction at the global level.

It is this perspective that highlights the key difference between the pragmatist and deliberative approaches to the institutionalisation of transnational democracy. Instead of seeing publics as constituted by responsible citizens who reason publicly on the basis of a distinctive form of communication, pragmatists see responsible action as emerging from publics constituted by persons who recognise a need for social cooperation in resolving common problematic situations. In the pragmatist view, publics are developing 'the traits of a state' when they develop strong organisational and decision-making capabilities and seek to make their concerns authoritative in global politics (Dewey 1991). Pragmatism therefore does not hold to the strict state-civil society separation that fundamentally shapes the deliberative approach. Beyond nation-states with sharply defined constitutional structures, the desire to maintain a strict separation between opinion-formation in the public sphere and will-formation in formal representative institutions seems to neglect the requirement for some kind of connective tissue between them, or at least assumes that the translation of opinions into decision-making will occur through an underlying discursive shift that changes the context in which formal decisions are reached. Deliberative democrats thus privilege informal procedures of truth-seeking (that are never power-free or completely non-strategic) over political voice in formal institutions. Dryzek is obviously concerned about the co-option of oppositional civil society – which is certainly an ever-present threat and one to be taken seriously – but in many global and transnational contexts this threat tends to be overstated and fails to acknowledge the strategic character of 'publics' themselves. As Cochran (1999: 535) points out, despite the blurring of the state-society divide, co-option is unlikely to be ever fixed or complete. Additionally, not all weak publics seek permanent or even minimal levels of inclusion in existing formal institutions, preferring to focus on contestation or developing alternative forums. Ultimately, pragmatic cosmopolitanism argues that in many contexts of contemporary global politics the need to realise change through access to formal decision-making outweighs the risk of co-option. One such context I discussed earlier centres on the contemporary climate change negotiations, where a wide variety of non-governmental actors attempt to influence states in formal institutions by 'channelling up' the concerns of excluded publics, while at the same time monitoring the negotiations and 'channelling down' information to broader transnational and domestic constituencies.[13]

However, the concern of deliberative democrats to maintain the authenticity and vibrancy of critical voices does accord with pragmatic cosmopolitanism in the sense that it sees transnational publics as the primary motor of critical publicity in global politics. In thinking about institutionalisation, we should recall Dewey's argument that publics are *politically organised* through representatives that 'care for' the interests of those affected by indirect consequences of social transactions. As *institutions* of representation, then, 'strong' publics require organisational processes for making, judging and contesting claims made by those representing affected constituencies. In this sense, political institutionalisation involves developing organisational rules for recognising the validity of representative claims and procedures for generating authoritative decisions based on critical inquiries that interrogate and weigh these claims. In modern democratic states, electoral institutions provide the most important rules for recognising the representative legitimacy of political actors. In transnational and global contexts, however, the challenge is to create institutions that provide different types of actors (states, international organisations, experts, NGOs, individuals, etc.), claiming to represent different and overlapping constituencies, with the opportunity to participate in critical inquiries that generate authoritative decisions about common problems.

In this regard, many important questions remain concerning how we move from the formulation and recognition of shared problems to the development of democratic institutions that test representative claims and generate decisions that resolve these problems. Here, we might draw lessons from successful cases like the international campaign to ban landmines, where a weak public with growing moral influence eventually became a broad coalition of actors (including states) responsible for creating the Ottawa Convention prohibiting the production and use of anti-personnel landmines (Cameron *et al.* 1998). One important lesson in this instance was the critical role of leadership in publicising the landmine problem and mobilising widespread support for a comprehensive treaty. The early stages of the campaign owed much to the efforts of NGOs working in post-war Cambodia in the 1980s; organisations like the UN and the International Committee of the Red Cross; US Congressmen (the United States did not sign the treaty); activists like 1997 Nobel Peace Prize Winner Jody Williams and the late Princess Diana; and, crucially, states like Canada, France and Norway, which gave the movement legitimacy and provided sites for its meetings (Tarrow 2005: 174). This instance of pragmatic cosmopolitanism is, of course, just one oft-cited example of successful transnational cooperation among many other instances of failure. But it effectively demonstrates the potential trajectories of transnational democracy. Specifically, it demonstrates that flourishing transnational publics are the most promising vehicles for the democratic reconstruction of global governance.

Conclusion

The perspective of pragmatic cosmopolitanism envisages the development of transnational democracy in and through the representative practices of cross-border problem-solving publics. This view recognises that global political space is today comprised of interrelated issues rather than an integrated demos – and that 'governance' in this context refers to coordinated action appropriate to the solution of specific problems (Rosenau 1998: 30–32; Urbinati 2003: 80). In this article, I grounded this approach in a Deweyan ethics that highlighted the indispensability of critical intelligence and imaginative representation in generating transnational democratic publics. I also argued that this ethics implies an equal right to the social conditions of intelligent self-transformation and that this principle of justice provides the normative warrant for global democratisation. Using this contingent foundation, I provided a set of normative responses to the problems faced by democrats in conceiving and realising democracy beyond nation-states, which are summarised and compared with the liberal cosmopolitan and deliberative approaches in Table 11.1 below.

This article extends the work already done by pragmatist scholars in at least three ways: (1) it offers a comprehensive Deweyan framework that directly addresses the main problems with conceiving and realising transnational democracy; (2) in doing so, it focuses attention on the important role of political leadership in constituting transnational publics, an important issue that is neglected in the literature on global and transnational democracy; and (3) it brings to light the central role of representative practices in the formation, maintenance and political agency of these publics. By connecting transnational democracy with processes of representative claim-making, pragmatic cosmopolitanism brings actors and agency back into conceptions of the public sphere by focusing attention on who is making claims and for what purpose.

Of course, the ethics of pragmatic cosmopolitanism is unlikely to satisfy those who want a more definitive blueprint for constructing global or transnational democracy. One might argue that pragmatic cosmopolitanism does not help us to make *categorical* statements about what constituencies are to be privileged, what specific social activities ought to be democratised, or the concrete institutional forms of critical publics. But that is precisely my point: pragmatic cosmopolitanism as a philosophically grounded approach to transnational democracy does not provide a fixed and universal rule book that must be mechanically applied to the world. In contrast, it provides a method for engaging in problematic situations (in this case democratic deficits), which involves an analysis of the conditions required for democratic reconstruction and the advocacy of particular ideals that can be used as critical tools in ameliorating these situations. To be sure, moral life does not exist in a power vacuum and we are sometimes faced with tragic moral choices that defy our demands for neat solutions. But to recognise our embeddedness in power relations and the complexity of moral life is not a good reason to abandon a commitment to critical inquiry that holds out the promise of improving the quality of present experience.

Table 11.1 Approaches to global and transnational democracy

	Liberal Cosmopolitanism (Held)	Deliberative Democracy (Dryzek)	Pragmatic Cosmopolitanism
Constituency	What should serve as the *primary* basis for delineating political constituencies?	Legal jurisdictions constituted by all those *significantly* affected	Discursive constituencies of all-affected	Problem-solving communities
Democratic Scope	What range of actions or institutions should be regulated by democratic processes?	Actions that violate individual autonomy	Existing transnational discourses	No *a priori* limits, but assumes a publicly recognised problem
Social Prerequisites	What social prerequisites need to be cultivated for democracy beyond the nation-state?	Cosmopolitan citizenship; resource redistribution	Informed and active citizens; *transnational* communication	Inter alia, leadership that fosters a consciousness of shared responsibility and cooperation
Practical Institutionalisation	How should global or transnational democracy be practically instituted?	Multi-level formal representative institutions; subsidiarity	Decentralised *networks* of civil society acting across state boundaries	Transnational institutions of critical inquiry *representing* all affected

Ultimately, then, we must recognise that democratic reconstruction involves political struggle. In this regard, the central insight of pragmatic cosmopolitanism is that these struggles involve harnessing the moral resources of democratic ideals in response to specific problems, and they require leadership to help generate the self-awareness and political agency of transnational publics. I demonstrated the importance of this political leadership in the current climate change negotiations and the campaign to ban landmines. What these reflections suggest is that advances in democratising global governance will likely be more piecemeal and issue-focused than many advocates of global democracy would like. Advances will likely come as a result of collective action focused on particular transnational problems, rather than through a movement advancing a particular model of democracy. They will likely involve coalitions of states, international organisations, NGOs, prominent individuals, professional and amateur activists, and (dare I say it) public intellectuals and social scientists. In emphasising the contextual possibilities for democratic reconstruction along these lines, pragmatic cosmopolitanism eschews the state-centrism of realist democrats and avoids the comprehensive prescriptions of a fixed model of global democracy.

Notes

1 Sidney Tarrow (2005: 25) defines internationalisation in terms of three interrelated trends: (1) 'An increasing horizontal density of relations across states, governmental officials and nonstate actors'; (2) 'Increasing vertical links among the subnational, national and international levels'; and (3) 'An enhanced formal and informal structure that invites transnational activism and facilitates the formation of networks of non-state, state, and international actors.'

2 There are, of course, other approaches that envisage democracy beyond nation-states, but the liberal cosmopolitan and deliberative approaches have dominated the normative literature in recent times. For an examination of some other approaches see McGrew (2002). The literature also features prominent contributions by those who are sceptical of global or transnational democracy. They tend to dispute: (1) the *empirical* accounts of globalisation that underpin global and transnational perspectives; (2) the *ontological* accounts of political community that envisage democracy outside the confines of thick national communities; and (3) the *normative* accounts of global democratisation that advance particular ethical principles as appropriate foundations of a new global order that at least partially transcends the modern state system. These are serious objections that must be addressed by cosmopolitan-minded democrats, but in this chapter I am primarily concerned with the arguments of the main advocates of global or transnational democracy and therefore do not address these objections in a systematic way.

3 This is certainly not the first attempt to use the work of John Dewey to develop an approach to global or transnational democracy. In recent times, Molly Cochran (2002) has explicitly articulated how Deweyan ideas provide ethical insights that can be harnessed to the project of transnational democracy. Hauke Brunkhorst (2002) has used Dewey's conception of a public to think about globalising democracy without a state. By focusing on leadership and representation in the framework of problems I outline below, this article significantly extends and deepens this work by offering a comprehensive theoretical framework that directly addresses the conditions for developing transnational democratic publics.

4 Dewey (1991: 147) writes: 'We are not concerned therefore to set forth counsels as to advisable improvements in the political forms of democracy ... The problem lies deeper; it is in the first instance an intellectual problem: the search for conditions under which the Great Society may become the Great Community. When these conditions are brought into being they will make their own forms. Until they come about, it is somewhat futile to consider what political machinery will suit them.'

5 According to Dewey (1991: 158), an 'omnicompetent individual' is someone who is 'competent to frame policies, to judge their results; competent to know in all situations demanding political action what is for his own good, and competent to enforce his idea of the good and the will to effect it against contrary forces'.

6 The most influential exponent is David Held (1995). For a survey of the ways in which the all-affected principle has been used to think about democracy in the context of globalisation see Agné (2006).

7 For example, see Gould (2006); Saward (2000); and Whelan (1983).

8 For a more comprehensive analysis of the concept of a 'representative claim' and its field of variations and effects, see Saward (2006).

9 Robert Goodin (2000) provides an assessment of four practical proposals that seek to adapt the ideals of deliberation to large-scale mass societies.

10 For another example of a context-sensitive approach to global democratisation see Patomäki and Teivainen (2004).

11 James Bohman (1999) uses the example of AIDS activism to propose that citizens can engage in public deliberation about the norms of cooperation between experts and lay principals.

12 The distinction between 'weak' and 'strong' publics was originally made and developed by Nancy Fraser (1992).

13 Robyn Eckersley (2007) writes about the 'channelling up' and 'channelling down' processes of transnational public spheres and provides another environmental example in her analysis of the tensions between environmental and trade regimes.

12 Conclusion: interrogating the dilemmas of democracy

Liberalism, cosmopolitanism and internationalism

James Bohman

In the last decade, liberal internationalism has undergone a revival, in the guise of democracy promotion abroad with the aspirations toward a new 'democratic peace', culminating in an expanding world organization of democracies. It is easy to think that this strand represents the continuation of Wilson's call to 'make the world safe for democracy'. One might think of other avowedly liberal forms of 'cosmopolitan' or 'transnational' democracy as continuation of this same project. Yet, even though they speak of liberal democracy or liberal rights, most of these forms of liberalism reject democracy promotion by force and other central ideas including the idea of the democratic peace as the means to achieving a new order. Liberal internationalism in the form of democracy promotion is hardly cosmopolitan in the sense of advocating for some overarching world organization that is a republic of republics. A liberal internationalism, if it exists, would see Wilson's adage as demanding a basic transformation of the political order. As Daniel Deudney puts it, the essential meaning of Wilson's call, as it resonates today, is to permit non-hierarchical polities to emerge and survive 'through the transformation of system level anarchy and unit level hierarchy' (2007: 186). Transnational liberalism is infused with a republican and cosmopolitan requirement of a just democratic order aiming at non-domination. This republican cosmopolitanism, as I have put it, is not the only transformation of liberal internationalism.

For theorists such as David Held and Jürgen Habermas, the changes brought about by global interdependence lead to a very different and more political institutional order, including a rich array of international institutions, new forms of constitutional and federal states and substate forms of organization. While many see new possibilities for democratic self-rule beyond the more limited scope of liberal internationalism, others see democracy functioning as a new form of exclusionary liberalism that hardly resolves the inherent tensions of its liberal internationalist predecessors. Liberal internationalism is the spectre haunting contemporary theories of global democracy. This lens is implicit in the contributions to this volume, often distorting the genuine differences in understanding the role of democracy in liberal international, contemporary cosmopolitan and transnational conceptions of democracy. In fact, contemporary theories of global democracy have a more fraught relationship to liberal internationalism, even if Held's position more closely resembles liberal internationalism than do most other theories. Inclusion on these views is defined in terms of a variety of ways in which citizens can gain access to influence over particular decisions that affect them. My goal in these remarks is to show that the contemporary landscape of theories of democracy is much more complex and variegated, the acknowledgement of which is required for genuinely interrogating democracy today. In this way I agree with Daniel Bray that for now 'democratising global governance will likely be more piecemeal and issue-focused', and thus does not necessarily require advancing a particular model of democracy. Nonetheless, the debates have gone far enough that such efforts should be informed by alternative conceptions of democracy beyond the state.

With this in mind, I will proceed in three steps. In the first section, I will provide a larger picture of the alternatives among contemporary cosmopolitan approaches, pointing out how they already seek institutional solutions to the problems so well diagnosed in Ian Clark's chapter. Similar issues are raised by Hobson's historical arguments against liberal cosmopolitanism. With some exceptions (Held and Bray in particular), this volume captures very little of the diversity of such approaches, all of which are too often cast as 'liberal' in some ahistorical sense. In the second section, I turn to historical and empirical objections to cosmopolitan theories of democracy, which are here primarily thought to simply reproduce liberal democracy. In most cases, these are historical claims about the presence or absence of particular conditions that are either required for robust democratic citizenship (Onuf and Onuf, Halperin) or for the lack of effective citizenship because of economic domination (Sassen). While they serve to point out conditions that promoted or inhibited democracy in the past, these claims do not provide either necessary or sufficient conditions for robust citizenship in the current form of politics. Finally, I consider more directly political objections to cosmopolitan projects (Mouffe, Hobson, Aradau and Huysmans). Their arguments propose alternative understandings, alternative practices and alternative subjects of democracy. While they develop alternative forms and possibilities, they seem to sacrifice the core of democracy, the capacity for self-rule, for conceptions that substitute the penumbra for the core and thus stylize democracy as essentially counter-institutional rather than institutional, a move which begins to undermine the crucial issues of democracy today, such as the question of the relevant constituency. It is no surprise that I agree with Bray when he argues that pragmatism can accomplish such a transformative form of democratic politics. But in order to judge among various, hypothetical transformations of existing practices, various tests of adequacy and feasibility need to be developed, such as increased capacity to solve deep problems like climate change that cut across local, transnational and global levels. Such forward-looking thinking is often absent in these contributions, with little basis for developing alternatives. While different theoretical proposals are mentioned and criticized, no systematic account of the various alternatives is provided. Before turning to the central issues around which these contributions revolve, I want to develop the main arguments of the three most significant proposals that aim at transforming democracy in the global era and then offer an alternative.

Cosmopolitanism and democracy: some theoretical alternatives

In this section, I consider the main theories of cosmopolitan and transnational democracy beyond the nation state. Each of these three positions represents a plausible account of the sort of institutional mechanisms that could successfully convert the outcomes of democratic political processes into a framework of appropriate political power. While opposed substantively to each other, each of these theories fails for complementary reasons. An alternative account can be developed that incorporates the strengths of each while overcoming their fundamental weaknesses. Starting with David Held's seminal contributions, we shall see that each theory makes various moral, social and institutional assumptions: moral assumptions to the extent that they are concerned with individuals and their life opportunities; social assumptions to the extent that each makes associations and institutions central, and, finally, political assumptions to the extent that they focus on specifically legal and political institutions that are necessary for some particular conception of democracy.

David Held's work on cosmopolitan democracy provides a more complete account than the other two minimalist democratic positions – those of Habermas and Dryzek – that are explained below. It is also more closely tied to an empirical examination of the impacts of globalization than Habermas's conceptual claims, and thus does not so easily rely upon the metaphysical assumptions of a type of social contract theory. Not only does Held show how international society is already thickly institutionalized well beyond the systems of negotiation that Habermas makes central, he further recognizes that 'individuals increasingly have complex and multilayered identities, corresponding to the globalization of economic forces and the reconfiguration of political power' (Held 2002: 95). Such potentially overlapping identities are the basis for participation in global civil society, in non-governmental organizations (NGOs) and in other transnational civil associations, movements and agencies that create opportunities for political participation at the global level. The chief advantages of Held's approach over the other two approaches are thus threefold: an emphasis on a variety of institutions; a multiplicity of levels and sites for common democratic activity; and a focus on the need for organized political actors in international civil society to play an important role in a system of global democracy. For all these advantages, the self-legislating *demos* reappears in Held's explicitly Lockean insistence that 'the artificial person at the center of the modern state must be reconceived in terms of cosmopolitan public law' (1995: 234).

When does this artificial person become a *demos* with supreme power? In Held's view, this political subject becomes more abstract. It is not manifested in individual legislative acts, but in making the global political framework itself the subject of the popular will and consent. Once legitimated, this political subject emerges within a 'common structure for political action' (1995: 231) that enables individuals and groups to pursue their individual and collective projects. The framework itself functions as a would-be sovereign rather than a distributed process of will formation, since sovereignty is now 'an attribute of democratic public law'. In order to reconstitute the community as sovereign, Held argues that particular *demoi* must submit to the will of the global *demos*: 'cosmopolitan law demands the subordination of regional, national and local sovereignties to an overarching legal framework'. Held argues that such subordination is required so that an authoritative global *demos* can emerge (1995: 154; also, 236).

This overarching legal framework raises a potential democratic dilemma for such a global *demos*. In order to be *overarching*, the framework must instantiate a hierarchy of authority. In order to be *democratic*, the common framework will have to pass through the collective will and reason of its citizens, thereby recreating at the global level the contractual moment of a determinate 'people' granting each other their mutual rights. In willing the general framework, the exact character of the rights and obligations that the common structure of political action necessarily entails cannot be fully determined. At the same time, however, in order to be *enforceable*, these rights and duties must be specified in some way by an authoritative institution possessing the competence to do so, and thus it must act both legislatively and judicially. The dilemma can be put this way: if it acts judicially, it seems undemocratic; yet, if it acts legislatively, it has no special democratic status over other legitimately constituted legislative wills.

Held's demand for democratic control over 'the overarching general legal framework' creates a fundamental continuity between democracy within and beyond the nation state. But it does so at a high price. First, it makes second-order questions about the framework somehow different than first-order ones, matters to be settled impartially that somehow rise above the fray of everyday democratic conflicts. Higher-level international politics are thus adjudicative rather than deliberative. This introduces a fundamental disanalogy with other cases of democratic self-determination: no such separation exists in a constitutional democracy that institutionalizes reflexivity by its openness to revision and amendment. At best, this legal framework recreates the weakness of the state within a dispersed international society, centring rather than decentring and dispersing democratic authority. Even if such a body were to exist, and even if it were somehow adequately representative, its judgements would always be made in terms of the particular modes of institutionalized representation that abstract from the relations and networks that make up international society. Such a dispersed and diverse polity requires a much more differentiated democratic structure, insofar as it cannot exercise the power of the *demos* without being a potential dominator. Although Held more recently in *Global Covenant* (2004) emphasizes multi-level and polycentric governance as necessary in the short and medium term much more than global parliamentary institutions, he still employs the same conception of cosmopolitan self-legislation as fundamental to a long-term global democratic order. In a word, in a period when even democracy in the state is disaggregated and decentred, the cosmopolitan conception of democracy seems to be insufficiently transformative, and its standard democratic institutions leave the problems of legitimacy unresolved.

The second conception is associated with the work of Habermas and is more strongly democratic, to the extent that it is guided by a particular ideal of a self-determining people who govern themselves by acts of legislation. Democracy on the nation state model connects three central ideas: that the proper political community is a bounded one; that it possesses ultimate political authority; and that this authority enables political autonomy, so that the members of the *demos* may 'choose freely the conditions of their own association' (Held 1995: 145). The normative core of this conception of democracy is the conception of freedom articulated in the third condition: that the subject of the constraints of law is free precisely in being the author of the laws. Far from being an avowed liberal, Habermas argues for 'decentring' democracy under the conditions of pluralism and complexity. If this applies to the modern state, then it would seem that cosmopolitan democracy would take this trend even further. Yet, when discussing 'postnational' legitimacy, Habermas clearly makes self-determination by a singular *demos* the fundamental normative core of the democratic ideal.

In both *The Postnational Constellation* and more recent essays on the EU, Habermas seeks to accommodate wider institutional pluralism (2001: 113–93). Still, he cannot have it both ways. When considering various disaggregated and distributed forms of transnational political order, he describes them in non-democratic terms, as a 'negotiating system' governed by fair bargaining.[1] This is because he clearly and indeed surprisingly accepts that self-determination through legislation is the deciding criterion of democracy, leaving negotiation among democracies as the fundamental form of political activity at the transnational level. Even given that this *demos* is at best a civic one, he nonetheless links the possibility of a 'postnational democracy' to a shared and therefore particular political identity, without which, he contends, we are left with mere 'moral' rather than 'civic' solidarity. According to Habermas, even if such a political community is based on the universal principles of a democratic constitution, 'it still forms a collective identity, in the sense that it interprets and realizes these principles in light of its history and in the context of its own particular form of life' (2001: 107). Without a common ethical basis, institutions beyond the state must look to a 'less demanding basis for legitimacy in the organizational forms of an international negotiation system', the deliberative processes of which will be accessible to various publics and to organizations in international civil society (2001: 109).

More recently, he argues that regulatory political institutions at the global level could only be effective if they take on features of governance without government, even if human rights as juridical statuses must be constitutionalized in the international system (Habermas 2006: 135–9). This less demanding standard of legitimacy does not include a sufficient capacity to deliberate about the terms governing the political authority of the negotiation system itself. This position is transnational, but ultimately non-democratic, primarily because it restricts its robust deliberative democracy to the level of the nation state. The stronger criteria for democracy are not applied outside the nation state, where governance is only indirectly democratic and left to negotiations and policy networks. Furthermore, the commitment to human rights as legal statuses pushes him in the direction of David Held's fundamentally legal form of political cosmopolitanism.

The third position can be called 'transnational' rather than cosmopolitan, precisely because it rejects the traditional state model in favour of a 'bottom-up' strategy that promotes a robust transnational civil society as the non-juridical basis for an alternative to the subordination of citizens to a common framework of public law. This account rejects the analogy to democracy in the nation state *tout court*, seeing its development as one of an ever-declining democracy rather than a threshold to be met by international institutions. According to John Dryzek, its leading proponent, 'there are imperatives that all states must meet' that are located in the core areas of its functioning, including economic growth, social control and legitimation. These imperatives impose 'structural limitations' on the state's public orientation in matters of policy (Dryzek 2000: 93). Among these are the structural limitations of capital on redistributive policies, now exacerbated by the mobility of capital in globalization. In the international arena, Dryzek's approach is further supported by the increasing importance of NGOs and the emergence of transnational public spheres, consisting primarily of informal networks of association and communication.[2] It is also supported by the emergence of various international 'regimes', that is, agreements about the rules and decision-making procedures that regulate specific activities or domains, including commercial whaling, the rights of children, nuclear accidents, and so on.

As with Held's insistence on an 'overarching framework', this shift to informal networks and weak publics also comes at a high price for democracy. The complementary weakness to Held's juridical model derives from the fact that on Dryzek's account transnational democracy can only be 'contestatory'. Dryzek thus ends up with a kind of institutional minimalism that also elides the dimension of active and empowered citizenship. This is most evident in the following sort of claim: 'Most of the government that does exist (in the form of organizations such as the UN, WTO or the EU) is not at all democratic, which suggests that transnational democrats might usefully focus their efforts on governance' in which civil society already has a large contestatory and discursive role (Dryzek 2000: 133). But why should we call this mixture of formal and informal institutions 'democratic' even in some minimal sense? What is the alternative means by which those who suffer injustice in the current system can convert their claims into effective political power? Lacking any clear account of how the powerless are able to entrench their claims institutionally, contestation is not the proper activity that the dominated require. The same is true of Held's more maximalist account, since the kind of institutional framework that he develops, while differentiated and multi-levelled does not address the issue of the appropriate active powers of citizenship sufficient for democratization in the international sphere. The minimum here must be sufficient to contain within it not only the constitutive features of democratic citizenship, but also the necessary conditions for non-domination.

These criticisms of the range of possible theories of democracy beyond the state suggest a fourth, more adequate alternative: it must be institutional, political, democratic and transnational. The first two features are necessary for the theory to be of the appropriate type, minimal or not. The first question is then: should these institutions be cosmopolitan or transnational in scope? Cosmopolitan democracy does not sufficiently transform current international practice, precisely because its top-down account of fundamentally legal global institutions requires a new global *demos*, not a democracy of *demoi*. In this respect, transnational democracy is the preferred alternative. At the same time, Dryzek's bottom-up version does not provide any basis for an institutional elaboration of the context of transnational citizenship. A normatively richer alternative is to reject both bottom-up and top-down approaches in favour of an approach that emphasizes vigorous interactions between publics and institutions as the ongoing source of democratic change and institutional innovation. Here deliberation replaces contestation as the proper democratizing activity. An adequate theory must in this respect be more like Held's cosmopolitanism, with its well-articulated multi-levelled institutional structure. While I defend a different way of developing this basic sort of institutional structure, it is hard to see how any conception of transnational democracy can avoid using its general structural features. The best proposals for a distinctively multi-level and transnational democracy preserve the best features of these other conceptions, while overcoming their fundamental weaknesses.

Despite a pervasive scepticism about the scope of democracy that runs across many of the contributions to this book, I will consider the arguments made in the various chapters in order to further the construction of an achievable form of multi-level and transnational democracy. This procedure will include contributions that are critical of the very idea of cosmopolitan or transnational democracy, since these criticisms may help in interrogating the possibilities of a viable conception of democracy beyond the state. Of course, the different contributions are concerned with differing conceptions and aspects of democracy in world politics. There will also be methodological issues concerning just how we can interrogate the possibilities for a transformed conception of democracy. The contributions to this volume are very often sceptical of claims about democracy beyond the state. Yet, while these arguments often capture cogent criticisms of some particular conception of postnational democracy, they do not necessarily apply to all such conceptions. In fact, these criticisms generally tend to focus on 'liberalism' or particular versions of transnational or cosmopolitan democracy. With some exceptions (such as Clark and Onuf and Onuf), the failure to address the variety of postnational forms of democracy often leads to criticisms that leave the conception of democracy unclear and thus very often miss as many targets as they hit.

Democracy and international society

Even if theorists recognize that there is a variety of approaches to extending democracy beyond the state, an important issue concerns what it is that the new forms of democracy are supposed to be replacing. As Clark points out, democracy has not been the central concern of most of the international institutions for most of the twentieth century; it is not even mentioned in the charters of the League of Nations and the UN. The results of introducing democracy could bring 'acute tensions' in 'international society', manifesting 'a form of exclusion even when international society may have a preference for inclusion' (Clark, this volume). On the one hand, once the inclusive character of the international society norm of democracy becomes more widespread and potentially universal, it could be seen as the result of 'normative deepening and integration'. But in doing so, such a norm could undermine the pluralism that is the hallmark of international society and the basis of its attempt to create collective security among all states. Yet, as important as the ideal of an inclusive international society has been, the practice of these institutions has hardly followed this norm, as when it favours powerful states in decision-making bodies such as the Security Council. The net result of a fully inclusive international society within institutional arrangements might mean a net loss in problem-solving capabilities. At the same time, the creation of a core of democratic states in which democracy is more fully realized and a periphery of states whose democracies are deficient in some way undermines the ideal of inclusiveness. We might call this the 'internationalist dilemma' of Wilsonian international democracy as a basis for a peaceful and inclusive international society. An inclusive international society is fundamentally an informal requirement and permits actors to make claims directly on each other on the basis of widely shared and informal norms. Civil society is thus a central part of international society. It is, however, easy to mistake such recognition with the legal recognition of a capacity to make binding claims.

International society is but one of many competing conceptions of the basis for a peaceful world order. Kant proposed a distinctly cosmopolitan solution: the reorganization of political power in an international system organized through the constraints of cosmopolitan law. In one form or another, this realistic utopia of peace has informed the formation of the international system, culminating in the emergence of international law and a zone of peaceful relations among democracies since 1945. This conception does not see the emergence of democratic or republican states as sufficient for peace, and certainly war is not a plausible means to achieve it. Indeed, at this juncture the instrumental use of democracy as a cause of preventive war has served to undermine the democratic peace and even the democratic quality of the states that engage in such wars. In this situation a different end is required: the formation of institutions by which democratic states and the international system may become more democratic in a mutually reinforcing way.

The idea that democracy may be a just cause for war starts with some plausible premises. The first is that democracy has now become a genuinely universal value, capable of being realized anywhere in the world. As many of the chapters in this book point out, this claim usually focuses on a single, liberal form of democracy. While certainly plausible, this premise ignores the vast social scientific literature concerning the background conditions for establishing democracy, which led many previous discussions of 'development' to argue that democracy should be a long-term rather than a short-term goal. If overthrowing a tyrannous and non-democratic government could alone create democracy, then there seems to be no moral objection to doing so. Second, democratic states have an interest in making this come about: once they are democracies, these states no longer belong to the list of potential enemies. Finally, promoting democracy by force is also made possible by the overwhelming hegemonic power of the United States, as an effective agent for such change. As an additional justification of this policy of war on non-democracies as a means to promote security is the obvious benefit that such an outcome would bring to the citizens of new democracies. Daniele Archibugi has called this idea of the democratic peace 'universal democracy' (as opposed to a cosmopolitan democracy), in which the goal is for 'the whole world to become democratic', as Larry Diamond puts it.[3]

Clark's discussion of this movement away from sovereignty-based pluralism toward a normative style of international society shows the perils of exclusion for international society, making it 'more limited and certainly unequal' (this volume: 39). Furthermore, once the hierarchy becomes translated into a distinction between those inside the zone of democratic peace and those still in anarchy outside it, then the zone of peace will cease to expand across this frontier without the use of force. One of the great innovations of eighteenth-century republican theories of security was 'to refer to Europe as a whole as a republic' and to see it as 'a complex system for restraining both anarchy and hierarchy'.[4] The problem here is not so much with adopting normative criteria of membership, but with the very idea of a non-tyrannical and benevolent hierarchy, whether domestic or international, which is unrealistically utopian, especially as we move from relatively independent states to a globally interconnected world. In this sense, there is no obvious inherent tension between the universal inclusion of international society and the emergence of this kind of multi-level political order that is common to the political proposals of Held or Habermas. Such a political order would in the end provide a genuine political mechanism of inclusion and security only if it would promote rather than reduce the pluralism of international society. It is true that theorists like Held do not appeal to international society as a source of norms, and this makes his top-heavy juridical conception less attractive to the less powerful. Rather than something threatened by democratization, a robust international society would be more likely to flourish in a democratic multi-level order than it would within a democracy confined to a single state.

To make this point another way, consider a somewhat idealized picture of the European Union. The EU polity is not understood in terms of the self-governance of citizens as members of a single *demos*, but rather in terms of multiple and overlapping *demoi*; the regime is then not such that all must participate in the same set of institutions or suffer the consequences of a uniform policy. As a unit of other units, it is difficult to square the nature of the Europolity with democracy as it is standardly conceived, except by seeing all member states as collectively constituting the *demos* of a common regime, which is then split into various levels of increasing scale. More than simply adding a new layer of authority, the EU provides a way to redefine the interactive relationships among the local, the national and the supranational levels of scale. If this reconstruction of the process of European political integration is correct, it also follows that a more unitary democratic structure would be not be the best way to realize democracy in a multi-level polity. While transnational conceptions of democracy may be motivated by issues of security and violence, they need not embrace the idea of a Concert of Democracies or think that the democratic peace hypothesis ought to guide democratic practices. It leaves out the important role of informal norms that emerge in civil society in a variety of areas, such as in Northern Ireland where cross-cutting groups that were both local and international helped to sustain and support the eventually successful peace process. At the same time, pluralism runs up against its limits when international society faces issues such as climate change in the face of state inaction. Political integration seems unavoidable, so that the issue should be how to accomplish it in as democratic a way as possible.

Onuf and Onuf (this volume) focus some of their criticism on the naiveté of 'liberal' democratic peace theorists and argue that many have assumed that democracy is a means to social peace. In fact, following Tocqueville, they argue that the system of states that emerged from the transition to democratic states 'is war prone or indeed failing by virtue of its irrelevance to productive forces in the world economy, that the modern world has reached its limits and may indeed have already over reached itself' (this volume: 18). Neither IR theory nor liberal institutionalism has helped much in understanding where we have come. Their solution is to appeal to Tocqueville, for whom democracy did not 'carry the normative baggage that liberal institutionalists now impute to it as they imagine an emergent condition, with equality linked to rights, the rule of law and limited government'. More important than its constitutional government, 'the character of the people and not its constitutional contrivances alone explains the extraordinary coexistence and reciprocal reinforcement of equality and liberty in America' (this volume: 26). Rather than seeing democracy as ameliorative, Tocqueville, they claim, foresaw the emergence of national democratic regimes and a geopolitics of 'great nations' contending for domination. The new ameliorists similarly fail to see the state of the world made worse by naive cosmopolitan aspirations that falsely idealize the revolutionary past and do not take into account the violence inherent in democratic politics.

Onuf and Onuf would of course be correct to say that all the broadly cosmopolitan and transnational thinkers that I discussed in this and the last section attempt to rekindle the embers of the period of the democratic revolutions or endorse a form of liberal utopianism. Following Daniel Deudney, the history of the United States (or of Europe after the Second World War) could be told quite differently. Indeed, their analysis of US federalism 'blurring the line between the domestic and the international' (and for this reason seeming to be 'less than modern') could be told quite differently, as more than modern; the same is true for the structural institutional solutions to the problem of size that made it possible for the US to become a continental state that does not easily conform to the one-sided (Deudney 2007: 173), Toquevillian picture of the history of American democracy offered here. I do not have the space to develop the alternative account, but the emergence of aggressive democracies in the nineteenth and twentieth centuries can only first come into view as problematic for democracy in light of the republican and liberal forms cosmopolitan tradition that they simply dismiss. This tradition is not peripheral to the practices of the American republic, nor is it somehow benighted and impractical, but is at the core of the American republican tradition from Madison to Wilson to Roosevelt. Realizing shared liberty in a 'republic of republics' proved to be a difficult task and required nothing short of a new political order. Indeed, the American founders referred to a *novus ordo saeclorum*, a new order from the ages that was neither like early republican city state nor the 'bloated' states of Europe. I can only briefly sketch an alternative and cosmopolitan picture of the American republic.

Such a Union of States would be possible only if each were to become a republic, and if the Union itself overcame anarchy and developed into 'an alternative to the European Westphalian system rather than an oddly constituted state within it' (Deudney 2007: 362). Madison, Hamilton and others thought of themselves in a long line of republican thinkers whose innovations would overcome the limitations of the Roman Republic and other classical models while also avoiding the problem of the patterns of violence and conflict that had become regularized in the European system of states. As articulated by 'Publius' (the pen name for Madison, Hamilton and Jay) in the *Federalist Papers*, the American republic offered a solution to the problems of the Westphalian system of hierarchical states in which security can only be attained by sacrificing liberty. For the international relations theorist Daniel Deudney, the founding of the United States also decisively broke intellectually with the impasses of previous republics and 'was nothing less than the climax of early modern republican security theory' (2007: 161).

Accordingly, the republic of republics should not be thought of as a unitary entity, as Kant does, but as divided and distributed within a multi-level system. In a transnational federation of this sort, popular sovereignty could be distributed across many different processes and locations, some running in parallel as might be the case when many different bodies deliberate about the same problem. In fact, this very problem of the sovereignty of distinct peoples and states is already operating at various levels of organization and interdependence and is thus the very problem that motivates Madison's conception of a plural or 'compound republic', even as sovereignty and all authority rests with the people. In the next section, I argue that the forms of republicanism developed from the anti-imperial tradition aim at securing shared liberty for all and does so by reformulating classical modern republicanism as a kind of government without the state, even if its authority rests only in the people whose sovereignty is distributed throughout and across all of the institutions of the Union of republics. The enduring importance of these ideas can be found in a variety of forms of political cosmopolitanism, including liberal internationalism as a continuation of this republican tradition, in terms of which many of the Toquevillian arguments seem to tell a very incomplete story about the role of plural republics and liberal internationalism in shaping institutions that avoid the twin evils of anarchy and despotism. On the republican reading that I have sketched here, these developments show the US had failed to become a republic and instead became the very hierarchical European state it had tried to avoid.

Against liberalism

However different the various conceptions of global democracy on offer may be, the primary opponent of many of them is 'liberal democracy', some version of the more or less standard picture of democracy as consisting of a constitutional state based on elections with entrenched rights for citizens. Despite their aware-ness of different models of democracy beyond the state, Aradau and Huysmans insist that communicative and cosmopolitan models of 'global and regional democracy should be understood in terms of the question of whether or not and how it is possible to scale up national institutions' (this volume: 153). Similarly, for Mouffe, the only way out of our current predicament is by 'abandoning the claim that democratization should consist in the global implementation of the Western liberal democratic model', (this volume: 125) especially given the fact that in the development of the particular Western conception of human rights 'the Judeo-Christian tradition played a central role'. While it may be true, as Mouffe notes, that this particular model of democracy is not the only legitimate way of organizing human affairs, to argue that the origin of such a conception exhausts its validity risks committing the genetic fallacy. Indeed, liberal rights such as freedom of conscience have surpassed their religious and Western origins. Freedom of religion has only been recognized by the Catholic Church as recently as the twentieth century. Nor is it true, as Aradau and Huysmans claim, that cosmopolitan and communicative approaches to democracy respond to mobility and migration 'as socio-economic flows which create a need for scaling up democratic structures of accountability or discursive legitimation' (this volume: 153). It seems very plausible that democracy needs to be thought of 'in terms of relations of mobility themselves'. As a consequence, building new insti-tutional structure should instead be seen as essential to making novel democratic responses to mobility possible, where the rights of non-citizens are recognized and enforced. If mobility is to be thought of as a democratic practice and a chal-lenge to existing democracies, then its democratic effects will surely be institutional.

Similarly, Hobson urges that we go beyond liberalism by recognizing that we have lost sight of the fact that 'for the majority of democracy's past, opinion has generally sided with Disraeli, regarding it as a dangerous and unstable form of rule that inevitably led to anarchy or despotism' (this volume: 66). Liberalism is the main culprit in forgetting the past and constructing a narrative of inevitable progress, so that 'it is a *liberal* vision that largely structures our mental horizons of what democracy is, and can be' (Hobson, this volume: 66). Even as 'the end of history' fad seems to have lost all intellectual respectability, Hobson still sees its basic doctrines as informing the current liberal view of democracy in the present. His alternative offers a radical historization and relativization of democracy as dependent on contingency and accident rather than universal history, the first step of which is to revive 'the much longer tradition of thought which saw it as something deeply problematic, and very distinct from liberalism' (Hobson, this volume: 67). This same distinction is important to non-liberal accounts of democracy, such as republicanism, for whom the modern republic is neither simply liberal nor merely the rule of the many, but rather looks for ways in which popular sovereignty is distributed across institutional locations. There are already important strands of democratic theory that consider the case for democracy without appealing to liberalism. Anti-democratic traditions do not only reject liberalism, but democracy itself, and as such are much less useful in rethinking present practices.

To see this point against the anti-liberals, republican thinkers have long argued against the ways in which liberalism was unable to solve the problem of hierarchy at home and anarchy abroad. Liberalism, republicans argued, did not develop a robust enough conception of popular sovereignty. In republican constitutions the separation of powers and other procedures for voting and representation suggest that popular sovereignty is possible even in the absence of direct democracy or direct popular rule. In a transnational federation of this sort, popular sovereignty could be distributed across many different levels, processes and locations, some running in parallel as might be the case when many different bodies deliberate about the same problem. The freedom that it sought to establish is not liberal freedom from interference, but freedom from domination, that is, being subjected to the arbitrary will of another, including the potentially despotic multitude that exercises domination over non-citizens. Despite its recent revival and extendibility to cosmopolitan forms of government, republican thought is surprisingly absent here, despite its criticism of existing democracy as unable to realize freedom as non-domination.

By reintroducing the important ideal of freedom as non-domination, republicans such as Philip Pettit have altered the political landscape around democracy. For quite some time, cosmopolitanism has been associated with liberalism. While it is widely assumed that liberalism has a nationalist and a republican form, a similar conceptual space for cosmopolitan republicanism is only now being developed, even as many Enlightenment defenders of republicanism were long opponents of empires for their grave injustices, and for undermining political freedom and community at home and abroad. As historians such as Anthony Pagden and Sankar Muthu have shown, a striking feature of eighteenth- and nineteenth-century republican thought is the development of a transnational form of political community as an alternative to colonial empires; this rejection of European colonialism lead to an embrace of a much stronger and egalitarian form of democracy than early modern republicans. Enlightenment republicans saw a clear negative feedback relationship between the expansion of centralized and executive powers through colonialism and robust and active powers of citizenship within the borders of free states. Thus, this critique of the imperial tendencies of states had enormous practical significance for the institutional design of any contemporary republic and the location for the proper exercise of citizenship. Liberal democracy is but one form that emerges from the development of the modern republic.

From Mouffe's anti-universalist and agonistic approach to democracy in a multipolar world, a quite different problem emerges. Instead of a lack of determinacy, Mouffe wants to shape a multipolar world structured around large continental units, the purpose of which is to preserve the pluralism from the levelling uniformity cosmopolitan schemes. Cosmopolitanism of any sort is de facto inimical to diversity, so that only if we accept the premise of the parlance of hegemony will we 'realise that to accept a diversity of political forms of organisation will be conducive to peace and stability than the enforcement of a universal model' (this volume: 129). Because of its metaphysical commitment to objectivity, liberal rationalism 'cannot apprehend the process of the construction of political identity', which 'at the same time is the condition of the impossibility of a society from which antagonism would have been eliminated' (this volume: 119). Cosmopolitanism, she argues, negates this irreducible dimension of the political. But in articulating her alternative, the result is surprising: 'envisaging a world of hegemonic blocks requires relinquishing the idea that they need to be parts of an encompassing moral and political unit' (this volume: 122). Instead, they will be parts of particular hegemonic blocs in which reaching consensus is possible, primarily because they are based on shared culture and religion that become the basis of regional interpretations of democracy. Besides assuming the desirability of the absence of pluralism in various hegemonic blocs, Mouffe's proposal seems to reproduce the worst non-cooperative logic of the Cold War period.

It does not seem likely that the political relations across these hegemonic blocs will be peaceable. In fact, various cosmopolitan alternatives seem vastly better and less prone to internal and external violence. This kind of order seems to eliminate any hope for an international society and the creation of norms across the hegemonic regimes. Second, it seems less likely that pluralism will survive under these conditions, to the extent that internal antagonisms would likely be heightened by their religious character. In fact, it gives to religion a greater role than it currently plays in political life in much of the non-Western world. To put it another way, secularity is not somehow balanced by theocracy. It is hard to see how such an account, which promises to create new forms of religious diversity, would flourish under more universal forms of political organization in which freedom of conscience is recognized as a minimum condition. How might this kind of political subject be organized differently? Weiler ambiguously describes the EU as a community in first-personal terms as '*a* people, even if he immediately adds 'a people, if you wish, of others' (Weiler 1999: 268ff.). Thus, the requirements of a differentiated institutional structure hold for the same democratic reasons, so that regardless of the scale of the polity: the major difference is that the EU is 'a polity of others', a polity of *demoi* rather than a fictive religious demos. Most proponents of such forms of democracy now recognize the problems with the multi-level character of feasible forms of postnational democratic rule.

Historical analyses and empirical objections

An interesting feature of the interrogation of democracy through diverse social scientific perspectives is that it should be able to bring historical and empirical questions to bear upon the issues of new forms of democracy outside of the state. For example, Aradau and Huysmans attempt to show the importance of transnational mobility for democracy, where 'practices of mobility are not just flows or networks upon which democratic institutions act but that they are an immanent part of democratic politics', where mobility itself is 'a democratic practice'. Mobility becomes 'entwined with democracy' through a 'double inscription of equality via rights and mass mobilization' (Aradau and Huysmans, this volume: 154). Sassen argues that cosmopolitan and transnational democracy have forgotten about the fundamental deep structural inequality of workers in all existing forms of democracy, an inequality that has been a pervasive part of capitalism for centuries, including the forms of capitalism instituted in liberal democratic regimes. Brief periods of gain by workers in the twentieth century have become undone, so that we now should ask the question whether these 'foundational inequalities were indeed systemic, wired into the functioning of capitalism itself. One open question is whether they are also wired into the functioning of liberal democracy' (Sassen, this volume: 82) (once again). Yet, Halperin provides contrary evidence, that after 1914 'labour became unified through its mobilization, not for industry but for war, and this was decisive to the achievement of democracy' (Halperin, this volume: 47). Workers thus do not seem to be 'foundationally unequal subject[s]', but have made significant gains democratically by means of mass armies. Each of these gives us very different accounts of possible democratic futures. Whereas Halperin argues in republican fashion for electoral enfranchisement and oppositional rights, Sassen wants to extend rights to various kinds of collective actors. How could these rights be realized in such a way as to go beyond current democratic practices?

With regard to Aradau and Huysmans, a central issue turns on whether or not they have shown that mobility is a *democratic* practice, or a social phenomenon that is both made possible by democracy and that potentially transforms it. By analogy to money's capacity to realize 'egalitarian ideals and relations to the stranger at the heart of society' (this volume: 155), Aradau and Huysmans develop an account of the effects of mobility, 'in which it become[s] political through claims to abstract rights and mass or "mob" mobilisation' (this volume: 155). The analogy has a grain of truth, but seems to fail to capture the realities of either labour in capitalism or mass migration. Despite its abstraction, money does not abstract from concrete social relations sufficiently to challenge their domination. In the case of transnational mobilities, the abstraction is toward universal rights, where mobile people do 'disrupt structures of power by claiming rights upon private and public authorities' (this volume: 157). Yet, at the same time the reality of such people's lives is that they have the status of 'illegal persons' and without documentation are unable to make claims effectively or to obtain access to many government services and legal protections. By having no political statuses they are subject to domination and abuse by private individuals and public authority. In order to see mobility as an inherently democratic practice, it would be necessary to show the way in which mobile people still lack the capacity to make claims; indeed, basic norms of the rule of law are fundamentally violated when illegality is pervasive in a democratic society.[5] In this case, there are resources in the liberal constitutional tradition, in which all residents have the status of persons, as seen in the 14th Amendment of the United States Constitution and in the person amendments of the Bill of Rights. As David Weissbrodt warns us, even with an extensive framework in international law protecting the rights of non-citizens, 'there remains a disjuncture between prescribed rights and the realities that non-citizens must face' (2008: 2).

Perhaps it is possible that political subjects emerge that are not just rights-claiming individuals, but also the mob or the multitude that stands outside of social relations. It is hard to see just why the capacity of the masses 'to mobilise numbers into a political force that can disrupt the ruling state of affairs' (Aradau and Huysmans, this volume: 161) ought to be understood as democratic or even as aiming at democracy. It is certainly true that there are limits to the law in its capacity to incorporate rightless persons or to eliminate the structural possibility of domination of citizens over non-citizens. Even if an actor who engages in mobilization takes 'equality as a maxim of action' in some broad sense, that actor's aim is first of all to achieve a particular level of countervailing power. The multitude is outside the law and hence may be in a democracy, but not of democracy. Once they make demands of democracy, their maxim becomes equality, which in turn becomes a general demand for citizenship status. Rather something else is at stake, more akin to Hegel's more basic demand that individuals be treated as persons and be recognized as having the status of persons.

Issues related to the practices of mobility and mobilization also emerge in both Halperin's and Sassen's chapters, and their conclusions are remarkably different. Halperin argues that the mass mobilization of workers for the two world wars 'was decisive to the achievement of democracy' (this volume: 47) ensuring the extensions of the franchise and inclusive participation in the political process. Schumpeter agrees with this assessment, noting that the decisive shift was prepared by the Second World War. But for Sassen, such periods of equality are little more than momentary lapses of 'the foundational inequality built into the making and legitimating of those two subjects' (this volume: 82) that has survived all the various supposed transformations and democratizations. Halperin follows Polanyi and argues that this is not the result of the opening up of a market, but in 'embedding' the economy within a territory. Sasssen supplies impressive evidence in the law of the limited rights of labour, although most of this evidence is prior to the Second World War. The issue between them is this: is there a kind of deep structure of capitalist economies that produces class-specific inequalities? Each looks at different kinds of evidence: Halperin discusses statistics related to the well-being of workers, while Sassen shows the ways in which workers lacked basic legal and economic rights. It seems to me that the real issue now is whether or not the achievements of the world wars are sustainable, particularly when the labour processes are no longer embedded as they were for several decades after the Second World War. The way out of this problem is perhaps a new, non-territorial form of embedding, perhaps presaged by some of the ways in which the European Union protects economic rights at a Continental scale. If the presuppositions and exigencies associated with capitalist globalization always have in fact undermined the achievements of democracy, then the problem may be as much the continued acceptance of an inherited framework of territorially embedded national economies and bounded national citizenship that must be transformed.

Conclusion

To conclude, let me turn to the two chapters by Held and Bray. Except for these two chapters, the others have largely interrogated democracy within states or within the state-oriented international system. While these locations remain a necessary feature of any account of democracy today, they are no longer sufficient. While these institutional forms are not likely to disappear anytime soon, they are being transformed. If so, it is an important task for the social sciences of democracy to investigate the changes that are occurring within democratic states, such as new decision-making bodies and the increased prevalence of practices, such as mass mobility, which challenge democracy quite profoundly. Some of the chapters critically engage with cosmopolitan ideas, although they are usually cast entirely within the framework of criticisms of 'liberal democracy', and are often quite limited by this assumption. David Held was one of the first to point out these limitations and to expand the state conception of democracy. At the same time, his innovative work made it possible for there to be many alternative conceptions, the discussion of which has been going on among political theorists and philosophers for some time. Some of these proposals also reject certain forms of liberal democracy as unsuited to cosmopolitan thinking and take their orientation from republican thinking, giving central place to the ideal of freedom as non-domination.

Contemporary cosmopolitan republicanism ought to be guided by the fundamental principle of popular sovereignty, which has its antecedents in both European and American federalism. Federalists such as Madison and Arendt laid the groundwork for a conception of plural and distributed popular sovereignty that is still applicable to contemporary transnational orders such as the EU. By pooling their sovereignty, such states promote rather than lose their freedom from domination. They avoid the risk of achieving security at the cost of freedom. With the emergence of the EU, for all its flaws, a new version of such a transnational order has been realized, this time with a stronger emphasis on more direct deliberative processes than the federalists would have allowed. With increasing global interdependence, it is time to revive this strand of political thought, with its unique attempt to unite a peaceful transnational order with popular democratic self-rule. In this respect, Dewey stands out among pragmatists for exploring these possibilities of democracy that goes beyond the machinery of the state. While Bray is correct that pragmatists seek to promote democracy as a means to achieve 'the ability of affected people to perceive and act upon' the consequences of social transaction, it is wrong to say that democracy should simply be allowed to 'rise from below' (this volume: 178). Such capacity requires institutions to organize such deliberation and decision making, if citizens are to have opportunities to exercise influence. 'Democracy from below' is not a substitute for institutions that distribute popular sovereignty.

Except for Held, these studies largely ignore issues of new and sometimes novel institutional forms. The difficulties at stake have to do with its current basic structure: that is, as a system of *multi-level government*. Nick Bernard defines multi-level government as 'a system of organizing public power divided into two or more layers of government, where each layer retains autonomous decision-making power vis-à-vis the others' (2003: 3). In such a multi-level structure, there is no sovereignty in the classical sense: multi-level systems require abandoning the idea that there is but one supreme authority over a territory. On the standard view, a political unit is sovereign only if it has such a location from the exercise of 'supreme authority'. But this is precisely what Bernard's definition of multi-level systems denies, since power is instead divided, so that no other unit has final authority over the others; this means that there is no central locus of power and a clear hierarchy of levels (as there would be in a true federation. According to the account of transnational government as a multi-level system, there are now many different sources of law and lawmakers and in which there are many different constitutions rather than one overriding constitution as a whole. We can catch a glimpse of this possibility in Held's chapter, in his discussion of an adequate basic structure that generates the necessary conditions for common democratic action for all those affected. To achieve this, any cosmopolitan order must enact 'a set of procedural principles for political life'. The discussion between Held and Bray marks a fundamental tension within democratic institutions between political authority and popular sovereignty, a tension that remains constitutive of promising forms of multi-level democracy.

Notes

1 For an alternative account that sees such phenomena in terms of political networks, see Slaughter (2004).
2 This is precisely the theme of Dryzek's most recent book, in which he claims that 'deliberative and democratic global politics can most fruitfully be sought in the more informal realm of international public spheres'. See Dryzek (2006: vii). For further discussion of these types of cosmopolitan and transnational democracy, see Bohman (2007).
3 See Archibugi (2007); Diamond (2003b). On the dismal historical evidence for democratization by force, see Cox *et al.* (2000); also Pei and Kasper (2003).
4 On the republican tradition of understanding international insecurity concerned with the dangers of hierarchy, see Deudney (2007: 16; 28–30). Deudney also shows that federalist institutions aim primarily at restricting hierarchy through promoting mixtures of forms of power. On the political cosmopolitanism typical of eighteenth-century Enlightenment republicanism, see Bohman (2008: 190–206).
5 See Bohman (2009).

Bibliography

Abramowitz, M. and Pickering, T. (2008) 'Making Intervention Work', *Foreign Affairs*, 87: 100–8.

Abrams, P. (1963) 'The Failure of Social Reform: 1918–1920', *Past and Present*, 24: 43–64.

Acemoglu, D. and Robinson, J. (2006) *Economic Origins of Dictatorship and Democracy*, Cambridge: Cambridge University Press.

Ackerly, B. (2006) 'Deliberative Democratic Theory for Building Global Civil Society: Designing a Virtual Community of Activists', *Contemporary Political Theory*, 5: 113–41.

Adkins v. Children's Hospital, 261 US 525 (1923).

Agamben, Giorgio (1998) *Homo Sacer: Sovereign Power and Bare Life*, Stanford: Stanford University Press.

Agamben, Giorgio (2005) *State of Exception*, Chicago: University of Chicago Press.

Agné, H. (2006) 'A Dogma of Democratic Theory and Globalization: Why Politics Need not Include Everyone it Affects', *European Journal of International Relations*, 13: 433–58.

Agnew, John (1999) 'Mapping Political Power Beyond State Boundaries: Territory, Identity, and Movement in World Politics', *Millennium: Journal of International Studies*, 28: 499–521.

Albright, M.K. (2003) *Madam Secretary: Madeleine Albright*, London: Macmillan.

Albright, M.K. (2006) *The Mighty and The Almighty: Reflections on Power, God, and World Affairs*, London: Macmillan.

Alessandri, E. (2008) 'World Order Re-founded: The Idea of a Concert of Democracies', *The International Spectator*, 43: 73–90.

All Headline News (AHN) (2008) 'Gorbachev Calls McCain's "League of Democracies" a Mistake', 17 April, www.allheadlinenews.com/articles/7010675456 (accessed 2 July 2008).

Allen, John and Pryke, Michael (1999) 'Money Cultures after Georg Simmel: Mobility, Movement, and Identity', *Environment and Planning D*, 17: 51–68.

Amin, S. (1977) *Unequal Exchange*, New York: Monthly Review.

Anderson, E. (2005) *Dewey's Moral Philosophy*. www.plato.stanford.edu/entries/dewey-moral (accessed 5 October 2007).

Andreski, S. (1968) *Military Organization and Society*, Berkeley: University of California Press.

Ankersmit, F. (2002) *Political Representation*, Stanford: Stanford University Press.

Aradau, Claudia (2008) *Rethinking Trafficking in Women. Politics out of Security*, Basingstoke: Palgrave Macmillan.

Arblaster, A. (1984) *The Rise and Decline of Western Liberalism*, Oxford: Basil Blackwell.

Archer, Robin (1998) *Economic Democracy: The Politics of Feasible Socialism*, Oxford: Oxford University Press.

Archibugi, Daniele (1998) 'Principles of Cosmopolitan Democracy', in D. Archibugi, D. Held and M. Köhler (eds) *Re-imagining Political Community: Studies in Cosmopolitan Democracy*, Cambridge: Polity.

Archibugi, Daniele (2000) 'Cosmopolitical Democracy', *New Left Review*, 2: 137–50.

Archibugi, Daniele (2007), 'Can Democracy be Exported?', *Widener Law Review*, 13(2): 283–94.

Archibugi, Daniele (2008) *The Global Commonwealth of Citizens: Toward Cosmopolitan Democracy*, Princeton: Princeton University Press.

Archibugi, Daniele, Held, David and Köhler, Martin (eds) (1998) *Re-Imagining Political Community: Studies in Cosmopolitan Democracy*, Cambridge: Polity.

Aristotle (edited by S. Everson) (1996) *The Politics and the Constitution of Athens*, Cambridge: Cambridge University Press.

Ashley, Maurice (1961 [1952]) *England in the Seventeenth Century*, London: Penguin Books.

Bairoch, P. (1993) *Economics and World History: Myths and Paradoxes*, London: Harvester.

Baker, Gideon (2002) *Civil Society and Democratic Theory: Alternative Voices*, London: Routledge.

Baker, Gideon and Chandler, David (eds) (2005) *Global Civil Society: Contested Futures*, London: Routledge.

Baker, R.S. (1923) *Woodrow Wilson and World Settlement, Vol. 3*, London: Heinemann.

Baldwin, F.E. (1926) *Sumptuary Legislation and Personal Regulation in England*, Baltimore: Johns Hopkins University Press.

Balibar, Etienne (1997) *La Crainte des Masses. Politique et Philosophie Avant et Après Marx*, Paris: Galilée.

Barratt Brown, M. (1970) *After Imperialism*, London: Merlin Press.

Bartelson, J. (2001) *The Critique of the State*, Cambridge: Cambridge University Press.

Barry, B. (1999) 'International Society From a Cosmopolitan Perspective', in D. Mapel and T. Nardin (eds) *International Society: Diverse Ethical Perspectives*, Princeton: Princeton University Press.

Baudrillard, Jean (1983) *In the Shadow of the Silent Majorities*, New York: Semiotext(e).

Baudrillard, Jean (1987) *Forget Foucault*, New York: Semiotext(e).

Bauer, H. and Brighi, E. (eds) (2009) *Pragmatism in International Relations*, London and New York: Routledge.

Beaud, Michel (1981) *Histoire du capitalisme: 1500–1980*, Paris: Editions du Seuil.

Beck, Ulrich (1998) *Democracy without Enemies*, Cambridge: Polity.

Beetham, David (1999) *Democracy and Human Rights*, Cambridge: Polity.

Bell, D. (2007) *The Idea of Greater Britain: Empire and the Future of World Order, 1860–1900*, Princeton: Princeton University Press.

Bell, D. A. (2007) *The First Total War: Napoleon's Europe and the Birth of Warfare as We Know It*, Boston: Houghton, Mifflin.

Bellah, R.N., Madsen, R., Sullivan, W.M., Swidler, A., Tipton, S.M. (1985) *Habits of the Heart: Individualism and Commitment in American Life*, Berkeley: University of California Press.

Bellamy, A.J. (2002) 'Pragmatic Solidarism and the Dilemmas of Humanitarian Intervention', *Millennium: Journal of International Studies*, 31: 473–97.

Benhabib, S. (2006) *Another Cosmopolitanism*, New York: Oxford University Press.

Benson, L. (1989) *The Working Class in Britain, 1850–1839*, London: Longman.

Bernard, N. (2003) *Multilevel Governance in the European Union*, The Hague: Kluver Law International.

Bigo, Didier (2005) 'Frontier Controls in the European Union: Who Is in Control?', in Didier Bigo and Elspeth Guild (eds) *Controlling Frontiers: Free Movement into and within Europe*, Aldershot: Ashgate.

Bobbio, Norberto (1995) 'Democracy and the International System', in Daniele Archibugi and David Held (eds) *Cosmopolitan Democracy*, Cambridge: Polity.

Bobbio, Norberto (2005) *Liberalism and Democracy*, trans. M. Ryle and K. Soper, London: Verso.

Bobbitt, P. (2002) *The Shield of Achilles: War, Peace and the Course of History*, London: Allen Lane.

Bobbitt, P. (2008) *Terror and Consent: The Wars for the Twenty-First Century*, London: Allen Lane.

Bohman, J. (1999) 'Democracy as Inquiry, Inquiry as Democratic: Pragmatism, Social Science and the Cognitive Division of Labor', *American Journal of Political Science*, 43: 590–607.

Bohman, J. (2007) *Democracy across Borders: From Dêmos to Dêmoi*, Cambridge, MA: MIT Press.

Bohman, J. (2008) 'The Republic of Humanity: The Cosmopolitan Imperative of Democratic Non-domination', in C. Laborde and J. Maynor (eds) *Republicanism and Political Theory*, London: Basil Blackwell, pp. 190–216.

Bohman, J. (2009) 'Living without Freedom: Democracy and the Cosmopolitan Constitution', *Political Theory*, 37: 539–61.

Bohman, J. and Lutz-Bachmann, M. (eds) (1997) *Perpetual Peace: Essays on Kant's Cosmopolitan Ideal*, Cambridge, MA: MIT Press.

Bok, Derek S. (1971) 'Reflections on the Distinctive Character of American Labor Law', *Harvard Law Review*, 84: 1394–1463.

Booth, Ken (2001) 'Ten Flaw of Just Wars', in K. Booth (ed.) *The Kosovo Tragedy: The Human Rights Dimensions*, London: Frank Cass.

Boucher, D. (1998) *Political Theories of International Relations: From Thucydides to the Present*, Oxford: Oxford University Press.

Bourdieu, Pierre (1987) 'The Force of Law: Towards a Sociology of the Juridical Field', *The Hastings Law Journal*, 38: 814–53.

Bourne, H.R.F. (1969 [1876]) *The Life of John Locke*, Vol. 2, Aalen: Scientia Verlag.

Boyce, R.W.D. (1987) *British Capitalism at the Crossroads, 1919–1932*, Cambridge: Cambridge University Press.

Breitman, R. (1981) *German Socialism and Weimar Democracy*, Chapel Hill: University of North Carolina Press.

Briggs, Asa (1959) *The Making of Modern England 1783–1867: The Age of Improvement*, New York: Harper and Row.

Briggs, Asa (1984) *A Social History of England*, New York: Viking.

Brogan, H. (2006) *Alexis de Tocqueville: A Biography*, London: Profile Books.

Brown, C. (1992) *International Relations Theory: New Normative Approaches*, New York: Columbia University Press.

Brown, C. (1999) 'Towards a Neo-Aristotelian Resolution of the Cosmopolitan-Communitarian Debate', in J.-S. Fritz and M. Lensu (eds) *Value Pluralism, Normative Theory and International Relations*, Basingstoke: Palgrave Macmillan.

Brown, C. (2002) *Sovereignty, Rights and Justice: International Political Theory Today*, Cambridge: Polity.

Brown, E.H.P. (1968) *A Century of Pay*, London: Macmillan.

Brunkhorst, H. (2002) 'Globalising Democracy Without a State: Weak Public, Strong Public, Global Constitutionalism', *Millennium: Journal of International Studies*, 31: 675–90.

Brunkhorst, H. (2005) *Solidarity*, Cambridge, MA: MIT Press.

Bryce, J. (1921) *Modern Democracies*, Vol. 1, London: Macmillan.

Buchanan, A. and Keohane, R. (2004) 'The Preventative Use of Force: A Cosmopolitan Institutional Proposal', *Ethics and International Affairs*, 18: 1–22.

Buergenthal, T. (1997) 'The Normative and Institutional Evolution of International Human Rights', *Human Rights Quarterly*, 19: 703–23.

Buergenthal, T. (1990) 'The Copenhagen Meeting: A New Public Order for Europe', *Human Rights Law Journal*, 11: 217–32.

Bukovansky, M. (2002) *Legitimacy and Power Politics: The American and French Revolutions in International Political Culture*, Princeton: Princeton University Press.

Bull, H. (1977) *The Anarchical Society*, London: Macmillan.

Bull, H. and Watson, A. (eds) (1984) *The Expansion of International Society*, Oxford: Clarendon Press.

Burgess, A. (2001) 'Universal Democracy, Diminished Expectation', *Democratization*, 8: 51–74.

Burke, E. (1999) *Select Works of Edmund Burke*, Vol. 2, Indianapolis: Liberty Fund.

Burton, J. (1990) *Conflict: Human Needs Theory*, New York: St Martin's Press.

Burton, J. (ed.) (1993) *Conflict: Human Needs Theory*, Basingstoke: Palgrave Macmillan.

Bush, G.W. (2003) 'President Delivers "State of the Union"', The White House, 28 January, www.washingtonpost.com/wp-srv/onpolitics/transcripts/bushtext_012803.html (accessed 2 September 2010).

Bush, G.W. (2006) 'President Thanks U.S. and Coalition Troops in Afghanistan', The White House, 1 March, http://georgewbush-whitehouse.archives.gov/news/releases/2006/03/20060301-3.html (accessed 2 September 2010).

Bush, G.W. (2008a) 'State of the Union Address', 28 January, www.whitehouse.gov/news/releases/2008/01/20080128-13.html (accessed 25 July 2008).

Bush, G.W. (2008b) 'The Importance of Freedom in the Middle East', 13 January 2008, www.whitehouse.gov/news/releases/2008/01/20080113-1.html (accessed 25 July 2008).

Cameron, M.A., Lawson, R.A. and Tomlin, B.W. (eds) (1998) *To Walk without Fear: The Global Movement to Ban Landmines*, Toronto and New York: Oxford University Press.

Canfora, L. (2006) *Democracy in Europe: A History of an Ideology*, trans. S. Jones, Malden: Blackwell.

Canovan, M. (1996) *Nationhood and Political Theory*, Cheltenham: Edward Elgar.

Canzler, W., Kaufmann, V. and Kesselring, S. (2008) *Tracing Mobilities: Towards a Cosmopolitan Perspective*, Aldershot: Ashgate.

Cardoso, F.H. and E. Faletto (1979) *Dependency and Development in Latin America*, Berkeley: University of California.

Carnegie Endowment (2008) 'Is a League of Democracies a Good Idea?', Transcript of Meeting, Carnegie Endowment for International Peace, 29 May, www.carnegieendowment.org/pubs (accessed 1 August 2008).

Carothers, T. (2008) 'An Unwanted League', *Washington Post*, 28 May, www.washingtonpost.com/wp-dyn/content/article/2008/05/27 (accessed 2 July 2008).

Carr, E.H. (1947) *The Soviet Impact on the Western World*, New York: Macmillan.

Carruthers, Bruce (1996) *City of Capital: Politics and Markets in the English Financial Revolution*, Princeton: Princeton University Press.

Carstairs, A. (1980) *A Short History of Electoral Systems in Western Europe*, London: Allen & Unwin.

Casanova, Jose (2006) 'Rethinking Secularization: A Global Comparative Perspective', *Hedgehog Review*, 8: 7–22.

Chandler, David (2002) *From Kosovo to Kabul: Human Rights and International Intervention*. London: Pluto Press.

Chandler, David (2003) 'New Rights for Old? Cosmopolitan Citizenship and the Critique of State Sovereignty', *Political Studies*, 51: 339–56.

Chandler, David (2004a) *Constructing Global Civil Society: Morality and Power in International Relations*, Basingstoke: Palgrave.

Chandler, David (2004b) 'Building Global Civil Society "From Below"', *Millennium: Journal of International Studies*, 33: 313–39.

Chandler, David (2007) 'Deriving Norms from "Global Space": The Limits of Cosmopolitan Approaches to Global Civil Society Theorizing', *Globalizations*, 4: 283–98.

Chandler, David (2009) *Hollow Hegemony: Rethinking Global Politics, Power and Resistance*, London: Pluto.

Chas. Wolff Packing Co. v. Court of Ind. Relations of State of Kansas, 262 US 522 (1923).

Ching, F. (2008) 'Asian Arc of Democracy', *Korea Times*, 24 February, www.koreatimes.co.kr/www/news (accessed 26 June 2008).

Chirot, D. (1977) *Social Change in the Twentieth Century*, New York: Harcourt, Brace Jovanovich.

Christophersen, J. (1966) *The Meaning of 'Democracy' as used in European Ideologies from the French to the Russian Revolution*, Oslo: Universitetsforlaget.

Chua, A. (2003) *World on Fire: How Exporting Free Market Democracy Breeds Ethnic Hatred and Global Instability*, New York: Anchor Books.

Clark, I. (2001a) *The Post-Cold War Order: The Spoils of Peace*, Oxford: Oxford University Press.

Clark, I. (2001b) 'Another "Double Movement": The Great Transformation after the Cold War?', *Review of International Studies*, 27: 237–56.

Clark, I. (2005) *Legitimacy in International Society*, Oxford: Oxford University Press.

Clark, I. (2007) *International Legitimacy and World Society*, Oxford: Oxford University Press.

Clemons, S. (2008) 'Concert of Democracies as a Shell Game', *The Washington Note*, 24 April, www.thewashingtonnote.com/archives/2008/04/concert_of_demo/ (accessed 24 June 2008).

Clough, S.B. (1940) *Economic History of Europe*, Boston: D.C. Heath and Co.

Coates, D. (2000) *Models of Capitalism*, Cambridge: Polity.

Cochran, M. (1999) *Normative Theory in International Relations: A Pragmatic Approach*, Cambridge: Cambridge University Press.

Cochran, M. (2002) 'A Democratic Critique of Cosmopolitan Democracy', *European Journal of International Relations*, 8: 517–48.

Cohrs, P.O. (2006) *The Unfinished Peace after World War I: America, Britain and the Stabilisation of Europe 1919–1932*, Cambridge: Cambridge University Press.

Colas, Alejandro (2002) *International Civil Society: Social Movements in World Politics*, Cambridge: Polity.

Collier, R. (1999) *Paths Towards Democracy*, Cambridge: Cambridge University Press.

Collier, R. and Collier, D. (1991) *Shaping the Political Arena*, Princeton: Princeton University Press.

Collins, H. and Abramsky, C. (1965) *Karl Marx and the British Labour Movement*, New York: Macmillan.

Commonwealth v. Pullis, Mayor's Court of Philadelphia (1806).

Commonwealth v. Hunt, 45 Mass. 111 (1842).

Conference on Security and Cooperation in Europe (CSCE) (1990) *Charter of Paris for a New Europe*, 21 November, Paris.

Connolly, William (2001) 'Cross-State Citizen Networks: A Reply to Dallmayr', *Millennium: Journal of International Studies*, 30: 349–55.

Connolly, William (2005) *Pluralism*, Durham, NC: Duke University Press.

Council for a Community of Democracies (CCD) (2006) *The First Five Years 2001–5*, Washington DC, www.ccd21.org (accessed 2 July 2008).

Cox, Archibald, Bok, D., Gorman, R. and Finkin, M. (2001) *Cases and Materials on Labor Law*, 13th edn, St Paul, MN: West Publishing.

Cox, M. (1998) 'Rebels Without a Cause? Radical Theorists and the World System Aafter the Cold War', *New Political Economy*, 3: 445–60.

Cox, M., Ikenberry, J. and Inoguchi, T. (2000) *American Democracy Promotion. Impulses, Strategies, and Impacts*, Oxford: Oxford University Press.

Cresswell, Tim (2006) *On the Move: Mobility in Modern Western World*, London: Routledge.

Cronin, B. (2003) *Institutions for the Common Good: International Protection Regimes in International Society*, Cambridge: Cambridge University Press.

Cronin, J. (1982) 'Labor Insurgency and Class Formation: Comparative Perspectives on the Crisis of 1917–1920 in Europe', in J.E. Cronin and C. Sirianni (eds) *Work, Community and Power: The Experience of Labor in Europe and America, 1900–1925*, Philadelphia: Temple University Press.

Crouch, C. (2004) *Post-Democracy*, Cambridge: Polity.

Cunningham, F. (2002) *Theories of Democracy: A Critical Introduction*, London and New York: Routledge.

Daalder, I. (2004) 'An Alliance of Democracies: Our Way or the Highway', *Financial Times*, 6 November, www.brookings.edu/opinions/2004/1106globalgovernance (accessed 2 July 2008).

Daalder, I. and Kagan, R. (2007) 'The Next Intervention', *Washington Post*, 6 August, www.washingtonpost.com/wp-dyn/content/article/2007/08/05 (accessed 26 June 2008).

Daalder, I. and Lindsay, J. (2007) 'Democracies of the World Unite', *Public Policy Research*, 14: 47–58.

Dahl, R. (1998) *On Democracy*, New Haven: Yale University Press.

Davis, L.E. and Huttenback, R.A. (1988) *Mammon and the Pursuit of Empire*, New York: Cambridge University Press.

Deane, P. (1979) *The First Industrial Revolution*, 2nd edn, Cambridge: Cambridge University Press.

Der Spiegel (2008) 'Waves of Would-Be Immigrants Target EU Shores', www.spiegel.de/international/europe/0,1518,561711,00.html (accessed 1 October 2008).

Deudney, Daniel (2007) *Bounding Power*, Princeton: Princeton University Press.

Deutsch, Karl *et al.* (1957) *Political Community and the North Atlantic Area*, Princeton: Princeton University Press.

Dewey, J. (1948) *Reconstruction in Philosophy*, Boston: Beacon Press.

Dewey, J. (1991) *The Public and Its Problems*, Athens: Swallow Press.

Dewey, J. (1998a) 'The Need for a Recovery of Philosophy', in L.A. Hickman and T.M. Alexander (eds) *The Essential Dewey: Volume 1: Pragmatism, Education, Democracy*, Bloomington and Indianapolis: Indiana University Press.

Dewey, J. (1998b) 'What I Believe', in L.A. Hickman and T.M. Alexander (eds) *The Essential Dewey: Volume 1: Pragmatism, Education, Democracy*, Bloomington and Indianapolis: Indiana University Press.

Dewey, J. (1998c) 'Time and Individuality', in L.A. Hickman and T.M. Alexander (eds) *The Essential Dewey: Volume 1: Pragmatism, Education, Democracy*, Bloomington and Indianapolis: Indiana University Press.

Dewey, J. (1998d) 'The Moral Self', in L.A. Hickman and T.M. Alexander (eds) *The Essential Dewey, Volume 2: Ethics, Logic, Psychology*, Bloomington and Indianapolis: Indiana University Press.

Dewey, J. (1998e) 'Moral Judgment and Knowledge', in L.A. Hickman and T.M. Alexander (eds) *The Essential Dewey, Volume 2: Ethics, Logic, Psychology*, Bloomington and Indianapolis: Indiana University Press.

Diamond, L. (2003a) 'Universal Democracy?', *Policy Review*, 119, www.policyreview.org/jun03/diamond_print.html (accessed 10 August 2004).

Diamond, L. (2003b) *Can the Whole World Become Democratic? Democracy, Development, and International Policies*, Irvine: Center for the Study of Democracy.

Diamond, L. (2008) *The Spirit of Democracy*, New York: Times Books.

Dickstein, M. (1998) 'Introduction: Pragmatism Then and Now', in M. Dickstein (ed.) *The Revival of Pragmatism: New Essays on Social Thought, Law and Culture*, Durham and London: Duke University Press.

Diehl, J. (2008) 'A "League" by Other Names', *Washington Post*, 19 May, A17.

Dobb, M. (1963) *Studies in the Development of Capitalism*, New York: International Publishers.

Donnelly, J. (2006) 'Sovereign Inequalities and Hierarchy in Anarchy: American Power and International Society', *European Journal of International Relations*, 12: 139–70.

Douzinas, Costas (2007) *Human Rights and Empire: The Political Philosophy of Cosmopolitanism*, London: Routledge Cavendish.

Downing, B. (1997) *The Military Revolution and Political Change in Early Modern Europe*, Princeton: Princeton University Press.

Doyle, M.W. (1983) 'Kant, Liberal Legacies, and Foreign Affairs', *Philosophy and Public Affairs*, 12: 205–35.

Doyle, M.W. (1986) 'Liberalism and World Politics', *The American Political Science Review*, 80: 1151–69.

Dryzek, John S. (1999) 'Transnational Democracy', *The Journal of Political Philosophy*, 7: 30–51.

Dryzek, John S. (2000) *Deliberative Democracy and Beyond: Liberals, Critics, Contestations*, Oxford: Oxford University Press.

Dryzek, John S. (2006) *Deliberative Global Politics: Discourse and Democracy in a Divided World*, Cambridge: Polity.

Duffield, Mark (2007) *Development, Security and Unending War: Governing the World of Peoples*, Cambridge: Polity.

Dunne, T.J. (1998) *Inventing International Society: A History of the English School*, Houndmills: Macmillan.

Duplex Printing Press Co. v. Deering, 254 US 443 (1921).

Eckersley, R. (2007) 'A Green Public Sphere in the WTO?: The Amicus Curiae Interventions in the Transatlantic Biotech Dispute', *European Journal of International Relations*, 13: 329–56.

Edwards, Martin (1999) *Future Positive: International Co-operation in the 21st Century*, London: Earthscan.

Eichengreen, B. and Leblang, D. (2006) 'Democracy and Globalisation', BIS Working Papers No. 219, Bank for International Settlements, Basel: Switzerland.

Ellis, G. (2000) 'The Revolution of 1848–1849 in France', in R.J.W. Evans and H. Strandmann (eds) *The Revolutions in Europe 1848–1849: From Reform to Reaction*, Oxford: Oxford University Press.

Elman, C. and M.F. Elman (eds) (2001) *Bridges and Boundaries: Historians, Political Scientists and the Study of International Relations*, Cambridge, MA: MIT Press.

Ely, James W. Jr. (1992) *The Guardian of Every Other Right: A Constitutional History of Property Rights*, New York: Oxford University Press.

Engels, Friedrich (1892 [1845]) *The Condition of the Working-Class in England in 1844*, London: Allen and Unwin.

Etzioni, A. (ed.) (1998) *The Essential Communitarian Reader*, Lanham, MD: Rowman and Littlefield.

Etzioni, A. (2004) *From Empire to Community: A New Approach to International Relations*, New York: Palgrave Macmillan.

Evans, P. (1979) *Dependent Development*, Princeton: Princeton University Press.

Eversley, D.E.C. (1967) 'The Home Market and Economic Growth in England, 1750–1780', in E.L. Jones and G.E. Mingay (eds) *Land, Labour, and Population in the Industrial Revolution*, London: Arnold.

Falk, Richard A. (1995) *On Humane Governance: Toward a New Global Politics*, Cambridge: Polity.

Fasolt, C. (2004) *The Limits of History*, Chicago: University of Chicago Press.

Feinman, Jay M. (1976) 'The Development of the Employment at Will Rule', *American Journal of Legal History*, 118: 126–7.

Feldman, Noah (2008) *The Fall and Rise of the Islamic State*, Princeton: Princeton University Press.

Festenstein, M. (1997) *Pragmatism and Political Theory*, Cambridge: Polity Press.

Festenstein, M. (2002) 'Pragmatism's boundaries', *Millennium: Journal of International Studies*, 31(3): 549–71.

Finkin, Matthew W., Goldman, Alvin L. and Summers, Clyde W. (1989) *Legal Protection for the Individual Employee*, St Paul, MN: West Publishing.

Finnemore, Margaret and Sikkink, Kathryn (1998) 'International Norm Dynamics and Political Change', *International Organization*, 52: 887–917.

Fligstein, Neil (1990) *The Transformation of Corporate Control*, Cambridge, MA: Harvard University Press.

Floud, R. (1997) *The People and the British Economy, 1830–1914*, New York: Oxford University Press.

Flynn, G. and Farrell, H. (1999) 'Piecing Together the Democratic Peace: The CSCE, Norms, and the Construction of Security in Post-Cold War Europe', *International Organization*, 53: 505–35.

Forbath, William E. (1991) *Law and the Shaping of the American Labor Movement*, Cambridge, MA: Harvard University Press.

Forsyth, M. (1987) *Reason and Revolution: The Political Thought of Abbé Sieyes*, New York: Holmes & Meier.

'Forum on the State as a Person' (2004) *Review of International Studies*, 30: 255–316.

Foucault, Michel (2003) *'Society Must Be Defended': Lectures at the Collège de France 1975–1976*, London: Allen Lane/Penguin.

Foucault, Michel (2007) *Security, Territory, Population: Lectures at the Collège de France 1977–1978*, Basingstoke: Palgrave.

Foucault, Michel (2008) *The Birth of Biopolitics: Lectures at the Collège de France 1978–1979*, Basingstoke: Palgrave.

Fourier, Charles (1932 [1829]) *Le nouveau monde industriel et societaire ou inventaire du procédé d'industrie attrayante et naturelle distribuée en séries passionnées*, Paris: Alcan.

Fox, G.H. (2004) 'Democratization', in D.M. Malone (ed.) *The UN Security Council: From the Cold War to the 21st Century*, Boulder, Co: Lynne Rienner.

Franck, T.M. (1992) 'The Emerging Right to Democratic Governance', *American Journal of International Law*, 86: 46–91.

Franck, T.M. (1995) *Fairness in International Law and Institutions*, Oxford: Oxford University Press.

Fraser, N. (1992) 'Rethinking the Public Sphere: A Contribution to the Critique of Actually Existing Democracy', in C. Calhoun (ed.) *Habermas and the Public Sphere*, Cambridge, MA and London: MIT Press.

Fukuyama, F. (1989) 'The End of History?', *The National Interest*, 16: 3–18.

Fukuyama, F. (1992) *The End of History and the Last Man*, London: Hamish Hamilton.

Fukuyama, F. (2008) 'They Can Only Go So Far', *Washington Post*, 24 August, www.washingtonpost.com/wp-dyn/content/article/2008/08/22/AR2008082202395.html (accessed 12 March 2010).

Fukuyama, F. (2010) 'Is the Age of Democracy Over?', *The Spectator*, 10 February, www.spectator.co.uk/spectator/thisweek/5766228/is-the-age-of-democracy-over.html (accessed 12 March 2010).

Gallie, W.B. (1964) *Philosophy and the Historical Understanding*, London: Chatto and Windus.

Galtung, J. (1969) 'Violence, Peace, and Peace Research', *Journal of Peace Research*, 6: 167–91.

Galtung, J. (2000) 'Alternative Models for Global Democracy', in B. Holden (ed.) *Global Democracy: Key Debates*, London: Routledge.

Gerschenkron, A. (1962) *Economic Backwardness in Historical Perspective*, Cambridge: Harvard University Press.

Gershman, C. (2005) 'Democracy as Policy Goal and Universal Value', *The Whitehead Journal of Diplomacy and International Relations*, 6: 19–38.

Godkin, E. (1898) *Unforeseen Tendencies of Democracy*, Westminster: Archibald Constable & Co.

Godwin, William (1976 [1798]) *Enquiry Concerning Political Justice, and Its Influence on Modern Morals and Happiness*, Harmondsworth, Middlesex: Penguin.

Goldstein, R. (1983) *Political Repression in Nineteenth Century Europe*, London: Croom Helm.

Gong, G. (1984) *The Standard of 'Civilization' in International Society*, Oxford: Oxford University Press.

Goodin, R. (2000) 'Democratic Deliberation Within', *Philosophy and Public Affairs*, 29: 81–109.

Gore, C. (2000) 'The Rise and Fall of the Washington Consensus as a Paradigm for Developing Countries', *World Development*, 28: 789–804.

Gosnell, H. (1930) *Why Europe Votes*, Chicago: University of Chicago Press.

Gould, C.C. (2004) *Globalizing Democracy and Human Rights*, Cambridge: Cambridge University Press.

Gould, C.C. (2006) 'Self-determination Beyond Sovereignty: Relating Transnational Democracy to Local Autonomy', *Journal of Social Philosophy*, 37: 44–60.

Gourevitch, P. (2002) 'Domestic Politics and International Relations' in W. Carlsnaes, T. Risse and B.A. Simmons (eds) *Handbook of International Relations*, London: Sage.

Greenfeld, L. (1992) *Nationalism: Five Roads to Modernity*, Cambridge: Harvard University Press.

Guild, Elspeth (2003) 'Exceptionalism and Transnationalism: UK Juridical Control of Detention of Foreign "International Terrorists"', *Alternatives*, 28: 491–515.

Guild, Elspeth (2004) *The Legal Elements of European Identity. EU Citizenship and Migration Law*, The Hague: Kluwer Law.

Guilhot, N. (2005) *The Democracy Makers: Human Rights and International Order*, New York: Columbia University Press.

Guizot, F. (1849) *Democracy in France*, 3rd edn, London: John Murray.

Gunnell, J.G. (1993) *The Descent of Political Theory: The Genealogy of an American Vocation*, Chicago: University of Chicago Press.

Gutman, Herbert (1976) *Work, Culture, and Society in Industrializing America: Essays in American Working-class and Social History*, New York: Knopf.

Haas, Ernst B. (1968) *The Uniting of Europe: Political, Social and Economic Forces 1950–1957*, Stanford: Stanford University Press.

Habermas, J. (1996) *Between Facts and Norms: Contributions to a Discourse Theory of Law and Democracy*, Polity Press: Cambridge.

Habermas, J. (1999a) 'Bestialität und Humanität', *Die Zeit*, 29 April, Franz Solms-Laubach trans. available at: www.theglobalsite.ac.uk/press/011habermas.htm. (accessed 7 October 2010).

Habermas, J. (1999b) 'The European Nation-state: On the Past and Future of Sovereignty and Citizenship', in *The Inclusion of the Other: Studies in Political Theory*, Cambridge: Polity.

Habermas, J. (2001) *The Postnational Constellation. Political Essays*, translated by Max Pensky, Cambridge: Polity.

Habermas, J. (2006) *The Divided West*, Cambridge: Polity Press.

Hall, J.A. (1993) 'Consolidation of Democracy', in David Held (ed.) *Prospects for Democracy*, Stanford: Stanford University Press.

Halliday, F. (1987) 'The State and Society in International Relations: A Second Agenda', *Millennium: Journal of International Studies*, 16: 215–29.

Halperin, M.H. (1993) 'Guaranteeing Democracy', *Foreign Policy*, 91: 105–22.

Halperin, S. (1997) *In the Mirror of the Third World: Capitalist Development in Modern Europe*, Ithaca, New York: Cornell University Press.

Halperin, S. (2004) *War and Social Change in Modern Europe: The Great Transformation Revisited*, Cambridge: Cambridge University Press.

Hannam, K., Sheller, M. and Urry, J. (2006) 'Mobilities, Immobilities and Moorings' [Editorial], *Mobilities*, 1: 1–22.

Hansard, T.C. (1859) *Hansard's Parliamentary Debates*, 3rd series, Vol. 153, London: Cornelius Buck.

Hardt, Michael and Negri, Antonio (2001) *Empire*, New York: Harvard University Press.

Hardt, Michael and Negri, Antonio (2006) *Multitude: War and Democracy in the Age of Empire*, London: Penguin.

Hartwell, Roland M. (1971) *The Industrial Revolution and Economic Growth*, London: Methuen.

Harwood, G. (1882) *The Coming Democracy*, London: Macmillan.

Hawkins, D. and Shaw, C. (2008) 'Legalising Norms of Democracy in the Americas', *Review of International Studies*, 34: 459–80.

Heater, D. (2002) *World Citizenship*, London: Continuum.

Heisbourg, F. (2007) 'Democracies of the World Unite: A Response', *The American Interest*, Jan–Feb., www.the-american-interest.com/ai2/article (accessed 26 June 2008).

Held, D. (1995) *Democracy and the Global Order: From the Modern State to Cosmopolitan Governance*, Cambridge: Polity.

Held, D. (1997) 'Democracy and Globalization', *Global Governance*, 3: 251.

Held, D. (1998) 'Democracy and Globalisation', in D. Archibugi, D. Held and M. Köhler (eds) *Re-imagining Political Community: Studies in Cosmopolitan Democracy*, Cambridge: Polity.

Held, D. (2000) 'The Changing Contours of Political Community: Rethinking Democracy in the Context of Globalization', in B. Holden (ed.) *Global Democracy: Key Debates*, London: Routledge.

Held, D. (2002) 'Law of States, Law of Peoples', *Legal Theory*, 8: 1–44.

Held, D. (2003) 'Cosmopolitanism: Globalisation Tamed?', *Review of International Studies*, 28: 465–80.

Held, D. (2004) *Global Covenant*, Cambridge: Polity.

Held, D. (2005) 'Principles of Cosmopolitan Order' in G. Brock and H. Brighouse (eds) *The Political Philosophy of Cosmopolitanism*, Cambridge: Cambridge University Press.

Held, D., McGrew, A., Goldblatt, A. and Perraton, J. (1999) *Global Transformations: Politics, Economics and Culture*, Cambridge: Polity.

Hersh, A., Scott, R. and Weller C. (2001) 'The Unremarkable Record of Liberalized Trade', Economics Policy Institute Briefing Paper, https://www.policyarchive.org/bitstream/handle/10207/8163/sept01inequality.pdf?sequence=1 (accessed 15 January 2010).

Hobbes, T. (1975) *Thucydides*, New Brunswick: Rutgers University Press.

Hobsbawm, E. (1968) *Industry and Empire*, London: Weidenfeld and Nicolson.

Hobson, C. (2008a) 'Democracy as Civilisation', *Global Society*, 22: 75–95.

Hobson, C. (2008b) 'Revolution, Representation and the Foundations of Modern Democracy', *European Journal of Political Theory*, 7: 465–87.

Hobson, C. (2009) *Democracy and International Politics: A Conceptual History, 1776–1919*, PhD dissertation, Australian National University.

Hobson, J.A. (1902) *Imperialism: A Study*, London: Allen and Unwin.

Hobson, J.A. (1934) *Democracy and a Changing Civilisation*, London: John Lane.

Holden, B. (ed.) (2000) *Global Democracy: Key Debates*, London: Routledge.

Honneth, A. (1998) 'Democracy as Reflexive Cooperation: John Dewey and the Theory of Democracy Today', *Political Theory*, 26: 763–83.

House of Lords Debates (2008), 24 June, www.theyworkforyou.com/lords/?id=2008–06–24a.1329.0 (accessed 2 July 2008).

Howard, M. (1961) *The Franco-Prussian War: The German invasion of France, 1870–1871*, London: Rupert Hart-Davis.

Hume, David (1955) 'Essays on Economics', in E. Rotwein (ed.) *Writings on Economics*, Madison: University of Wisconsin Press.

Hunt, A. (1996) *Governance of the Consuming Passions*, Basingstoke: Macmillan.

Huntington, S.P. (1991) *The Third Wave: Democratization in the Late Twentieth Century*. Norman: University of Oklahoma Press.

Hurrell, A. (2007) *On Global Order: Power, Values, and the Constitution of International Society*, Oxford: Oxford University Press.

Hutchings, Kimberly (2008) *Time and World Politics: Thinking the Present*, Manchester: Manchester University Press.

Huysmans, Jef (2004) 'Minding Exceptions: Politics of Insecurity and Liberal Democracy', *Contemporary Political Theory*, 3: 321–41.

Ikenberry, G.J. (2009) 'Liberal Internationalism 3.0: America and the Dilemmas of Liberal World Order', *Perspectives on Politics*, 7: 71–87.

Ikenberry, G.J. and Slaughter, A.-M. (2006a) *Forging a World of Liberty under Law: US National Security in the 21st Century*, Princeton: The Woodrow Wilson School of Public and International Affairs, Princeton University.

Ikenberry, G.J. and Slaughter, A.-M. (2006b), 'A Bigger Security Council, with Power to Act', *International Herald Tribune*, 26 September, www.iht.com/articles/2006/09/26/opinion/edslaughter.php (accessed 26 June 2008).

Inglehart, R. and Welzel, C. (2005) *Modernization, Cultural Change, and Democracy: The Human Development Sequence*, Cambridge: Cambridge University Press.

In re Debs, 158 US 564 (1895).

Jabri, Vivienne (2007a) *War and the Transformation of Global Politics*, Basingstoke: Palgrave.

Jabri, Vivienne (2007b) 'Solidarity and Spheres of Culture: The Cosmopolitan and the Postcolonial', *Review of International Studies*, 33: 715–28.

Jensen, O.B. (2006) ' "Facework", Flow and the City: Simmel, Goffman, and Mobility in the Contemporary City', *Mobilities*, 1: 143–65.

Joas, H. (1993) *Pragmatism and Social Theory*, Chicago and London: The University of Chicago Press.

Jullien, François (2008) *Le Monde Diplomatique*, February.

Kagan, R. (2008a) *The Return of History and the End of Dreams*, London: Atlantic Books.

Kagan, R. (2008b) 'The Case for a League of Democracies', *Financial Times*, 13 May, www.carnegieendowment.org/publications/index (accessed 2 July 2008).

Kaiser, Karl (1969) 'Transnationale Politik. Zu Einer Theorie Der Multinationalen Politik', in Ernst-Otto Czempiel (ed.) *Die Anachronistische Souveränität*, Köln: Westdeutscher Verlag.

Kaldor, Mary (1999) 'Transnational Civil Society', in T. Dunne and N. J. Wheeler (eds) *Human Rights in Global Politics*, Cambridge: Cambridge University Press.

Kaldor, Mary (2001) *Analysis*. BBC Radio Four, 29 March.

Kaldor, Mary (2003) *Global Civil Society: An Answer to War*, Cambridge; Polity.

Kaldor, Mary (2007) *Human Security*, Cambridge: Polity.

Kant, I. (1970) *Kant's Political Writings*, H. Reiss (ed. and intro), Cambridge: Cambridge University Press.

Kant, I. (1983) *Perpetual Peace, and Other Essays on Politics, History, and Morals*, translated by T. Humphrey, Indianapolis: Hackett Pub. Co.

Kant, I. (1989) 'Perpetual Peace: A Philosophical Sketch', in H. Reiss (ed.) *Kant: Political Writings*, Cambridge: Cambridge University Press.

Katznelson, Ira (1985) 'Working-Class Formation and the State: Nineteenth-Century England in American Perspective', in P.B. Evans, D. Rueschemeyer and T. Skocpol (eds) *Bringing the State Back In*, Cambridge: Cambridge University Press.

Katznelson, Ira and Zolberg, Aristide R. (eds) (1986) *Working-class Formation: Nineteenth-Century Patterns in Western Europe and the United States*, Princeton: Princeton University Press.

Kaul, I, Conceição, P., Goulven, K. and Mendoza R. (eds) (2003) *Providing Global Public Goods*, Oxford: Oxford University Press.

Keane, John (2003) *Global Civil Society?*, Cambridge: Polity.

Keane, John (2009) *The Life and Death of Democracy*, London: Simon & Schuster.

Keck, M.E. and Sikkink, K. (1998) *Activists Beyond Borders: Advocacy Networks in International Politics*, Ithaca and London: Cornell University Press.

Keene, E. (2002) *Beyond the Anarchical Society: Grotius, Colonialism, and Order in World Politics*, Cambridge: Cambridge University Press.

Keohane, R.O., Macedo, S. and Moravcsik, A. (2009) 'Democracy-Enhancing Multilateralism', *International Organization*, 63: 1–31.

Kindleberger, C. (1964) *Economic Growth in France and Britain, 1851–1950*, Cambridge, MA: Harvard University Press.

Kissinger, H. (1957): *A World Restored: Metternich, Castlereagh, and the Problems of Peace, 1812–1822*, Boston: Houghton Mifflin.

Kloppenberg, James T. (1994) 'Democracy and Disagreement: From Weber and Dewey to Habermas and Rorty', in Dorothy Ross (ed.) *Modernist Impulses in the Human Sciences, 1870–1930*, Baltimore: Johns Hopkins University Press.

Koskenniemi, M. (1989) *From Apology to Utopia: The Structure of International Legal Argument*, Helsinki: Finnish Lawyers' Publishing Company.

Kuper, A. (2004) *Democracy Beyond Borders: Justice and Representation in Global Institutions*, Oxford: Oxford University Press.

Kuznets, S. (1964) *Postwar Economic Growth*, Cambridge, MA: The Belknap Press.

Kymlicka, W. (2001) *Politics in the Vernacular: Nationalism, Multiculturalism and Citizenship*, Oxford: Oxford University Press.

Laclau, Ernesto and Mouffe, Chantal (2001) *Hegemony and Socialist Strategy: Towards a Radical Democratic Politics*, 2nd edn, London: Verso.

Landes, D. (1969) *The Unbound Prometheus*, Cambridge: Cambridge University Press.

Laurie, Bruce (1997) *Artisans into Workers: Labor in Nineteenth-Century America*, Champaign: University of Illinois Press.

Lawlor v. Loewe, 235 US 522 (1915).

Le Bon, Gustave (1995 [1896]) *The Crowd. A Study of the Popular Mind*, Virginia: University of Virginia Library Electronic Text Center.

Lebow, R.N. (2010) *Forbidden Fruit: Counterfactuals and International Relations*, Princeton: Princeton University Press.

Lecky, W. (1899) *Democracy and Liberty*, Vol. 1, London: Longmans, Greed and Co.

Lenin, V.I. (1939) *Imperialism*, New York: International Publishers.

Levy, J. (1989) 'The Causes of War: A Review of Theories and Evidence', in P.E. Tetlock, J. Husbands, R. Jervis, P.C. Stern and C. Tilly (eds) *Behavior, Society, and Nuclear War*, Vol. 1, New York: Oxford University Press.

Lewis, Norman (1998) 'Human Rights, Law and Democracy in an Unfree World', in T. Evans (ed.) *Human Rights Fifty Years On: A Reappraisal*, Manchester: Manchester University Press.

Lieven, D. (1992) *The Aristocracy in Europe, 1815–1914*, New York: Macmillan.

Lincoln, A. (1860) Speech at Hartford, CT, 5 March (*Daily Courant* version), in R.P. Basler (ed.), *The Collected Works of Abraham Lincoln*, 8 vols, New Brunswick, NJ: Rutgers University Press (1953–5), 4: 8. *Collected Works* available online at http://quod.lib.umich.edu/l/lincoln/.

Lincoln, A. (1861) Address to the New Jersey Senate, 21 February, in Basler, *Collected Works of Lincoln*, 4: 236.

Lincoln, A. (1862) Annual Message to Congress, 1 December, in Basler, *Collected Works of Lincoln*, 5: 537.

Lincoln, A. (1863) Gettysburg Address, 19 November (newspaper version), in Basler, *Collected Works of Lincoln*, 7: 19–21.

Lind, M. (2007) 'For Liberal Internationalism', *The Nation*, 2 July, www.newamerica. net/publications/articles/2007/liberal_intern (accessed 2 July 2008).

Linklater, Andrew (1998) *The Transformation of Political Community*, Cambridge: Polity.

Lochner v. New York, 198 US 45 (1905).

Locke, John (1924 [1690]) *Of Civil Government: Two Treatises*, New York: E.P. Dutton.

Loewe v. Lawlor, 208 US 274 (1908).

Luhmann, N. (1990) 'The Future of Democracy', *Thesis Eleven*, 26: 46.

Lustig, R. (2008) 'How about a League of Democracies?', BBC Radio Four, 19 May, www. bbc.co.uk/blogs/worldtonight/2008/05/how_about_a_league (accessed 2 July 2008).

MacGilvray, E.A. (1999) 'Experience as Experiment: Some Consequences of Pragmatism for Democratic Theory', *American Journal of Political Science*, 43: 542–65.

MacGilvray, E.A. (2000) 'Five Myths About Pragmatism, or, Against a Second Pragmatic Acquiescence', *Political Theory*, 28: 480–508.

Madison, J. (2001) '10th Federalist Paper', in G. Carey and J. McClellan (eds) *The Federalist*, Indianapolis: Liberty Fund.

Mahbubani, K. (2007) 'Charting a New Course', *Survival*, 49: 201–9.

Maier, C. (1975) *Recasting Bourgeois Europe*, Princeton: Princeton University Press.

Maine, H. (1886) *Popular Government: Four Essays*, London: John Murray.

Maistre, J. (1996) *Against Rousseau: 'On the State of Nature' and 'On the Sovereignty of the People'*, trans. R. Lebrun, Montreal: McGill-Queen's University Press.

Mann, M. (1988) 'European Development: Approaching a Historical Explanation', in J. Baechler, J.A. Hall and M. Mann (eds) *Europe and the Rise of Capitalism*, Oxford: Basil Blackwell.

Mann, M. (1999) 'The Dark Side of Democracy: The Modern Tradition of Ethnic and Political Cleansing', *New Left Review*, I/235: 18–45.

Mansfield, E.D. and Snyder, J. (1995) 'Democratization and the Danger of War', *International Security*, 20: 5–38.

Mansfield, E.D. and Snyder, J. (2001) 'Democratic Transitions and War: From Napoleon to the Millennium's End', in C. Crocker, F.O. Hampson and P. Aall (eds) *Turbulent Peace. The Challenges of Managing International Conflict*, Washington, DC: United States Institute of Peace.

Mansfield, E.D. and Snyder, J. (2005) *Electing to Fight: Why Emerging Democracies Go to War*, Cambridge, MA: MIT Press.

Marchetti, R. (2008) 'Global Democracy and International Exclusion', *Review of International Studies*, 34: 207–24.

Marks, S. (2000) 'International Law, Democracy and the End of History', in G. Fox and B. Roth (eds) *Democratic Governance and International Law*, Cambridge: Cambridge University Press.

Marwick, A. (1980) *Image and Reality in Britain, France, and the USA Since 1930*, London: Collins.

Marx, Karl (1967) *Communist Manifesto*, London: Penguin.

Marx, Karl (1977 [1867]) *Capital*, New York: Vintage Books.

Marx K. and Engels, F. (1848) *The Manifesto of the Communist Party*, www.newyouth.com/ archives/classics/marxengels/communistmanifesto.html (accessed 27 August 2008).

Mathias, P. (1983) *The First Industrial Nation*, New York: Methuen.

Mattes, A. (2011) 'Citizens of a Common Intellectual Homeland', PhD dissertation, University of Virginia.

Maurer, Bill (2006) 'The Anthropology of Money', *Annual Review of Anthropology*, 35: 15–36.

Mazzini, G. (2001) *Thoughts upon Democracy in Europe (1846–1847)*, Centro Editoriale Toscano.

Mayall, J. (2000) 'Democracy and International Society', *International Affairs*, 76: 61–75.

McAdam, D., Tarrow, S. and Tilly, C. (2001) *Dynamics of Contention*, Cambridge: Cambridge University Press.

McCarthy, T. (1991) *Ideals and Illusions*, Cambridge, MA: MIT Press.

McFaul, M. (2004–5) 'Democracy Promotion as a World Value', *The Washington Quarterly*, 28: 147–63.

McFaul, M. (2010) *Advancing Democracy Abroad: Why We Should and How We Can*, Lanham: Rowman & Littlefield.

McGrew, A. (1997) 'Conclusion: Democracy Beyond Borders?: Globalization and the Reconstruction of Democratic Theory and Politics', in A. McGrew (ed.) *The Transformation of Democracy? Globalization and Territorial Democracy*, Cambridge: Polity/Open University.

McGrew, A. (2002) 'Transnational Democracy', in A. Carter and G. Stokes (eds) *Democratic Theory Today*, Cambridge: Polity.

McHenry, D.E. (1940) *His Majesty's Opposition*, Berkeley: University of California Press.

McNeill, W.H. (1974) *The Shape of European History*, London: Oxford University Press.

McNeill, W.H. (1986 [1949]) *History of Western Civilization*, Chicago: University of Chicago Press.

McWilliam, Rohan (1998) *Popular Politics in Nineteenth-Century England*, London: Routledge.

Melucci, Alberto (1988) 'Social Movements and the Democratization of Everyday Life', in J. Keane (ed.) *Civil Society and the State: New European Perspectives*, London: Verso.

Mezzadra, Sandro (2006) *Diritto Di Fuga. Migrazioni, Cittadinanza, Globalizzazione*, Verona: Ombre Corte.

Miller, David (1995) *On Nationality*, Oxford: Oxford UniversityPress.

Mitrany, David (1948) 'The Functional Approach to World Organization', *International Affairs*, 24: 350–63.

Mitrany, David (1966) *A Working Peace System*, Chicago: Quadrangle Press.

Mohan, C. Raja (1999) 'India and the Concert of Democracies', *The Hindu*, 5 August, www.indianembassy.org/press/New_Delhi_Press/August_1999 (accessed 2 July 2008).

Montag, Warren (1999) *Bodies, Masses, Power. Spinoza and His Contemporaries*, London: Verso.

Montag, Warren (2005) 'Who's Afraid of the Multitude? Between the Individual and the State', *The South Atlantic Quarterly*, 104: 655–73.

Montgomery, David (1980) 'Strikes in the Nineteenth Century', *Social Science History*, 4: 81–104.

Moore, B. (1966) *Social Origins of Democracy and Dictatorship*, Boston: Beacon.

Morantz, R. (1971) *'Democracy' and 'Republic' in American Ideology (1787–1840)*, unpublished thesis, Columbia University.

Morgan, E.S. (1988) *Inventing the People: The Rise of Popular Sovereignty in England and America*, New York: Norton.

Morris, C. and Adelman, I. (1988) *Comparative Patterns of Economic Development, 1850–1914*, Baltimore: Johns Hopkins University.

Mouffe, Chantal (1993) *The Return of the Political*, London: Verso.

Mouffe, Chantal (1999) 'Deliberative Democracy or Agonistic Pluralism?', *Social Research*, 66: 745–58.

Mouffe, Chantal (2000) *The Democratic Paradox*, London: Verso.

Mouffe, Chantal (2005) *On the Political*, Abigndon: Routledge.

Muller v. Oregon, 208 US 412 (1908).

Murdoch, W.W. (1980) *The Poverty of Nations: The Political Economy of Hunger and Population*, Baltimore: Johns Hopkins University Press.

Murphy, S. (1999) 'Democratic Legitimacy and the Recognition of States and Governments', *International and Comparative Law Quarterly*, 48: 545–81.

Nairn, T. (1981) *The Break-Up of Britain*, 2nd rev. edn, London: Verso.

Niebuhr, R. (1945) *The Children of Light and the Children of Darkness*, London: Nisbet & Co.

Niebuhr, R. and Sigmund, P. (1969) *The Democratic Experience: Past and Prospects*, New York: Frederick A. Praeger Publishers.

North, Douglass C. (1981) *Structure and Change in Economic History*, New York: W. W. Norton.

North, Douglass C. and Thomas, Robert (1973) *The Rise of the Western World: A New Economic History*, New York: Cambridge University Press.

North, Sir Dudley (1856 [1691]) 'Discourse upon Trade, Principally, Directed to the Cases of the Interest, Coynage, Clipping, Increase of Money', in J.R. McCulloch (ed.) *A Select Collection of Early English Tracts on Commerce*, London: Printed for Political Economy Club.

Nussbaum, A. (1954) *A Concise History of the Law of Nations*, rev. edn, New York: Macmillan.

Nyers, Peter (2006) 'Taking Rights, Mediating Wrongs: Disagreements over the Political Agency of Non-Status Refugees', in Jef Huysmans, Andrew Dobson and Raia Prokhovnik (eds) *The Politics of Protection. Sites of Insecurity and Political Agency*, London: Routledge.

O'Donnell, G. (1979) *Modernization and Bureaucratic-Authoritarianism*, Berkeley: University of California Press.

Olesen, T. (2005) 'World Politics and Social Movements: The Janus Face of the Global Democratic Structure', *Global Society*, 19: 109–29.

O'Loughlin, J. *et al.* (1998) 'The Diffusion of Democracy, 1946–1994', *Annals of the Association of American Geographers*, 88: 545–74.

Onuf, N. (1989) *World of Our Making: Rules and Rule in Social Theory and International Relations*, Columbia: University of South Carolina Press.

Onuf, N. (1998) *The Republican Legacy in International Thought*, Cambridge University Press.

Onuf, N. and P. Onuf (2006) *Nations, Markets, and War: Modern History and the American Civil War*, Charlottesville: University of Virginia Press.

Onuf, P. (2004) 'Nations, Revolutions, and the End of History', in M.A. Morrison and M. Zook (eds) *Revolutionary Currents: Nation Building in the Transatlantic World*, Lanham, MD: Rowman and Littlefield.

Onuf, P. (2007) 'Democrazia, rivoluzione e storiografia del mondo contemporaneo', *Contemporanea: Rivista do storia dell '800 e dell '900*, 10: 149–55.

Onuf, P. and N. Onuf (1993) *Federal Union, Modern World: The Law of Nations in an Age of Revolutions, 1776–1814*, Madison, WI: Madison House.

Palmer, R.R. (1959–1964) *The Age of the Democratic Revolution: A Political History of Europe and America, 1760–1800*, 2 vols, Princeton: Princeton University Press.

Panikkar, Raimundo (1982) 'Is the Notion of Human Rights a Western Concept?', *Diogenes*, 120: 81–2.

Pappas, G.F. (2008) *John Dewey's Ethics: Democracy as Experience*, Bloomington and Indianapolis: Indiana University Press.

Parekh, B. (1993) 'The Cultural Particularity of Liberal Democracy' in D. Held (ed.) *Prospects for Democracy: North, South, East, West*, Cambridge: Polity Press.

Paris, R. (2002) 'International Peacebuilding and the "Mission Civilisatrice" ', *Review of International Studies*, 28: 637–56.

Paris, R. (2004) *At War's End: Building Peace after Civil Conflict*, Cambridge: Cambridge University Press.

Patomäki, H. and Teivainen, T. (2004) *A Possible World: Democratic Transformation of Global Institutions*, London and New York: Zed Books.

Pei, M. and Kasper, S. (2003) *Lessons from the Past: The American Record on Nation Building*, Carnegie Endowment for International Peace: Policy Brief 23, 2–8.

Pentland, C. (1973) *International Theory and European Integration*, New York: Free Press.

Perlman, Selig (1928) *A Theory of the Labor Movement*, New York: Macmillan.

van der Pijl (1998) *Transnational Classes and International Relations*, London: Routledge.

Pirenne, H. (1966) *Economic and Social History of Medieval Europe*, New York: Harcourt, Brace and Co.

Plattner, M. (1988) 'Liberalism and Democracy: Can't Have One Without the Other', *Foreign Affairs*, 77: 171–80.

Plattner, M. (2007) *Democracy Without Borders? Global Challenges to Liberal Democracy*, New York: Rowman & Littlefield Publishers.

Polanyi, K. (1944) *The Great Transformation: The Political and Economic Origins of Our Time*, New York: Farrar and Rinehart.

Polanyi, K. (2001 [1944]) *The Great Transformation: The Political and Economic Origins of Our Time*, Boston: Beacon Press.

Porter, T.M. and Ross, D. (eds) (2003) *The Cambridge History of Science*, Vol. 7, *The Modern Social Sciences*, Cambridge: Cambridge University Press.

Portes, A. (1985) 'Latin American Class Structures: Their Composition and Change During the Last Decades', *Latin American Research Review*, 20: 7–40.

Price, R. (2003) 'Transnational Civil Society and Advocacy in World Politics', *World Politics*, 55: 579–606.

Przeworski, A. (1979) 'The Material Bases of Consent', *Political Power and Social Theory*, 1: 21–63.

Przeworski, A. and Wallerstein, M. (1992) 'Structural Dependence of the State on Capital', *American Political Science Review*, 82: 11–29.

Quesnay, François (1958 [1757]) 'Grains', in *François Quesnay et la Physiocratie*, Vol. 2, Paris: Institut National D'études Démographiques.

Rancière, Jacques (1995) *On the Shores of Politics*, London: Verso.

Rancière, Jacques (1999) *Disagreement. Politics and Philosophy*, translated by Julie Rose, Minneapolis: University of Minnesota Press.

Rancière, Jacques (2007) 'Does Democracy Mean Something?', in Costas Douzinas (ed.) *Adieu Derrida*, Basingstoke: Palgrave.

Rancière, Jacques, Guénoun, Solange and Kavanagh, James H. (2000) 'Literature, Politics, Aesthetics. Approaches to Democratic Disagreement', *SubStance*, 29: 3–24.

Rawls, J. (1985) 'Justice as Fairness: Political not Metaphysical', *Philosophy of Public Affairs*, 14: 223–51.

Ray, Douglas E., Sharpe, Calvin William and Strassfeld, Robert N. (1999) *Understanding Labor Law*, New York: M. Bender.

Reid, Julian (2006) *The Biopolitics of the War on Terror: Life Struggles, Liberal Modernity, and the Defence of Logistical Societies*, Manchester: Manchester University Press.

Rich, R. (2001) 'Bringing Democracy into International Law', *Journal of Democracy*, 12: 20–34.

Rischard, J.-F. (2002) *High Noon*, New York: Basic Books.

Risse, Thomas, Ropp, Stephen C. and Sikkink, Kathryn (eds) (1999) *The Power of Human Rights: International Norms and Domestic Change*, Cambridge: Cambridge University Press.

Roberts, A. and Zaum, D. (2008) *Selective Security: War and the United Nations Security Council since 1945*, London: Adelphi Paper 395, IISS.

Roberts, J. (1994) *Athens on Trial: the Antidemocratic Tradition in Western Thought*, Princeton: Princeton University Press.

Robin, Corey (2004) *Fear. The History of a Political Idea*, Oxford: Oxford University Press.

Robinson, W. (1996) *Promoting Polyarchy*, Cambridge: Cambridge University Press.

Rogers, Joel (1990) 'Divide and Conquer: Further Reflections in the Distinctive Character of American Labor Laws', *University of Wisconsin Law Review*, 1: 1–148.

Rosanvallon, P. (1995) 'The History of the Word "Democracy" in France', *Journal of Democracy*, 6: 140–54.

Rosenau, J.N. (1998) 'Governance and Democracy in a Globalising World', in D. Archibugi, D. Held and M. Köhler (eds) *Re-Imagining Political Community: Studies in Cosmopolitan Democracy*, Cambridge: Polity.

Rosenberg, J. (1994) *The Empire of Civil Society: A Critique of the Realist Theory of International Relations*, London and New York: Verso.

Rosenberg, J. (2000) *The Follies of Globalisation Theory: Polemical Essays*, London: Verso.

Ross, D. (ed.) (1994) *Modernist Impulses in the Human Sciences, 1870–1930*, Baltimore: Johns Hopkins University Press.

Rousseau, J.-J. (1997) *Of the Social Contract*, in *Rousseau:* The Social Contract *and* Other Later Political Writings, trans. V. Gourevitch, Cambridge: Cambridge University Press.

Royle, T. (1999) *Crimea: The Great Crimean War, 1854–1856*, Boston: Little Brown and Company.

Rubinstein, W.D. (1998) *Britain's Century: A Political and Social History 1815–1905*, New York: Arnold Publishers.

Rueschemeyer, D., Stephens, E.H. and Stevens, J.D. (1992) *Capitalist Development and Democracy*, Chicago: University of Chicago Press.

Ruggie, John G. (1993) 'Territoriality and Beyond: Problematizing Modernity in International Relations', *International Organization*, 47: 139–74.

Russett, B. (1993) *Grasping the Democratic Peace: Principles for a Post-Cold War World*, Princeton: Princeton University Press.

Sassen, Saskia (1988 [1997]) *The Mobility of Labor and Capital: A Study in International Investment and Labor Flow*. Cambridge: Cambridge University Press.

Sassen, Saskia (1999) *Guests and Aliens*. New York: New Press.

Sassen, Saskia (2008) *Territory, Authority, Rights: From Medieval to Global Assemblages*, updated 2nd edn., Princeton: Princeton University Press.

Sauvigny, G. (1962) *Metternich and his Times*, trans. P. Ryde, London: Darton, Longman & Todd.

Saward, M. (2000) 'A Critique of Held', in B. Holden (ed.) *Global Democracy: Key Debates*, London and New York: Routledge.

Saward, M. (2006) 'The Representative Claim', *Contemporary Political Theory*, 5: 297–318.

Scheffler, S. (1999) 'Conceptions of Cosmopolitanism', Utilitas, II.

Scheuerman, William E. (1994) *Between the Norm and the Exception. The Frankfurt School and the Rule of Law*, Cambridge, MA: MIT Press.

Schmidt, B.C. (1997) *The Political Discourse of Anarchy: A Disciplinary History of International Relations*, Albany, NY: SUNY Press.

Schmitt, C. (1988) *The Crisis of Parliamentary Democracy*, trans. E. Kennedy, Cambridge, MA: MIT Press.

Schmitt, C. (1996) *The Concept of the Political*, Chicago: University of Chicago Press.

Schmitt, C. (2003) *The Nomos of the Earth in the International Law of the Jus Publicum Europaeum*, New York: Telos Press.

Schmitz, H.P. and Sell, K. (1999) 'International Factors in Processes of Political Democratization: Towards a Theoretical Integration', in J. Grugel (ed.), *Democracy without Borders: Transnationalization and Conditionality in New Democracies*, London: Routledge.

Scholte, J.A. (2000) *Globalization: A Critical Introduction*, Basingstoke: Palgrave Macmillan.

Scholte, J.A. (2002) 'Civil Society and Democracy in Global Governance', *Global Governance*, 8: 281–304.

Schroeder, P.W. (1994) *The Transformation of European Politics 1763–1848*, Oxford: Clarendon Press.

Schumpeter, J.A. (1976) *Capitalism, Socialism and Democracy*, London: Routledge.

Seidel, Michael A. (1972) 'The Restoration Mob: Drones and Dregs', *Studies in English Literature, 1500–1900*, 12: 429–43.

Sen, A. (1999) 'Democracy as a Universal Value', *Journal of Democracy*, 10: 3–17.

Sewell, William H., Jr. (1980) *Work and Revolution in France: The Language of Labor from the Old Regime to 1848*, New York: Cambridge University Press.

Shaw, Martin (1994) *Global Society and International Relations: Sociological Concepts and Political Perspectives*, Cambridge: Polity.

Shoemaker, Robert B. (2004) *The London Mob: Violence and Disorder in Eighteenth-Century England*, London: Continuum.

Shorr, D. (2007) 'Legitimacy Synonymous with Democracy', *Democracy Arsenal*, 8 June, www.democracyarsenal.org/2007/06/legitimacy_syno.html (accessed 2 July 2008).

Sighele, Scipio (1901) *La Foule Criminelle. Essai De Psychologie Collective*, Paris: Félix Alcan.

Silver B. and Slater, E. (1999) 'The Social Origins of World Hegemonies', in G. Arrighi and B.J. Silver (eds) *Chaos and Governance in the Modern World System*, Minneapolis: University of Minnesota Press.

Simmel, Georg (1950 [1903]) 'Metropolis and Mental Life', in Kurt H. Wolff (ed.) *The Sociology of Georg Simmel*, New York: Free Press.

Simmel, Georg (1950) 'The Stranger', in Kurt H. Wolff (ed.) *The Sociology of Georg Simmel*, New York: Free Press.

Simmel, Georg (1955) 'The Web of Group-Affiliations' in Kurt H. Wolff (ed.) *Conflict*, London: Collier-Macmillan.

Simmel, Georg (1971a) 'The Poor', in Donald N. Levine (ed.) *Georg Simmel on Individuality and Social Forms*, Chicago: University of Chicago Press.

Simmel, Georg (1971b) 'The Problem of Sociology', in Donald N. Levine (ed.) *Georg Simmel on Individuality and Social Forms*, Chicago: University of Chicago Press.

Simmel, Georg (1978) *The Philosophy of Money*, translated by Tom Bottomore and David Frisby, London: Routledge & Kegal Paul.

Skidelsky, R. (2008) 'League of Democracies is a Frightening Thought', *Taipei Times*, 25 June, www.taipeitimes.com/News/editorials/archives/2008/06/25/2003415622 (accessed 2 July 2008).

Skinner, Q. (1973) 'The Empirical Theorists of Democracy and Their Critics: A Plague on Both Their Houses', *Political Theory*, 1: 287–306.

Skinner, Q. (1998) *Liberty before Liberalism*, Cambridge: Cambridge University Press.

Slaughter, A.-M. (1995) 'International Law in a World of Liberal States', *European Journal of International Law*, 6: 503–31.

Slaughter, A.-M. (2004) *A New World Order*, Princeton: Princeton University Press.

Smith, Adam (1976 [1759]) *The Theory of Moral Sentiments*, London: Printed for A. Millar.

Smith, T. (2007) *A Pact with the Devil*, New York: Routledge.

Snyder, J.L. (2000) *From Voting to Violence: Democratization and Nationalist Conflict*, New York: Norton.

Soysal, Y.N. (1994) *Limits of Citizenship. Migrants and Postnational Membership in Europe*, Chicago: University of Chicago Press.

Stanley, Amy Dru (1998) *From Bondage to Contract: Wage Labor, Marriage, and the Market in the Age of Slave Emancipation*, Cambridge: Cambridge University Press.

Staten, Henry (1985) *Wittgenstein and Derrida*, Oxford: Basil Blackwell.

Stedman, S.J. (2007) 'UN Transformation in an Era of Soft Balancing', *International Affairs*, 83: 933–44.

Steinfeld, Robert J. (1991) *The Invention of Free Labor: The Employment Relation in English and American Law and Culture*, Chapel Hill: University of North Carolina Press.

Steinfeld, Robert J. (2001) *Coercion, Contract, and Free Labor in the Nineteenth Century*, New York: Cambridge University Press.

Stivachtis, Y.A. (2008) 'Civilization and International Society: The Case of European Union Expansion', *Contemporary Politics*, 14: 71–89.

Strikwerda, K. (1993) 'The Troubled Origins of European Economic Integration: International Iron and Steel Migration in the Era of World War I', *American Historical Review*, 98: 1106–29.

Sunkel, O. (1993) 'From Inward-Looking Development to Development From Within', in O. Sunkel (ed.) *Development From Within: Toward a Neostructuralist Approach for Latin America*, Boulder, CO: Lynne Rienner.

Taithe, B. (2001) *Citizenship and Wars: France in Turmoil, 1870–1871*, London: Routledge.

Tan, K. (1998) 'Liberal Toleration in the Law of Peoples', *Ethics*, 108: 276–95.

Tarde, Gabriel (1901 [1989]) *L'opinion Et La Foule*, Paris: Presses Universitaires de France.

Tarrow, S. (2005) *The New Transnational Activism*, Cambridge: Cambridge University Press.

Taylor, Benjamin and Witney, Fred (1992) *U.S. Labor Relations Law: Historical Development*, Englewood Cliffs, NJ: Prentice Hall.

Taylor, C. (1998) 'The Dangers of Soft Despotism', in A. Etzioni (ed.), *The Essential Communitarian Reader*, Oxford: Rowman and Littlefield.

Teeple, G. (1995) *Globalization and the Decline of Social Reform*, New Jersey: Humanities Press.

Teune, Henry (2002) 'Global Democracy', *The ANNALS of the American Academy of Political and Social Science*, 581: 22–34.

Tharoor, S. (2008) 'This Mini-League of Nations Would Cause Only Division', *Guardian*, 27 May, www.guardian.co.uk/commentisfree/2008/may/27/unitednation (accessed 2 July 2008).

Thompson, E.P. (1963) *The Making of the English Working Class*, New York: Vintage Books.

Thompson, E.P. (1993) 'The Moral Economy of the English Crowd in the Eighteenth Century', Reprinted in *Customs in Common: Studies in Traditional Popular Culture*, New York: The New Press.

Thompson, J. (1992) *Justice and World Order: A Philosophical Inquiry*, New York: Routledge.

Tilly, C. (1991) *Durable Inequality*, Berkeley: University of California Press.

Tipton, F.B. (1976) *Regional Variations in the Economic Development of Germany During the Nineteenth Century*, Middletown, CT: Wesleyan University Press.

Tocqueville, A. de (1987) *Recollections: The French Revolution of 1848*, trans. G. Lawrence, New Brunswick, NJ: Transaction Publishers.

Tocqueville, A. de (2003) *Democracy in America and Two Essays on America*, trans. G.E. Bevan, London: Penguin Books.

Tocqueville, A. de (2004) *Democracy in America*, trans. A. Goldhammer, New York: Library of America.

Tomlins, Christopher L. (1993) *Law, Labor, and Ideology in the Early American Republic*, New York: Cambridge University Press.

Trebilcock, C. (1981) *Industrialization of the Continental Powers 1780–1914*, London: Longmans.

Tucker, R.C. (1981) *Politics as Leadership*, Columbia and London: University of Missouri Press.

Turgot, Anne Robert Jacques (1795 [1769–70]) *Reflections on the Formation and Distribution of Wealth*, London: E. Spragg.

UK Cabinet Office (2008) 'The National Security Strategy of the United Kingdom: Security in an Interdependent World', Norwich: Cm 7291, TSO.

Unger, Roberto Mangabeira (1983) 'The Critical Legal Studies Movement', *Harvard Law Review*, 96: 561–675.

United Nations (1992) 'United Nations Framework Convention on Climate Change', http://unfccc.int/resource/docs/convkp/conveng.pdf (accessed 5 December 2008).

United Nations Framework Convention on Climate Change (2008) 'Daily Programme for Friday', 12 December, (Cop14) (Cmp4), http://unfccc.int/resource/docs/2008/cop14/od11.pdf (accessed 5 January 2009).

Urbinati, N. (2003) 'Can Cosmopolitical Democracy be Democratic?', in D. Archibugi (ed.) *Debating Cosmopolitics*, London and New York: Verso.

—— (2006) *Representative Democracy: Principles and Genealogy*, Chicago: University of Chicago Press.

Urry, John (2000) *Sociology Beyond Societies. Mobilities for the Twenty-First Century*, London: Routledge.

—— (2007) *Mobilities*, Cambridge: Polity.

US National Security Strategy (2002) September. www.georgebush-whitehouse.archives. gov/nsc/nss/2002 (accessed on 7 February 2011).

Virno, Paolo (2004) *A Grammar of the Multitude*, New York: Semiotext(e).

Walker, R.B.J. (1993) *Inside/Outside: International Relations as Political Theory*, Cambridge: Cambridge University Press.

Wallerstein, Immanuel (1974) *The Modern World System*, New York: Academic Press.

Waltz, K.N. (1959) *Man, the State, and War: A Theoretical Analysis*. New York: Columbia University Press.

Waltz, K.N. (1979) *Theory of International Politics*, Reading, MA: Addison-Wesley.

Walzer, M. (1983) *Spheres of Justice. A Defense of Pluralism and Equality*, New York: Basic Books.

Wehler, H.-U. (1969) *Bismarck Und Der Imperialismus*, Cologne: Kiepenheuer.

Weiler, J.H.H. (1999) *The Constitution of Europe*, Cambridge: Cambridge University Press.

Weiner, M.J. (1982) *English Culture and the Decline of the Industrial Spirit, 1850–1980*, Cambridge: Cambridge University Press.

Weiss, J. (1977) *Conservatism in Europe 1770–1945*, New York: Harcourt, Brace Jovanovich.

Weissbrodt, David (2008) *The Human Rights of Non-citizens*, Oxford: Oxford University Press.

Werth, C. (2008) 'Robert Kagan: Why Should Democracy be Shy?', *Newsweek*, 31 May, www.newsweek.com/id/139403 (accessed 2 July 2008).

Wesseling, H.L. (1997) *Imperialism and Colonialism*, Westport, CT: Greenwood Press.

Whelan, F.G. (1983) 'Prologue: Democratic Theory and the Boundary Problem', in J.R. Pennock and J.W. Chapman (eds) *Liberal Democracy*, New York and London: New York University Press.

Wilentz, Sean (1984) 'Against Exceptionalism: Class Consciousness and the American Labor Movement, 1790–1920', *International Labor and Working Class History*, 26: 1–24.

Williams, D. and Young, T. (1994) 'Governance, the World Bank and Liberal Theory', *Political Studies*, 42: 84–100.

Williams, G. (1979) 'Imperialism and Development', *World Development*, 6: 925–36.

Wilson, W. (1965) 'The World Must be Made Safe for Democracy', in A. Fried (ed.) *A Day of Dedication: The Essential Writings and Speeches of Woodrow Wilson*, New York: Macmillan.

Witte, Edwin E. (1932) *The Government in Labor Disputes*, New York: McGraw Hill.

Wolin, S. (2001) *Tocqueville between Two Worlds: The Making of a Political and Intellectual Life*, Princeton: Princeton University Press.

Wolin, S. (2008) *Democracy Incorporated: Managed Democracy and the Specter of Inverted Totalitarianism*, Princeton: Princeton University Press.

Wood, E.M. (1996) 'Demos versus "We, the People": Freedom and Democracy Ancient and Modern', in J. Ober and C. Hedrick (eds) *Dēmokratia*, Princeton: Princeton University Press.

Woods, D.C. (1982) 'The Operation of the Master and Servant Acts in the Black Country, 1858–1875', *Midland History* 102: 93–115.

Wright, E. (2000) 'Workers' Power, Capitalist Interest and Class Compromise', *American Journal of Sociology*, 105: 957–1002.

Youngs, R. (2001) *The European Union and the Promotion of Democracy*, Oxford: Oxford University Press.

Zakaria, F. (1997) 'The Rise of Illiberal Democracy', *Foreign Affairs* 76: 22–43.

Zelizer, Viviana A. (1997) *The Social Meaning of Money: Pin Money, Paychecks, Poor Relief, and Other Currencies*, Princeton: Princeton University Press.

Žižek, S. (2008) *In Defense of Lost Causes*, London: Verso.

Zürn, M. (2000) 'Democratic Governance Beyond the Nation-state: The EU and Other International Institutions', *European Journal of International Relations*, 6: 183–221.

Index

Page numbers in *italics* denote tables.